Sports Media

Looking toward a future with increasingly hybridized media offerings, *Sports Media: Transformation, Integration, Consumption* examines sports media scholarship and its role in facilitating understanding of the increasingly complex world of sports media. Acknowledging that consumer demand for sports media content has influenced nearly every major technology innovation of the past several decades , chapters included herein assess existing scholarship while positing important future questions about the role sports media will increasingly play in the daily lives of sports fans worldwide. Contributions from well-known scholars are supplemented by work from younger researchers doing new work in this area.

   Developed for the Broadcast Education Association's Research Symposium series, this volume will be required reading for graduate and undergraduate students in communication studies, sociology, marketing, and sports management, and will serve as a valuable reference for future research in sports media.

Andrew C. Billings arrived at the University of Alabama in 2011, where he assumed the role of the Ronald Reagan Chair of Broadcasting. He is the author of six books, including *Olympic Media: Inside the Biggest Show on Television* (Routledge, 2008). Additionally, he is also the author of over 50 refereed journal articles and book chapters and his work has won numerous awards from organizations such as the National Communication Association and the Broadcast Education Association. His work in the classroom at Clemson University also earned him many teaching awards. He has consulted with many sports media agencies and is a past holder of the Invited Chair of Olympism at the Autonomous University of Barcelona.

Electronic Media Research Series

SPONSORED BY THE BROADCAST EDUCATION ASSOCIATION

Donald G. Godfrey, Series Editor

Media and Social Life
Edited by Mary Beth Oliver, Arthur A Raney

Media Management and Economics Research in a Transmedia Environment
Edited by Alan B. Albarran

Media and the Moral Mind
Edited by Ron Tamborini

Sports Media

Transformation, Integration, Consumption

Edited by
Andrew C. Billings

Routledge
Taylor & Francis Group

NEW YORK AND LONDON

First published in paperback 2014
by Routledge
711 Third Avenue, New York, NY 10017

Simultaneously published in the UK
by Routledge
2 Park Square, Milton Park, Abingdon, Oxon OX14 4RN

Routledge is an imprint of the Taylor & Francis Group, an informa business

© 2011 & 2014   Routledge, Taylor and Francis

Typeset in Bembo by Taylor & Francis Books

The right of Andrew C. Billings to be identified as author of this work has been asserted by him in accordance with sections 77and 78 of the Copyright, Designs and Patents Act 1988.

Library of Congress Cataloging in Publication Data
A catalog record has been requested for this book

ISBN13: 978-0-415-88368-9 (hbk)
ISBN13: 978-0-415-70332-1 (pbk)
ISBN13: 978-0-203-83279-0 (ebk)

Printed and bound in Great Britain by TJ International Ltd, Padstow, Cornwall

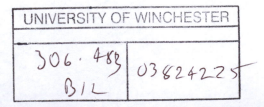

Contents

Series editor's foreword

In 2008, the Broadcast Education Association initiated a new program promoting original research. The result was the creation of the BEA Research Symposium and publications. The annual symposium forums, chaired by national scholars, are organized presentations, papers and discussion of leading-edge research within the BEA Annual Conference.

The purpose of the BEA Symposium is as a catalyst for future research. It honors leading scholars of the discipline and features their work along with new and upcoming scholarship.

New to the BEA Symposium in 2010 is a partnership with Taylor and Francis to publish symposium research through the newly established Electronic Media Research Series, created for this purpose. Along with the BEA Research Symposium Series, this publication provides a keystone research text for those researching within the discipline. It will bring the reader up to date relative to the topic, and it reflects the current work within the field as well as providing a comprehensive bibliography and index, facilitating future research.

The BEA launches this Symposium Publication Series with Andrew C. Billings, *Sports Media: Transformation, Integration, and Consumption*. It is the first in the BEA Electronic Media Series and will be a milestone for all future research in sports media.

Sincerely,

Donald G. Godfrey, Ph.D.
BEA Research Committee Chair
Symposium Series, Executive Editor

Preface and acknowledgements

When I first agreed to be the 2010 Broadcast Education Association Research Symposium Chair, I did not realize a book was attached to the project. When I found out that the fruits of the Symposium on *Sports Media: Transformation, Integration, Consumption* would result in a forward-thinking volume of the same name, I was simultaneously overwhelmed and exhilarated by the prospect. Ultimately, the exhilaration superseded any trepidation I felt about advancing a project of this scope. What you ultimately read here should be a minority-portion of "assessment of the field" mixed with a heavier dose of "trends and future directions." I am honored and proud of the work people contributed to this book that collectively sets a tone for future editions in this BEA/Routledge series.

Sports Media: Transformation, Integration, Consumption is, at its core, a fusion project. Contributions are made by scholars who have been central to sports media discussions for decades, but contributions are also included by newly minted Ph.D.'s and, in one case, a talented and ambitious graduate student. This is also a fusion of disciplinary understandings, as sports media is a field that has been parsed out among many different schools of thought and epistemological underpinnings. The chapters complement each other while, hopefully, exuding a sense of scope for a field that has many tentacles and a rapidly increasing profile.

The dichotomous nature of traditional and new media offerings is certainly present in the subjects explored in the book. What we ultimately know is that new media are doing more to expand the sports media universe than they are being used to replace some traditional venues for sport consumption, namely radio and television. Chapters 1–6 are offered by senior scholars who were invited to the day-long symposium offered by the Broadcast Education Association on April 15, 2010. I selected people for a variety of reasons that range from diversity of scholarship to the ability of their work to transcend national boundaries and provide insight about nations in the plural sense. I also selected them because they are key contributors to the scholarly discussion and have been for quite some time. The topics and approaches of their scholarship are quite diverse, but what remains uniform is the rigor of their efforts; it is all of the highest quality. Chapters 7–10 were competitively selected papers from a national competition and were vetted by the senior scholars mentioned for Chapters 1–6. Together, they offer a wider range of scholarship as it relates to new media influences, while also giving any "fan" of sports media an opportunity to note the promise of many scholars in the earlier stages of their careers. The future is, indeed, quite bright. Chapter 11 is then a piece I wrote that attempts to survey the field and offer directions for years to come; a shorter version of it served as the closing address for the symposium. The book concludes with a compilation of seminal works in the field, again as broad and diverse as one would imagine for a subject as interdisciplinary as sports media.

In the end, what I hope this book provides is a seminal work appropriate for graduate courses in sports media while also being a guidebook for anyone wishing to embark upon scholarship in this academic area. The goal of any edited volume is to impart a wide variety of insights that no single person could possibly accomplish. I believe we have attained that lofty objective.

Finally, there are so many people to thank. I will attempt to do so knowing that words will not do justice to the mix of support, insight, and enthusiasm they exhibited that ultimately gave me a sense of direction and confidence in a unity of purpose. Typically, when I first hear about a potential project, I take at least a few days – often a few weeks – to determine whether the project is worth the amount of time and effort that will be necessary. When Glenda Williams called me to query if I would be willing to be the Broadcast Education Association Research Symposium Chair, I broke that general rule, eagerly agreeing to the task immediately. While I saw it as an honor to be selected, what really appealed was the opportunity to work with great people (inside BEA and out) and to advance a sub-discipline within our field that I believe to be of great import. Not once did I regret my decision to serve, as the experience has been tremendous. I must thank not only Glenda Williams but also Donald Godfrey, who has been a steady resource while always allowing me a great deal of editorial latitude, and to Heather Birks, who could always answer my questions (and there were many) effectively and immediately. The BEA is in great hands with leaders like this. Couple that with the positive words and constant advocate that is Linda Bathgate at Routledge and my experience has been quite blessed.

I also must acknowledge the tremendous work of seven senior scholars who aided the process every step of the way, including time-consuming tasks such as evaluating the submissions for the paper competition. Those scholars are: Jennings Bryant, Walter Gantz, Marie Hardin, Arthur Raney, Michael Real, David Rowe, and Lawrence Wenner. Their works are represented in this volume not only in their contributed chapters but also with their insights on other chapters and with the extended reference list I compiled at the end. I see a great deal of growth in the

BEA Research Symposium and believe it will continue to grow in scope, participation, and readership in the years to come. This volume begins an annual contribution to the state of the discipline; in establishing this series, BEA and Routledge have partnered for something that should be seminal reading for people in broadcasting and electronic media.

Andrew C. Billings
2011

Contributors

Dr. Vince Benigni (Ph.D., University of Georgia) is an Associate Professor of Communication at College of Charleston and Director of the Graduate Program in Organizational and Corporate Communication. He has authored a number of studies on sport and media, as well as public relations pedagogy. He is author of *True Maroon* (2008), a history of intercollegiate athletics at College of Charleston.

Dr. Andrew C. Billings (Ph.D., Indiana University) is Professor of Communication Studies and Director of the Pearce Center for Professional Communication at Clemson University. He is the author of over 40 journal articles and six books related to communication and sport, including *Olympic Media: Inside the Biggest Show on Television* (Routledge, 2008).

Dr. Walter Gantz (Ph.D., Michigan State University) is Professor of Telecommunications and Chair of that department at Indiana University. He has been studying sports fans for nearly 30 years as part of his interest in the ways media fit into the context of daily life.

Dr. Marie Hardin (Ph.D., University of Georgia) is Associate Professor of Journalism and Women's Studies and Associate Dean for Graduate Studies and Research at Penn State University. She is the author of over 40 journal articles, book chapters and reports related to communication and sport, most of which focus on gender-related issues.

Dr. Jeffrey W. Kassing (Ph.D., Kent State University) is an Associate Professor in the Division of Social and Behavioral Sciences at Arizona State University. He researches parent–child and coach–athlete interactions in youth sports and fan–athlete interaction via new media. His work has appeared in *Communication Yearbook*, the *Western Journal of Communication*, and the *International Journal of Sports Communication*.

Dr. Lindsey J. Meân (Ph.D., University of Sheffield, UK) is Assistant Professor in the Division of Social and Behavioral Sciences at Arizona State University. Her research typically focuses on the impact of discourses, identities and ideologies across sport production, organization, consumption, and participation. Most of her published work concerns gender-related issues. She recently co-edited a special issue on sport of the *Journal of Language and Social Psychology*.

Dr. Lance Porter (Ph.D., University of Georgia) is an Associate Professor of Mass Communication and the Advertising Area Head in the Manship School of Mass Communication at Louisiana State University. He holds a joint appointment with the Center for Computation and Technology, and has focused on digital media since 1995, when he built his first commercial Web site. He researches how digital media affect communication and culture.

Dr. Arthur A. Raney (Ph.D., University of Alabama) is Associate Professor of Communication and Director of Doctoral Studies in the School of Communication at Florida State University. His research examining the relationships between morality and media consumption has been published in a variety of scholarly journals and anthologies. He is also the lead editor of *Handbook of Sports and Media* (Lawrence Erlbaum Associates, 2006).

Dr. Michael R. Real (Ph.D., University of Illinois) is Professor of Communication and Culture at Royal Roads University in Victoria, BC, Canada. His books include *Exploring Media Culture*, *Super Media*, and *Mass-Mediated Culture*. He has written scores of scholarly and general publications, including more than three decades of research on media and sports. He has also directed local and international research projects, and hosted television and radio programs. His work focuses on media, culture, and social responsibility.

Dr. David Rowe (Ph.D., University of Essex, UK) is Professor of Cultural Research at the University of Western Sydney (Australia). He is author of over 90 journal articles and author/editor of eight books related to media and popular culture, including *Sport, Culture and the Media* (2004).

Jimmy Sanderson (M.A., Arizona State University) is a doctoral student in the Hugh Downs School of Human Communication at Arizona State University. His research focuses on sports communication, particularly how social media and computer-mediated communication affects sporting practices. His work has appeared in journals such as *American Behavioral Scientist*, *International Journal of Sport Communication*, *Journal of Computer-Mediated Communication*, and *Western Journal of Communication*.

Dr. Lauren Reichart Smith (Ph.D., University of Alabama) is an Assistant Professor of Public Relations at Auburn University. Her research focuses on media portrayals, specifically within the realm of sports. She has research forthcoming in the *Journal of Sports Media.*

Dr. Lawrence A. Wenner (Ph.D., University of Iowa) is the Von der Ahe Professor of Communication and Ethics in the College of Communication and Fine Arts and the School of Film and Television at Loyola Marymount University in Los Angeles. He is former editor of the *Journal of Sport and Social Issues* and his books include *MediaSport* and *Media, Sports, and Society.* His most recent book (with Steven Jackson) is *Sport, Beer, and Gender: Promotional Culture and Contemporary Social Life.*

Dr. Chris Wood (Ph.D., University of Georgia) is Owner and President of JWA Public Communications in Athens, Georgia. He has 20 years of professional experience researching, planning, executing and evaluating public communications campaigns, which often provide stimuli for scholarly work. In addition, he has published a handful of conference papers, journal articles, and/or book chapters, while teaching part-time and serving on the advisory board of the Grady College of Journalism and Mass Communication at the University of Georgia.

INTRODUCTION

Andrew C. Billings

CLEMSON UNIVERSITY

Perhaps the most telling formula for the success of a popular culture artifact regards the pairing of two concepts: ordinary person, extraordinary circumstance. Films such as *Titanic,* television shows such as *Lost,* and virtually every John Grisham novel have utilized the formula to great effect as they take a group of highly relatable people and place them in a situation far removed from the viewers' daily lives. We want the people to be like us (in a way that allows us to almost place ourselves within the narrative) but we want the circumstances to be epic and unique (to allow us to imagine what we would do in a similar predicament). The formula is time-tested and proves out in the billions of dollars that funnel through the system of popular culture each year. Fiction writers know how effective the premise of ordinary person/extraordinary circumstance works in a multitude of genres.

The nonfiction equivalent plays out quite effectively as well … in sports media. Parasocial relationships (see Horton & Wohl, 1956 and later Auter & Palmgreen, 2000) form between the consuming audience and the narratives that take place within the mass mediated sports event. Sports fans seek any sort of connection to the players, ranging from the simplest of casual conversations to a piece of autographed memorabilia to, more recently, following their favorite athletes on websites and through social media such as Twitter and Facebook. We shower our favorite athletes with praise, offering comments about how they are "down to earth" or a "normal guy" or are just "cool." Yet they are our heroes not just because they are down to earth, but also because they tend to enact unearthly feats rather routinely. Ordinary person; extraordinary circumstance. Snowboarder Shaun White became the epitome of "cool" at the 2006 and 2010 Winter Olympics because he seemed so approachable – and then proceeded to nail a backside 1080 halfpipe trick. Indy racer Danica Patrick rose to fame by embodying an attractive feminine persona while racing at 220 miles per hour in a cluttered straightaway. We love them because they could be us, yet decidedly, in their actions, are not us.

All of this relates to this volume entitled *Sports Media: Transformation, Integration, Consumption* because, at its core, this book is about analyzing what appeals and what doesn't, what sells and what doesn't, what works and what doesn't, what is fair and what isn't. This book incorporates many points of view that jointly explore the power inherent in a sports event, whether it is a megasports event such as the Olympics or World Series that is viewed by millions, or a niche sports event such as a college volleyball game that still has been found to have a demonstrable and loyal following. Wenner (1998) coined the term "mediasport" to represent the fusion of these two entities. This book evolves from Wenner's conception, as it covers the national and the international, the male and the female, the athlete and the fan, the traditional and the new. Nevertheless, within all of these wide-ranging issues, the book still underscores information that answers fundamental questions for academics, including:

- Who consumes mediasport?
- Why do they consume mediasport?
- What are the perceived benefits from consuming mediasport?
- What is the difference between watching and consuming mediasport?
- How do traditional media interact with new media to form modern notions of mediasport?
- What trends are increasing within mediasport?
- What trends are dissipating within mediasport?
- What are the effects of mediasport within modern society?

And, perhaps most importantly:

- What can the academic community do to advance the understanding and knowledge base within mediasport scholarship?

The contributors in the book range from senior scholars who have been inter-rogating these complex issues for decades to new assistant professors who build on this scholarship in new and fascinating ways. They all have some sort of grounding in the communication discipline, yet they almost all interact (at academic conferences) and incorporate (in their scholarly writings) a merged interdisciplinary approach. A topic such as sports media necessitates such a broad understanding. This book advances that understanding in useful ways simultaneously theoretical and applied.

The book opens with a different type of chapter from the others that follow – a broad-view assessment of the field by Walter Gantz in Chapter 1. Gantz has been working in the field of sports communication for several decades, often positing the difficult questions about measuring and understanding audiences for sports media telecasts. The chapter sets the table for what Gantz calls the "feast" that is to come in the rest of the chapters. First, he offers a sense of context – both for the state of sport scholarship and also the current place in which convergence media (the combination of traditional, new, social, and user-generated) has come to the fore at the time of this writing in 2010. Gantz offers a top 10 list for mediasport research that is informed by the seminal transactional model offered by Wenner (1989) that includes: (a) the media sports production complex, (b) the content of media sports, (c) the audience, and (d) the social system in which these elements relate to one another. Gantz then rightly blurs these issues, noting that "expanded options, shifting demographics, and advances in technology are likely to affect each of the elements." The result is an informed and forward-thinking chapter that sets the stage for the various research chapters to come.

Chapter 2 features a detailed sense of history and theory offered by Michael Real. The pairing of sport and television is portrayed as one of maximum convenience and impact, essentially arguing for a synergy that made the fit between sport and television so beneficial in the latter part of the 20th Century. Real queries, "What do we find when we deconstruct the components of this arranged marriage?" The answer offered in the chapter involves notions of suspense, intimacy, intertextuality, and more that result in the "enriching the sense of witnessing, understanding, and feeling the physical reality."

Chapters 3 and 4 mesh nicely with each other, examining the role of gender in divergent and yet ultimately complementary manners. First, Chapter 3 is written by Marie Hardin, focusing on the creators and authors behind prominent women's sports blogs. Incorporating the work of Michel Foucault, Hardin interviews contributors to Women's Talk Sports, a blog collective devoted to the advancement and promotion of women's athletics. Deflecting direct notions of who is to blame for the diminishment of women's sports within mainstream media, the respondents ultimately gauge equity in many ways, asking questions such as "Does it flip?" when bloggers ask whether certain depictions or narratives could ever be applied to men athletes. Hardin concludes that such forms of new media allow both men and women to reshape traditional notions about feminism, "reforming their own identities, engaging in ethical practices, and countering technologies of power" in the process.

Lawrence Wenner's writings offer a natural transition in Chapter 4, as he tackles gender from the perspective of the potential impact on perceptions of masculinity. Wenner notes that "narrative constructions of the sports fan, alongside those of other kinds of fans, continue to pathologize fanship as obsessive, hysterical, or as a form of psychological compensation." This becomes one area in which mediasport being predominantly male results in a mocking of the sports fan that is inherently masculinized. Wenner uses popular television advertisements as the artifacts to create five archetypes, exploring the commodified male sports fan as: (1) nut case, (2) loser, (3) juvenile, (4) relationally deficient, and (5) emasculated. The result is a highly compelling case for "the strategic use of the mocked sports fan in advertising narratives to help sell to those being mocked," namely the male sports fan.

Chapter 5 introduces the corollary often integrated into many sports narratives: the infusion of morality into the layered discussions that surround how we interpret sport. Using well-known examples such as Zinadine Zidane's famous head butt in the 2006 World Cup and Pete Rose's gambling on baseball, Arthur Raney offers a unique examination of subjective morality that often is in play within mediasport. He writes that while we can all "long for the day when the ideals preached to athletes – integrity, honor, loyalty, compassion, respect, humility – are universally adopted by their fans," this is not likely to occur. Given that, scholarship must address the function and enactment of morality within modern interpretations of sport.

Offering a much internationalized perspective, Australian sport researcher David Rowe contributes Chapter 6, which focuses on an examination of the past in order to understand an increasingly muddied outlook for the future of mediasport. Noting this potential turn, Rowe notes that "if the era of TV sports hegemony is passing into history, the regime that will replace it – if any – is by no means yet installed." Consequently, he addresses the trajectory of sports on television, concluding that sport offers an irreplaceable opportunity to "move freely across national cultural formations" and into the sphere noted in his chapter title: beyond broadcasting, beyond sports, beyond societies.

The combination of Jimmy Sanderson and Jeffrey Kassing results in Chapter 7, the first of two specific looks at the social media sensation, Twitter. More specifically, Sanderson and Kassing offer a contrast between what was offered in the past, in which players and fans were "actors in and consumers of the storyline, but uninvolved in how those stories get shaped and presented" and what is the case now with the advent of social media. In a series of mini case studies involving professional athletes such as Curt Schilling and Allen Iverson, Sanderson and Kassing illuminate how athletes can attempt to control information dissemination as well as frame media stories about themselves. Relatedly, fans exert control of the narratives, whether this involves the validation or vilification of the athlete or team about which they are "tweeting." The authors stress the sense of the inevitability of mainstreaming social media outlets, finding them "transformative and adversarial, while also being integrative and community building."

The book then transitions to a Chapter 8 focus on new media communities on the Internet by Lance Porter, Chris Wood, and Vince Benigni. The three scholars delve into the world of Fan-Based Internet Sports Communities (FBISCs), finding a space in which fans find empowerment without a diminished sense of enjoyment. They empirically test the motives for fan consumption, finding that these communities are where the "hard-core" sports fans reside, meaning they are sometimes the epicenter of what it means to be a modern and avid sports fanatic. As the authors conclude, FBISCs have evolved into places that "keep the active, vociferous sports fan coming back for more."

Chapter 9 continues the new media theme, looking at the social media phenomenon of Twitter explained previously in Chapter 7, but this time with a gender-specific lens. Lauren Reichart Smith utilizes past traditional mediasport examinations to determine whether gender biases remain within the boundaries of Twitter-based communication in college sports. As she notes, "traditional media platforms are limited by constraints of space, time and money ... [but with Twitter] the only restriction set forth is the 140 character limit of posts." Previous gender inequities in mediasport have been traced back to the notion of choice – gatekeepers choosing to cover men's sports over women's sports because of a finite amount of space. Smith's chapter ultimately underscores how hard-wired these gender differences can be, as she uncovers diminishment of female athlete and sport coverage that is similar to traditional media studies of the past.

Of course, a book on mediasport would be remiss without a focus on ESPN, the giant of all media outlets. This contribution is offered in Chapter 10 by Lindsey Meân. ESPN is truly a widespread media giant, offering content in virtually every conceivable domain, ranging from television to radio to magazines to Internet and mobile applications. Meân sets her gaze on ESPN.com, the most popular sport-related website in the United States. In uncovering how discourses and ideologies are revealed on the site, Meân finds an "illusionary collaboration" in which consumers of the site feel empowered and yet ultimately helped ESPN "deploy familiar narratives that re/produced sport within the narrow traditional discourses of sport and its rituals."

Chapter 11 is a self-authored synthesis chapter in which I attempt to aggregate the collective contributions of the past 30 years of mediasport scholarship and then identify avenues for fruitful future academic pursuits. While my conclusion about the past 30 years is that "the amount of seminal sport communication scholarship produced over the past three decades is astounding and, moreover, exceeds the overarching systemic structures that should support it," I also note new trends that could help to systematically advance the field in the very near future. Six themes are then articulated for future study: (1) Sporting community in the age of fragmentation, (2) Primary consumption beyond the sporting performance, (3) Defining identity beyond one-shot variable analyses, (4) Recognizing the interdisciplinary nature of sport without losing sports media identity, (5) Stressing the impact factor, and (6) Emphasizing the value of distraction. The chapter concludes by emphasizing the double-edged sword that is always prevalent in mediasport scholarship as scholars attempt to be interested without being a fan, and critical while not losing sight of the ultimate good sport can offer myriad constituencies.

Finally, the Appendix offers a very distinctive opportunity to synthesize past works through the constitution of an extended reference list for the field. When one attempts to offer a list claiming to be "comprehensive" in any manner, there is an inevitable perspective in which the project ultimately falls short in the mind of the reader. The citations in this chapter are a noble effort to compile the works of the past 30 years in the area of mediasport. The majority of seminal works are likely to be found, yet there is no question that undiscovered and valuable outliers remain. Thus, what is offered is a fairly comprehensive account of scholarly endeavors, yet it should never be regarded as a fully exhaustive listing. Several other clarifications must also be made. First, the reference list represents seminal works in sports media, a subset of study within the convergence area that is communication and sport. The preponderance of the works directly ties to sports media theory and implications, yet others impact the field through more secondary linkages. Second, this focus on sports media scholarship inherently required a wide uncovering of interdisciplinary works, meaning that this list not only covers journals traditionally connected to the communication discipline but also to other fields (including sociology, marketing, and many more) that have provided influential insights to the manner in which we discuss sports media today. Finally, one will likely notice a relative paucity of book chapters on this list; this is largely because many of the key chapter contributions arose within a book on sport that was listed as a single entry. For instance, Arthur Raney and Jennings Bryant's contribution in the form of the edited *Handbook of Sports and Media* is immense, yet rather than listing each of these chapters, they are all included in the single citation for the book. In the end, the goal of the Appendix was to create a comprehensive list of citations that anyone wishing to or currently studying sports media could potentially consult and use as a heuristic for future work.

In sum, it is my sincere hope that this 12-chapter volume offers a truly useful blend of insights and uses, as it was my aim for the book to be useful for both academicians and industry experts, both empiricists and rhetoricians, both traditional scholars and new media scholars. The goal is to provide a practical and valuable glimpse as to the state of the joint fields of sport and media at the end of the first decade of the 21st Century. Thanks to the generous and insightful contributions of all of these contributors, I feel confident this aim has been accomplished within the pages you are about to read.

References

Auter, P.J. & Palmgreen, P. (2000). Development and validation of a parasocial interaction measure: The audience-persona interaction scale. *Communication Research Reports, 17*(1), 79–89.

Horton, D. & Wohl, R.R. (1956). Mass communication and para-social interaction. *Psychiatry, 19*, 215–29.

Wenner, L.A. (Ed.). (1989). *Media, sports, and society*. Newbury Park, CA: Sage.

Wenner, L.A. (Ed.). (1998). *MediaSport*. New York: Routledge.

1

KEEPING SCORE

Reflections and suggestions for scholarship in sports and media

Walter Gantz

INDIANA UNIVERSITY

Mediated sports communication is a burgeoning, rapidly maturing, and increasingly sophisticated and nuanced field of inquiry. In this chapter, I will offer a sweeping overview and assessment of the field, argue that the mediated sports landscape has changed in ways that demand our attention, and focus on research I would like to see conducted over the next decade.

Overview

Let me begin with the obvious: The academic field of media and sport (dubbed mediasport by Wenner, 1998) is enormous and reflects the work of psychologists, sociologists, anthropologists, economists, physiologists, historians, communication scientists, rhetorical and cultural/critical scholars. We are housed in a variety of liberal arts departments as well as in schools of health, marketing and business, the arts, physical education, and recreation. Like faculty in many communication programs, we are an extraordinarily diverse lot, bringing remarkably different theories, methods, and interests to sports. What we have in common is the intersection of mediasport, yet we may have little awareness of each other's efforts. Much of our work is presented at conferences and then published in journals that reflect our disciplines. Let me illustrate how wide that is: For this book, Billings prepared a list of *significant* work over the past 30 years in sports and media. That list contains over 400 entries, including articles in over 70 journals. Time constraints and long-standing disciplinary silos limit our interest and vision. None of us will get to all those journals. We are, as I noted, an enormous field: no single talk, annual conference, book, journal, grand theory or applied method can fully capture the scope of the descriptive and theory-based work in mediasport. At the same time, I think conceptual frameworks provide important structure and offer a way at looking at what we know and have yet to study.

As systematic scholarship on mediated sports was picking up steam, Wenner (1989) offered a transactional model for studying media and sports, one that featured four primary elements: (a) the media sports production complex, (b) the content of media sports, (c) the audience, and (d) the social system in which these elements relate to one another. Relatively little has been written about the ways in which sports leagues – and the International Olympic Committee – negotiate with broadcast, cable, satellite and mobile distribution outlets – or about the spreadsheets that guide those negotiations; about the pressures local and regional governments face when trying to keep or lure a professional franchise; about the current dance between the sports leagues and media outlets as the sports leagues develop networks of their own; about the government's bully-pulpit role in trying to establish a playoff system for Division I college football; or about the ways in which the professionalism of selected collegiate sports may be shaping undergraduate life (e.g. Grant, Leadley, & Zygmont, 2008; Gratton & Solberg, 2007; Sperber, 2000; Zimbalist, 1999). Instead, and perhaps because of ease of access to data, much of the work on mediasport – certainly much relying on social science and cultural methods – has focused on content and audiences.

Dozens of content analyses have examined how gender, race, nationality, and nationalism have been covered in sporting events, sportscasts, and print coverage of sports (Billings, 2008; Duncan, 2006; Grainger, Newman, & Andrews, 2006; Hundley & Billings, 2010). We know that although coverage has improved, women's sports still are underrepresented; that there is gender marking and a hierarchy of naming; that in sports programming and ads on those shows, women are presented and described in ways that emphasize their gender and belittle their passion, commitment, and excellence as athletes; and that female sports journalists still face hurdles their male counterparts do not. We know that coverage of minorities has improved; that Black players are being portrayed as successful because of their intelligence, work ethic, and leadership skills, and that there are more minorities on the set as sports reporters and anchors – but that we have yet to enter a post-racial world. We know that the Olympics remains a bastion of quiet nationalism although we see greater coverage of women's sports than elsewhere.

Hundreds of studies have examined the audience for sports – and with good reason. Although mediasport represents a multi-billion dollar industry, with annual rights fees for the NFL alone in the billions of dollars, there would be no media–sports production complex without the apparent growing base of fans who attend games, watch televised sports at home, in dorms, and at bars, and follow news of their favorite players and teams on television, newspapers, magazines, online, and now with mobile devices. Sports programming delivers large, attractive and elusive audiences to advertisers – and those in the industry know exactly who that audience is.

Perhaps because academics lack access to comprehensive sets of ratings and sales data, many of us have focused on the origins and nature of fanship, the exposure experience, and the consequences of following mediated sports (Cialdini et al., 1976; Gantz & Wenner, 1995; Hirt, Zillmann, Erickson, & Kennedy, 1992; Raney,

2006; Wann & Branscombe, 1990; Wann et al., 2006; Zillmann, Bryant, & Sapolsky, 1979). We know that environmental and personality factors shape one's interest in sports; that fans for sports appear more invested in this activity than fans for other genres of programming; that there are a wide range of reasons for watching sports, headed by entertainment and eustress motivations; that context, companionship, content, and level of fanship affect the viewing experience; that while male fans still outnumber female fans, the fanship experience generally cuts across gender lines; that fanship is extended to fantasy sports; that loyalties run deep; that winning and losing matters and affects fan self-perceptions in a variety of ways; that fan behaviors can sometimes be dysfunctional; and that, occasional headlines to the contrary, fanship does not appear to significantly disrupt long-standing relationships or lead to domestic violence.

All this we know – sort of, and I will come back to that shortly – but expanded options, shifting demographics, and advances in technology are likely to affect each of the elements in Wenner's transactional model – and also highlight the *transactional* nature of the relationships. There is critical interplay across elements in the mediated sports complex, with the audience increasingly active and central to the decisions made by sports organizations and content providers.

The changing landscape

First, the media landscape is now cluttered with local, regional, and national sports networks and online sites that compete for audience attention. Proliferation of sports – and other entertainment options – simultaneously fragments the audience and makes sports more valuable as little else (currently, TV programs such as *American Idol*, *Dancing with the Stars*, and *The Mentalist*) draws significant audiences. After an over-time ratings dip that must have worried the major professional leagues and the networks carrying them, ratings were up in 2009 and early 2010, at least for major sporting events (Master, 2009), suggesting an audience with an almost insatiable appetite for sports – or at least one that hungers for extraordinary human interest match-ups (e.g., the 2010 Super Bowl between New Orleans and Indianapolis) and sports events (e.g., the 2010 Masters, featuring Tiger Woods' return to golf after a self-imposed break from competition – and prying press).

Second, the audience for some sports – like baseball – is aging (Gallup, 2005) and, as it ages, becomes less attractive to advertisers who, we are told, remain wed to reaching the 18–34, 18–49, or 25–54 demographic. To lure an audience raised on MTV, rock music blares from stadium loudspeakers, the Olympics includes exciting sports like the snowboard half-pipe that thrill young adults, and the Super Bowl featured slightly edgy entertainment, at least until Justin Timberlake met Janet Jackson in the 2004 Super Bowl and, deliberately or not, momentarily exposed a portion of her breast.

Third, digital video recorders (DVRs), streaming video, interactive and online programming, social media, and mobile technologies have moved the audience from back to front seat. Make no mistake about it: While new media boast about record attention and suggest that linear, non-interactive media are on their last legs, television is still king and commands the lion's share of time spent using the media, even for children and adolescents. Indeed, the average American spends more time watching television (35 hours per week) than ever before (Nielsen, 2010). But, today's audience time-shifts, multitasks, views programming across a variety of screens, creates content, and expects to have its voice heard. The media sports production complex knows that and is scrambling to catch the audience with cross-platform campaigns and content – and scrambling to measure it, too: witness Nielsen's three-screen report and ESPN's cross-platform (TV, radio, the Internet, mobile, and print) research initiative, ESPN XP, for the 2010 World Cup.

These three changes affect each of the components in Wenner's transactional model and are likely to serve as a springboard for research on mediasport. I expect and welcome research that describes the demography of those who turn to inter-active and mobile sports media outlets; that captures the uses, gratifications, and effects of exposure to those outlets; that measures the interplay between the fan's voice and that of the journalist; that determines if the money spent on sports makes dollars and sense – are rights and naming fees worth the money? Is the fan's pocket-book elastic? Are publicly funded stadiums worth the opportunity costs? All these issues merit study – but I must admit, like late night talk show host David Letter-man, I have my top ten list. It is a list that reflects longstanding personal interests as well as goals – and frustrations – I believe many of us share. As you will see, my list starts with explication and measurement, two issues central to solid research.

Agenda

First, we need to take more care of the way we define and measure sports fanship. What does it mean – and what does it take – to be counted as a fan? And, does the participant or the researcher make that decision? When asked on public opinion polls, most Americans say they are sports fans. But, are they really, at least as some of us consider fanship? I am uncomfortable with self-proclamation, particularly on dichotomous option questions (e.g., "Do you consider yourself a sports fan?"). At least from my perspective, this results in overestimations of the nation's fan base and includes those who are more casual with their fanship, those who jump on band-wagons for short periods of time and are no more interested in following some sports activity than they are for a TV program they occasionally enjoy watching or talking about. On the other hand, what does it take to be a fan? What criteria do researchers use to separate fans from non-fans or segment fanship based on responses to an item or index? There is no magic number that delineates fans from non-fans (or serious fans from those less serious) primarily because fanship is not a dichotomous concept. Instead, people can be placed on a fanship continuum. This is fine for correlational analyses that link fanship levels with outcome variables, but not helpful for fan/non-fan comparisons. For that, cuts must be made. Many researchers rely on frequency distributions, means, and standard deviations for those cuts; they are data-based but still arbitrary decisions. For example, Wenner and I constructed a fanship index based on responses to questions that measured interest in watching TV sports, perceived knowledge of one's favorite sport, and exposure to sports programming on weekdays and weekends – and then used the top and bottom quartiles to create fan and non-fan groups (Gantz & Wenner, 1995). We created separate distributions for men and women and used the appropriate quartile cuts with each distribution, all the while knowing that it took less to be a "fan" for women in our sample than it did for men.

I do not expect researchers to arrive at a universally used measure of fanship, in part because there is a difference between fanship for a player, a team, a university, a league, a sport, or an event like the Olympics or World Cup. There also may be a difference between identification with a team (e.g., one's school team) and being a sports fan. As a result, and at a minimum, we will need to employ measures that reflect the research questions under consideration and provide critical reference points for those being studied. A survey about NFL fans ought to operationalize fanship differently than one about fanship for the FIFA World Cup – but even with that, ambiguity with the term "fan" will add error into our measurement. The term itself is vague rather than confusing, much as "exercise" is understood but needs to be described in order to maximize shared meaning across respondents (Fowler, 1992).

I also know that research involves trade-offs, that survey research can be quite costly, and that many of us who study the concomitants and consequences of fanship use time-consuming multidimensional measures and indices for those variables. We may not have the time or money for multi-item measures of fanship – and respondents may not have the interest to work through a thorough assessment of fanship and then all the other questions we wish to ask. Respondent fatigue is a factor that plays into the measurement equation. As a result, I am not suggesting we adopt a 40 or 50 item measure of fanship. It may not be worth the trade-offs. But, much as we cannot measure media exposure with a single item on a questionnaire (even though people sometimes try, e.g., "How much television would you say you watch on an average week?"), I wonder if we can get a valid measure of fanship using a single item that inevitably squelches variability.

Three quick points here: First, let's recognize that fanship is not a dichotomous variable and that, at a minimum, we need to move past the easy yes/no set of responses. Sutton, McDonald, Miline, and Cimperman (1997) found three types of fans: the social, the focused, and the vested – and even that is greatly simplifying the issues. For that reason, I applaud ESPN's study on the life cycle of sports fans where fanship was measured on an 11 point scale (ESPN, 2009). Similarly, an online study of fans sponsored by the Norelco Consumer Products Company merits credit for its assessment: die-hard fan, avid fan, casual fan, and championship fan, with descriptions for each option (Wann, Friedman, McHale, & Jaffe, 2003). Respondents were asked to select from four options that described their level of sports fanship: Second, we also need to recognize that fanship is not a unidimensional concept, that it cannot be fully captured by a single item with whatever scale is attached to it. Here, the ESPN and Norelco measures fall short. To a point, Wann's work on sports fanship serves as an exemplar (Wann, 2002). His five-item measure taps into self and social domains of fanship, recognizes that sports is enjoyable entertainment, and that sports may be central to an individual's sense of self. Yet, in not defining the term "sport fan," Wann leaves it up to respondents to interpret it as they wish – and adding, I would argue, measurement error into the mix. Third, we should recognize that, from the questions asked to the cut points employed, our measures of fanship will affect our findings. Here, we simply need to be vigilant and carefully consider measures when evaluating results. Fortunately, most journals provide detailed information about methods. Unfortunately, the same cannot be said about the trade press, a potentially valuable source of information. We need to educate and encourage these outlets to provide measurement information, even though it may be important to a small subset of their readers.

Second, we need to recognize that fanship is not a static state phenomenon. ESPN's study on the life cycle of sports fans suggests that sports avidity peaks for men between the ages of 12 and 24. According to ESPN, slightly more than half of those 12–17 and 18–24 (52% and 51%, respectively) are avid fans. This declines to 47% among 25–34 year-old men, 41% among those 35–49, and 36% among 50+ men, even though as men age, they watch more sports on television. A different – and curvilinear – pattern emerged for women, with sports avidity highest among females 2–17, lowest between 18 and 49, and then modestly up again for women 50+.

It is not surprising that fanship is strong by adolescence. Extrinsic factors such as parental, sibling, and peer interest in mediated sports – as well as their participation in sports – help shape fanship (Dietz-Uhler, End, & Jacquemotte, 2000; Wann, 2006). Intrinsic factors such as level of competitiveness matter, too (Gantz, Wilson, Lee, & Fingerhut, 2008). Yet, avidity is not constant. Why is it that avidity declines over time? ESPN's report suggests that extrinsic factors such as career and family commitments – and fiscal issues associated with raising a family – shift attention and passion elsewhere, that adults no longer have the time or energy to care as much as they did. Intrinsic factors are likely to be at work, too. It may be that as we age, our interests, values, and passions shift, that our sense of self-worth is no longer tied to the fortunes of athletes increasingly younger than us (younger than our children, too), and that we tire of headlines that trumpet the latest indiscretions of twenty-something professional athletes.

Age is a developmental and social construct that shapes our interests, goals, expectations, behaviors, and attitudes about our lives; we are defined, described, limited, given certain privileges and perhaps even freed by age (Atkinson, 2009). Being a sports fan – participating in sports, too – may have different meanings for young and old. Why is it, for example, that the fan base for major league baseball is aging, or at least older than the fan base for other major sports? Is it because baseball was more prominent years ago, because the game unfolds at a slower pace than sports like football, because, for older fans, it serves as a reminder of times past

(Krizek, 2002)? Just as the motivational structure for following sports varies somewhat from sport to sport, motivations for following sports – responses to sports, too – may vary by age.

As the expected lifespan for humans has increased, scholars and health practitioners (marketers, too) have paid heed to the aging process and the lives of older adults. Using an array of methods (e.g., surveys for attitudes and behaviors, fMRIs for brain activity), many have studied life satisfaction, happiness, and psychological well-being and uncovered variations – similarities, too – across age groups (Ryff, 1995; Yang, 2008). Those who study mediated sports should do the same. We need to examine how cognitive, affective, physiological, behavioral and social factors associated with the life cycle affect the arc of fanship.

Third, we should pay more attention to the social dimension of fanship. The rise and popularity of sports bars points to functions that this particular social setting serves. Eastman and Land (1997) observed and spoke with sports bar patrons who said sports bars gave them access to an important membership community and offered an opportunity for easy-to-start social interaction. Weed (2007) described English pubs as a safe venue for watching football (soccer) in the physical presence of others; that the communal experience was a critical component of patron participation and enjoyment. The social dimension of mediated sports is important for non-fans, too. Indeed, watching sports because friends or family members are watching resonates more strongly among non-fans than among fans (Gantz & Wenner, 1995). Perhaps for that reason, women are more likely to watch sports with others than are men – and when they watch with others, it's typically with men (ESPN, 2009).

Today, fans do not need to be physically alongside one another to share the experience. With digital and mobile technology, fans text and call, tweet, Facebook chat and blog – while they watch – in ways that enrich the viewing experience. What proportion of viewers engage in such behaviors and what are they like demographically and psychographically? What are those texts and calls and tweets and chats about? Are fans gloating, predicting, critiquing, complaining, commiserating – or just staying in touch, as so many college students do as soon as they step outside the classroom? And, what are the consequences of those behaviors? Do they create wider fanship networks and simultaneously infuriate those who just want to sit and watch or be done with sports when the game is over? I am comfortable with descriptive studies here – and, admittedly, elsewhere, too – although I suspect a wealth of psychological factors predict and correlate with these behaviors.

Fourth, we should pay close attention to fantasy sports. Fantasy sports draws millions of players (an estimated 27 million Americans now play annually; Fantasy Sports Trade Association, 2009), mostly fans, who enjoy the opportunity to pick a team, showcase their general manager-like sports-acumen, and perhaps win some money as well. I find two possible allegiance-related outcomes particularly interesting here. Because of vested interests, fantasy sports players may watch more sports. This seems reasonable as, collectively, these fans spend more than a billion minutes on fantasy websites (Kimball, 2008). Increased exposure to televised sports would be good for the networks as it delivers a very desirable audience: According to a fantasy sports industry group, the average fantasy sports player is an 18–49-year-old male with upscale demographic attributes (Baerg, 2009). At the same time, increased exposure sets up allegiance conflicts when one's fantasy sports players are playing against one's favorite team. In these situations, who does the fan root for and does the conflict adversely affect the entertainment value and enjoyment of the experience? Beyond that, and over the long run, I wonder if devotion to fantasy sports – and here, I am going to include video games and online massive multiplayer games – might erode fanship for one's hometown team and curtail the media use patterns – perhaps game attendance as well – associated with fanship for a team.

Fifth, we need to move away from studying college students, especially those fresh from high school who attend college on a full-time basis. I am not knocking college students. They are great fans with deep-seated and full-throttled loyalty to their institution. Scores of terrific studies have relied on their participation. Indeed, much of what we know about the correlates and consequences of fanship is based on college student samples. And, when we're studying loyalty to an institution's sports teams, we should start with this group. But, for the most part, college is an age-related cocoon, perhaps an economic one, too, that tells us little, descriptively, about the vast majority of sports spectators and fans. Do those in the work force at 18 share sports-viewing motivations, interests, and reactions with college students, or is the mediated sports experience different and functionally related to the disparate opportunities and experiences each group has? And, if there is an age-related arc to fanship, we won't capture it with those in our classes. We may do better with students attending community colleges, especially those in urban areas, as they offer a broader array of age groups and life experiences than those typically found at four-year institutions.

We are going to have to work harder to reach the sports audience and it will be more costly. Phone interviews now have very low response and completion rates although they provide access to the (adult) population at large. Relying on the Internet – and programs like Survey Monkey – help matters but recruiting participants is not easy. Here, too, I write from recent personal experience where posting messages on scores of message boards – and offering the possibility of a reward, too – led to a sample below my expectations. Rules vary across message boards; some do not permit posting requests for survey participation until the user (the researcher) has participated in current discussions. Messages also quickly move off the radar as threads evolve. To maximize exposure, requests must be re-posted – if permitted – on a near daily basis. This requires considerably more work than handing out questionnaires in class or handing off the interviewing task to survey research firms. Reliance on Internet sites and message boards also is likely to limit samples to fans – of a sport, a school, a team, a player, or a writer whose insights and opinions users enjoy. In turn, this limits generalizations and fan non-fan comparisons, although it may provide qualitative and quantitative insights that merit attention.

Sixth, we need to conduct more work in the field, be it at bars and restaurants, stadiums, homes, health and social clubs, OK, even in the dorms. Sports media content – all programming, actually – is consumed everywhere, including on the go, on second, third, and fourth screens. Nielsen now documents exposure to all four screens. We cannot beat Nielsen here but since the exposure context matters, it would be informative to learn how the sports consumption experience varies across distribution modalities. For several decades, scholars – many in psychology – have used beepers and PDAs to signal respondents throughout the day to describe what they are doing and how they are feeling. Using "the experience sampling method" where, over the course of a week, participants filled out a brief questionnaire every time they were beeped, Kubey and Csikszentmihalyi (1990) documented the television viewing experience and compared it to other routine activities. Television did not fare well on a number of measures including affect, concentration, and challenge, although many looked forward to watching TV. We could follow their lead, using texting, and capture the essence of the sports experience without the impact of memory and recall coming into play.

Seventh, we should triangulate when possible and, as appropriate, integrate qualitative and quantitative methods. I love numbers, believe in shared meanings, am comfortable generalizing from samples and overall, have a strong quantitative orientation. Yet, I recognize that numbers can fall short, especially when we move from head counts to describing the nature of the mediated sports experience. Numbers outline the skeleton. Qualitative descriptions provide bulk and resonate in ways numbers may not. Years ago, I used four methods to assess television's fit in marital life (Gantz, 2001) – a forerunner to message boards (newsgroups on Usenet), face-to-face intensive interviews, focus groups, and survey research. Survey research provided the numbers but the open-ended nature of the other methods added substance, illustrations, that were not captured on the phone. Today, perhaps wrongly, and that is a concern with qualitative data, I remember an unhappy woman's plaintive description of being deceived by her husband – she learned only after they were married that he was an avid sports fan quite happy watching sports all weekend – and need to remind myself that for most couples, conflicts about television were minor and easily resolved.

As I prepared for this chapter – and thought about the arc of fanship – I was struck by a qualitative study about University of Florida football fans, people who ranged in age from 30 to 78, people who had been following the Gators for from 7 to 51 years (Gibson, Wilming, & Holdnak, 2002). Much as politicians weave in stories of average Americans to hammer home their point about the state of our economy or health care system, Gator fan stories gave meaning to the concept of life-long fanship – and the influence of the family life cycle – in ways mean scores and standard deviations cannot. Qualitative and quantitative work can go hand in hand. Let's spend some time observing and listening and add that to what we know from the survey numbers we crunch out.

Eighth, we should encourage the sports industry to participate in collaborative research and, without jeopardizing their standing or revenue-streams, share data that academics otherwise would not have. Nielsen cannot give away its data and the networks are not likely to share proprietary insights that give them a leg up in the marketplace. But, ratings and marketing data have limited shelf life. Year-old data have little value to networks, stations, advertisers, and ad agencies as they focus and make deals based on new numbers. For academics, year-old data are almost brand new. Some marketing research corporations offer year-old data to academics at steeply discounted prices, prices institutions and individual researchers can afford to purchase. We should encourage other firms to do the same, all the while hoping for unfettered access to "old" data so academics can run correlational and regression analyses central to their research questions and hypotheses.

Beyond this, academics and sports industry personnel share an interest in understanding audience behavior. The sports industry has money, access to great data, and some really smart people, too (some from the ranks of academe). But, the insights we have, the measures and measurement tools we have created, and the research facilities we have constructed can contribute to the sports industry's understanding of their audience as we describe, explain, and predict sports fanship. Academics can, for example, encourage the use of measures that adequately tap fanship. ESPN has begun partnerships with academic institutions – e.g., with the University of Pennsylvania's Wharton School to study consumer behavior associated with global sports events such as the 2010 FIFA World Cup.

Ninth, we should continue to monitor sports content and, in doing so, gently encourage gender-, sex-, race-, and nationality-neutral coverage. This is not to say that every sport, every team, and every athlete merits equal or uncritical coverage. Far from it. But because words and images matter, because they contribute to the way we think of athletes and sports, nations too, we should continue to chart sports content – and do the same for fan-based content, likely to be far more inflammatory, especially on the web, than that offered by national, regional, and local sports organizations. Analyses of web-based content pose sampling challenges more vexing than those for traditional media, but these have been addressed elsewhere (Jordan & Manganello, 2009) and can be applied here.

Finally, and I admit this is more of an administrative than research goal, we should create an organization with an annual conference, periodic electronic newsletter, and a database open to all. Like the International Communication Association, the National Communication Association, the Association for Education in Journalism and Mass Communication and the Broadcast Education Association (these reflect my interests; I am sure I have left out other major, broad-based academic organizations relevant to sports scholars), the organization would serve as a big tent and would feature divisions that reflect the interests and epistemological sensibilities of its members. It would deliberately set up a broader base than existing organizations that focus on sports (e.g., North American Society for the Sociology of Sport). An executive committee has been formed for such an organization, so this represents a gentle nudge to go forward. All of us also would benefit from an electronic database of relevant information, perhaps including abstracts, for conference papers, research articles, monographs, and books – plus whatever reports the industry is willing to share. Because we are such an eclectic and diverse group of scholars, that database may bridge gaps, knock down some silos, and enhance our understanding of mediated sports.

That's my agenda. I hope it has given you at least a snack's worth of food for thought. There is a feast in the chapters that lie ahead. Read and enjoy.

References

Atkinson, J.L. (2009). Age matters in sport communication. *Electronic Journal of Communication,* *19*(3 & 4).

Baerg, A. (2009). Just a fantasy? Exploring fantasy sports. *Electronic Journal of Communication,* *19*(3 & 4).

Billings, A.C. (2008). *Olympic media: Inside the biggest show on television.* New York: Routledge.

Cialdini, R.B., Borden, R.J., Thorne, A., Walker, M.R., Freeman, S., & Sloan, L.R. (1976). Basking in reflected glory: 3 (football) field studies. *Journal of Personality and Social Psychology,* *34*(3), 366–75.

Dietz-Uhler, B., End, C., & Jacquemotte, L. (2000). Sex differences in sports fan behavior and reasons for being a sport fan. *Journal of Sport Behavior,* *23,* 219–31.

Duncan, M.C. (2006). Gender warriors in sport: Women and the media. In A.A. Raney & J. Bryant (Eds.), *Handbook of sports and media* (pp. 313–30). Mahwah, NJ: Lawrence Erlbaum Associates.

Eastman, S.T. & Land, A. (1997). The best of both worlds: Sports fans find good seats at the bar. *Journal of Sport & Social Issues,* *21*(2), 156–78.

ESPN. (2009). The life cycle of the sports fan – 2008.

Fantasy Sports Trade Association. (2009). Homepage. Retrieved on January 5, 2009 from www.fsta.org

Fowler, F.J. (1992). How unclear terms affect survey data. *Public Opinion Quarterly,* *56*(2), 218–31.

Gallup. (2005, February 4). Six in 10 Americans are pro-football fans. Retrieved May 20, 2010 from gallup.com/poll14812/Six-Americans-Pro-Football-Fans.aspx

Gantz, W. (2001). Conflicts and resolution strategies associated with television in marital life. In J. Bryant & J.A. Bryant (Eds.), *Television and the American family* (2nd Ed., pp. 289–316). Mahwah, NJ: Lawrence Erlbaum Associates.

Gantz, W. & Wenner, L.A. (1995). Fanship and the television sports viewing experience. *Sociology of Sport Journal,* *12*(1), 56–74.

Gantz, W., Wilson, B., Lee, H., & Fingerhut, D. (2008). Exploring the roots of sports fanship. In L.W. Hugenberg, P.M. Haridakis & A.C. Earnheardt (Eds.), *Sports mania* (pp. 63–77). Jefferson, NC: McFarland & Company.

Gibson, H., Wilming, C., & Holdnak, A. (2002). "We're Gators … not just Gator fans": Serious leisure and University of Florida football. *Journal of Leisure Research,* *34*(4), 397–425.

Grainger, A., Newman, J.I., & Andrews, D.L. (2006). Sport, the media, and the construction of race. In A.A. Raney & J. Bryant (Eds.), *Handbook of sports and media* (pp. 447–68). Mahwah, NJ: Lawrence Erlbaum Associates.

Grant, R.R., Leadley, J., & Zygmont, Z.X. (2008). *The economics of intercollegiate sports.* Singapore and Hackensack, NJ: World Scientific.

Gratton, C. & Solberg, H.A. (2007). *The economics of sports broadcasting.* London and New York: Routledge.

Hirt, E.R., Zillmann, D., Erickson, G.A., & Kennedy, C. (1992). Costs and benefits of allegiance: Changes in fans' self-ascribed competences after team victory versus defeat. *Journal of Personality and Social Psychology,* *63*(5), 724–38.

Hundley, H.L. & Billings, A.C. (2010). *Examining identity in sports media*. Los Angeles: Sage Publications.

Jordan, A.B. & Manganello, J. (2009). Sampling and content analysis: An overview of the issues. In A.B. Jordan, D. Kunkel, J. Manganello & M. Fishbein (Eds.), *Media messages and public health* (pp. 67–87). New York: Routledge.

Kimball, B. (2008, December 22). Growing interest in make-believe. *USA Today*.

Krizek, B. (2002). The grayer side of the game: Baseball and the "older" fan. In G. Gumpert & J. Drucker (Eds.), *Take me out to the ballgame: Communicating baseball* (pp. 401–28). Cresskill, NJ: Hampton Press.

Kubey, R.W. & Csikszentmihalyi, M. (1990). *Television and the quality of life: How viewing shapes everyday experience*. Hillsdale, NJ: Lawrence Erlbaum Associates.

Master, S. (2009, December 18). The world is watching more than ever. *Nielsenwire*. Retrieved May 20, 2010 from nielsen.com/nielsenwire/consumer/game-on-the-world-is-watching-more-than-ever/

Nielsen. (2010). *Three screen report*.

Raney, A.A. (2006). Why we watch and enjoy sports. In A.A. Raney & J. Bryant (Eds.), *Handbook of sports and media* (pp. 313–30). Mahwah, NJ: Lawrence Erlbaum Associates.

Ryff, C.D. (1995). Psychological well-being in adult life. *Current Directions in Psychological Science, 4*(4), 99–104.

Sperber, M.A. (2000). *Beer and circus: How big-time college sports is crippling undergraduate education* (1st Ed.). New York: H. Holt.

Sutton, W.A., McDonald, M.A., Miline, G., & Cimperman, J. (1997). Getting and fostering fan identification in professional sports. *Sports Marketing Quarterly, 6*, 15–22.

Wann, D.L. (2002). Preliminary validation of a measure for assessing identification as a sport fan: The sport fandom questionnaire. *International Journal of Sport Management, 3*, 103–15.

Wann, D.L. (2006). The causes and consequences of sport team identification. In A.A. Raney & J. Bryant (Eds.), *Handbook of sports and media* (pp. 331–52). Mahwah, NJ: Lawrence Erlbaum Associates.

Wann, D.L. & Branscombe, N.R. (1990). Die-hard and fair-weather fans: Effects of identification on BIRGing and CORFing tendencies. *Journal of Sport & Social Issues, 14*(2), 103–17.

Wann, D.L., Friedman, K., McHale, M., & Jaffe, A. (2003). The Norelco sports fanatics survey: Examining behaviors of sports fans. *Psychological Reports, 92*, 930–36.

Wann, D.L., Koch, K., Knoth, T., Fox, D., Aljubaily, H., & Lantz, C.D. (2006). The impact of team identification on biased predictions of player performance. *Psychological Record, 56*(1), 55–66.

Weed, M. (2007). The pub as a virtual football fandom venue: An alternative to "Being there." *Soccer & Society, 8*(2/3), 399–414.

Wenner, L.A. (1989). Media, sports, and society: The research agenda. In L.A. Wenner (Ed.), *Media, sports, and society* (pp. 13–48). Newbury Park, CA: Sage.

Wenner, L.A. (Ed.). (1998). *MediaSport*. New York: Routledge.

Yang, Y. (2008). Social inequalities in happiness in the United States, 1972 to 2004: An age-period-cohort analysis. *American Sociological Review, 73*(2), 204–26.

Zillmann, D., Bryant, J., & Sapolsky, B. (1979). The enjoyment of watching sports contests. In J.H. Goldstein (Ed.), *Sports, games, and play: Social and psychological viewpoints* (2nd Ed., pp. 241–78). Hillsdale, NJ: Lawrence Erlbaum Associates.

Zimbalist, A.S. (1999). *Unpaid professionals: Commercialism and conflict in big-time college sports*. Princeton, NJ: Princeton University Press.

2

THEORIZING THE SPORTS–TELEVISION DREAM MARRIAGE

Why sports fit television so well

Michael Real

ROYAL ROADS UNIVERSITY

For more than 50 years, television has been the primary vehicle through which Americans and much of the world access sports events. During this period, both television and sports have grown continuously in size and influence – expanding their audiences, increasing their profits, and occupying a central position within culture and society (Real, 2005). What are the formal elements that constitute television that map so closely with the elements that constitute sports events? Formal theories of what makes television *"television"* work from concepts of light, movement, and sound often combined with concepts of liveness, narrative structure, genre conventions, and the pleasure of the text. Even within the new mix of digital media, television retains its primacy in American lives, with Nielsen (Petterle, 2009) reporting increases in hours of television viewing along with increased DVR and online access. From the beginning, sports have seemed a perfect match for television. What do we find when we deconstruct the components of this arranged marriage?

Sports exemplify the central concepts of television theory

Television as "light"

In developing his theory of television phenomenology, Paddy Scannell (2009) asks the question: What is present when a television is flipped on that is not present when it is off? One obvious difference is the presence of the lighted television picture, a visible difference. Sports, because they are bodily activities, are distinctly visual and visible. A tennis serve, a diving catch, a pinpoint pass, breaking the tape, sinking an undulating putt – all are physical activities that can be watched. The light of the television picture reproduces these physical acts, instantly and at a distance. It is a dream come true for the sports fan who cannot be physically present at an event; the event comes to him or her through the light of the television screen. Unlike a written version of the event, even online, television brings the event simultaneously to the viewer, usually in real time. Unlike radio, it is multisensory in reaching the eye as well as the ear and enriching the sense of witnessing, understanding, and feeling the physical reality of what is going on.

Television and "movement"

As an art form, television contrasts with photography, painting, sculpture, architecture, and the plastic arts by capturing and transmitting motion, the actual movement of human bodies. The image is not static but dynamic, as in theater or film, allowing the viewer to access exactly how the athlete moves, turns, stretches, and interacts with others. As aesthetically pleasing as they are, the classic Greek statue of the discus thrower or the 1924 George Bellows painting of Jack Dempsey boxing against Luis Angel Firpo can only suggest but not include movement. The movement of race cars, basketball players, and all sports is captured and transmitted with complexity and fluidity by the light of the television picture.

Television and "sound"

Heightening the realism of television's representation is the quality of sound that both reproduces the original crack of the bat, grunt of the tennis player, or ping of the club on the golf ball, and lays on additional levels of sound both diagetic as in natural crowd noise and non-diagetic as in announcer comments and musical enhancements. NBC's famous 1980 experiment of a Jets–Dolphins telecast without announcers has never been repeated, despite the praise of some football and television purists (Hollander, 2008). The international television feed of Olympic events provides the natural sound from the venue, but the national services that purchase and distribute the feed add their own announcers. (This announcer-free version of some Olympic events is available on the IOC website.) Television's ability to transmit visual and auditory signals completes the sensation of being present at the game, even as it adds layers of graphics, interpretation, and commodification.

The power of "liveness"

Early television writers were taken by television's ability to transmit live events. In 1956, *New York Times* TV critic Jack Gould famously praised the liveness of television:

> Live television ... bridges the gap instantly and unites the individual at home with the event afar. The viewer has a chance to be in two places at once.

Physically, he may be at his own hearthside but intellectually and, above all, emotionally, he is at the cameraman's side.

(cited in Corner, 1999, p. 26)

Until Ampex developed the first video recorder in 1956, television was only either live or on celluloid film, with its "liveness" setting it apart from the movies and previous moving image technology. Like radio, television takes the audience to the event as it happens. But unlike radio's verbal description of the event, television enables the audience to visually witness the event itself. The television image has a reality of its own, an ontological character, but it is directly related to what it depicts – the spinning skater, the leaping rebounder, the diver in midair. As Gould noted, live television makes the viewer present at the event as it happens. Each televised World Series game in the first decade of mass television, the 1950s, brought millions of Americans into Yankee Stadium and other parks in ways never before possible. Even with today's 24/7 news cycles, liveness and immediacy remain important. The Olympics suffer a significant drop in American television ratings and rights fees because of the time delay whenever they take place in a distant time zone in Asia or Europe rather than North America. NBC sports producers found the 15–18 hour delay in broadcasting the 2000 Sydney Olympics prevented the enormous ratings they had hoped for (Billings, 2008, p. 52). For sports fans, liveness matters.

"Suspense" and open-ended drama

Essential to the demand for live viewing of sports events is the open-ended dramatic, narrative sequence of the event. Most of television programming is scripted and recorded in advance, with the ending predetermined by the script and known to those producing it. Today's reality TV programming is a controversial mix of scripting and unknown endings as in the live competitions for *American Idol* and *Dancing with the Stars*. Sports are the quintessential "reality TV" in that they are unscripted and are acted out in real time by people who by their actions actually determine the outcome. Sports are, in fact, more "real" than many types of reality programming because the sporting event is not created only for television and has an existence prior to its being televised, unlike a group of strangers assembled on a remote island for videotaped survivor exercises. The dynamics and outcome of a sporting event are not determined by scriptwriters and producers. No one knows in advance who will win the Super Bowl, not even the players and coaches, even though the two weeks preceding it are filled with endless prognostication. This quality of sports television more recently has been labeled the "suspense" factor and has been the subject of empirical studies by Zillman (1996), Bryant and Raney (2000), Raney (2003), and others (e.g., see Westerwick et al. 2009). The uncertainty of the outcome combines with a negative psychological affect in the fear of loss and a positive affect in the hope of victory, making live sports drama a powerfully emotional television experience, just as Gould noted more than a half century ago.

The "intimacy" of television

Early television theorists were forced to confront the reduction in live programming as 1960s hit shows featured filmed dramas (*Bonanza*) and heavily edited comedies (*Laugh-In*). In addition to liveness, theorists began to distinguish television, from cinema in particular, by noting how small the television screen was and how domestic most viewing sites were, both in sharp contrast to the movie theater. Newcomb's (1974) pioneering work, *TV: the Most Popular Art* called this quality of television "intimacy" and argued that it, along with television's unique qualities of "continuity" and "formulaic" history, more accurately defined television whether live or recorded: "The smallness of the television screen has always been its most noticeable physical feature. ... Such smallness suits television for intimacy; its presence brings people into the viewer's home to act out dramas" (Newcomb, 1974, p. 245) In recent years, Amanda Lotz has argued for the continued relevance of Newcomb's insights. She writes (2007, p. 256): "The same aesthetic elements Newcomb outlines continue to characterize television story-telling – and in some cases are even more pronounced now." As we show below, increased screen size has not eliminated television's essential continuity and formulaic historicity; even television's intimacy can be rediscovered on the small screens of mobile devices.

Intimacy, it might be argued, is not generally a quality of large-scale spectator sports. But led by Roone Arledge, television in the 1960s confronted this challenge. Arledge was dedicated to moving beyond the few fixed cameras that gave comprehensive but unexciting views of sporting events. Boxing and wrestling had become popular in the first decade of television at least partially because they were intimate – two men fighting in a closed space – and easy to follow on the small screen. In a long memo for ABC, Arledge (2003, pp. 30–31) pitched how more complex sports could be done better, specifically college football.

> We will utilize every production technique that has been learned in producing variety shows, in covering political conventions, in shooting travel and adventure series to heighten the viewer's feeling of actually sitting in the stands and participating personally in the excitement and color of walking through a college campus to the stadium to watch the big game.
>
> ... In addition to our fixed cameras we will have cameras mounted in Jeeps, on mike booms, in risers or helicopters, or anything necessary to get the complete story of the game ... all the excitement, wonder, jubilation, and despair that make this America's number one sports spectacle, and a human drama to match bullfights and heavyweight championships in intensity.
>
> In short – WE ARE GOING TO ADD SHOW BUSINESS TO SPORTS!
>
> (*Emphasis in original*)

Turning the tension between intimacy and spectacle into a strength, Arledge personalized the sport viewing experience even as he vastly expanded its technology and reach. Games played before millions on television nevertheless feature profiles of the personal lives of participants, slow-motion close-up replay of action, and insider discussions of action and strategy, often by former players and coaches. Today one of the most personalized, "intimate" expressions of fandom is the fantasy league, an involving and immersive blend of interactive digital technology within the context of television coverage of the events (PRWeb, 2008).

"Continuity" in television content

Newcomb's concept of television's "continuity" also fit sports especially well. Films, despite frequent sequels, are usually a one-off affair. In contrast, television thrives on the series, the recurring weekly program. One setting, whether domestic (*I Love Lucy*), work (*The Mary Tyler Moore Show*), or exotic (*Star Trek*), a stable cast, a regular time slot, a faithful audience – continuity became the bread and butter of television profits in the network era. Continuity enhances intimacy. Newcomb (p. 253) noted: "The sort of intimacy described here creates the possibility for a much stronger sense of audience involvement, a sense of becoming a part of the lives and actions of the characters they see. ... made possible by the creation of continued series."

What could more closely parallel the loyalty of a sports fan to a team or player or even a given sport than the idea of "continuity," of involvement that joins the lives and actions of the fan with the lives and actions of the athletes? Today fans can experience an intimate, informed continuity with their favorites even if they live on a different continent; "moving images meet de-territorialized viewers" (Appadurai, 1996, p. 4) in fans' connection to a geographically distant sports team. Television enables fans dispersed across a continent to buy or access a satellite or cable package which, combined with online access to team and player information as well as reporter and fan comments, ensures a complete continuity in their intimate identification with their team.

Television's formulaic use of history

From a shared history, collective memory creates a set of widely shared expectations. These we call formulas, or as Newcomb (1974) writes, "The television formula requires that we use our contemporary concerns as subject matter" (p. 258). But television formulas draw heavily on the past for answers to the present, especially the past as popularly remembered. History, tradition, and inherited know-how become the reassuring staple of television series and formulas. Before television, spectator sports were experienced through live attendance at sporting events and their recounting in radio and newspapers. But the televised version eventually became the official version, the remembered account of American sports, the for-mulaic history. The remembered past of a sports aficionado may be punctuated with a photograph, perhaps sprinter Usain Bolt breaking the tape or soccer player Brandy Chastain kneeling in triumph. But the bulk of sports memory today is of the television version. We remember the last six decades of sports through the filters of television formulas and historical contextualizing.

Just as television formulas reflect a "mythology" of domestic bliss in American homes, of frontier freedom, of the all-powerful crime fighter, so do television sports celebrate a historical mythology of Joe Montana in the Super Bowl, Michael Jordan in the championship final, Billy Jean King defeating Bobby Riggs, Willie Mays racing deep into the 480-foot center field at the Polo Grounds to catch Vic Wertz's drive and then whirl around to throw a strike to the infield. Every sporting event resides within a deep reservoir of historical facts and mythologies, a well from which players, announcers, and fans can pull up great performances and powerful narratives. When *Sunday Night Football* is the second-highest rated program of the fall 2009 television season, between *NCIS* and *Dancing with the Stars* (Reiter, 2009), when the Super Bowl is the number one annual spectacle in America and when televised sports stars command $100 million-plus multi-year contracts, there can be no doubt that the intimacy and continuity of narratives and mythologies of sport lie close to the heart of the American psyche.

The television "image" and editing

Initially, the television image was considered remarkable because it could reproduce at a distance the objects and movement within the physical world. But, because the television image also has a reality of its own, as noted above, that image can be manipulated, modified, and reproduced in endlessly different forms. Television editing moved the image from direct reproduction to highly manipulated versions as the medium matured toward today's fast-paced, heavily cut and edited images with super-imposed data and graphics together with insertions of frequent replays and modified images. Sports offer a satisfying playing field for such manipulations, with the inter-relationships, associations, and connections within a contest, between contests, and between the contest and external materials, including promos and commercials, all waiting to be juxtaposed with each other. Also, this television image, unlike film or print, supports a direct form of address that works well for sports: "Let's go down on the sideline with Pam Oliver"; "Watch how the tight end seals off the outside in this replay." Such address adds an additional layer of connectivity, intimacy, and continuity to the live and edited imagery.

Television's text, intertextuality, and the politics of representation

Television program versus television "text"

Stuart Hall (1973/1980), John Fiske (1987) and many since have stressed the importance of distinguishing the television program that is produced from the television text that is "read" by the viewer. The produced program is a document that presents, that makes available, organized images and sounds to the viewer. It becomes a television "text" when it is viewed, when its latent meanings are activated, expanded upon, even opposed by the "reader." The program is static; the text dynamic. Nothing illustrates this better than the viewing of televised sports. Even the seemingly passive viewer, the couch potato, carries on internal monologues with the game: "Hmm, what a clever play … oops, bad call … ow, great hit." The involved sports fan becomes a hyperactive reader of the text, yelling at the screen, arguing with coaches and officials, complaining about the announcers, agonizing over the suspense, directly influenced by the manner of presentation (see Zillman, 1996; Bryant, Zillmann, & Raney, 1998; Bryant & Raney, 2000; Raney, 2003). In the process of making meaning in the reading of television, the viewer experiences the rich polysemy and intertextuality of the text.

Reading the "polysemic" television text

Reception theorists (Fiske, 1987; Morley, 2004) argue that there is no one meaning or canonical reading in a text. Texts are, instead, polysemic (literally "many signs"). Barthes (1977) called this "the death of the author" because no one, not even its creator, has a monopoly on what a text can mean to a reader. "Meaning" is realized only when the socially situated viewer makes it, in interaction with the text. An Alabama fan will realize a quite different reading than will a Florida fan for the same title game, in terms of both meaning (polysemy) and evaluation (polyvalence).

The way the reader "fills gaps" in the text will vary with culture, group experiences, and individual psychology, and falls into three categories. First, "text-activated" reading, favored by Metz (1974), Eco (1970), and the semiologists, sees the signs and codes within the text as dominating the reader's interpretation. Second, "reader-activated" reading, in the New Criticism of Stanley Fish (1980), places the personal concerns of the reader ahead of anything in the text. Finally, "context-activated" reading, preferred by many television scholars (Fiske, 1987; Harris & Alexander, 1998; Abelman & Atkin, 2002; Wilson, 2004; Sandvoss, 2005; Gray, Sandvoss, & Harrington, 2007), sees both text and reader as proactive in determining the meaning realized from a text. It is not too difficult to see print journalists inclining toward the more cautious and public text-activated readings, while sports talk shows lean toward the more subjective reader-activated readings and the rest of us wander among the three in varying circumstances. It is also easy to find Hall's (1980) preferred, negotiated, and oppositional readings in a sports fan's response to the text of a game. One of the most important consequences of accepting texts as polysemic is the resulting ability to employ intertextuality in their reading.

"Intertextuality" and television

"Intertextuality" is the term coined by Julia Kristeva (1973, 1980) to account for how texts draw their meanings from other texts. The television viewer has a range of pre-existing textual knowledge that he or she brings to bear on the immediate television text. For example, confronted by "skicross" racing for the first time in the Olympics in the 2010 Vancouver Games, the viewer makes meaning by calling up knowledge of similar texts. The obvious intertextual reference in this case is to snowboardcross, which is, like skicross, also a four-person side-by-side racing event, one introduced in the 2006 Olympics. But another type of viewer will call up a different intertextual reference, one to motocross bike racing texts, and yet another type will draw on Alpine downhill competitions, speedskating, or even running races. The sports fan has a vast range of intertextual knowledge to call on, texts visualizing past games or performances, texts of statistics and data, texts of an individual or team history, texts of an opponent's roster and history, and so on. Intertextuality makes each specific televison sports text "resonate" through association with innumerable other texts. The non-fan finds the same text flat because it evokes no intertextual resonance for him or her.

Fiske (1987) distinguishes *primary* intertextuality in which texts link through genre, character, or content. Sports are a genre in television, but each sport is also rich with its own primary intertextual links in content, whether volleyball, soccer or triathlon. Sports superstars provide primary intertextuality, links familiar to many because of saturation television coverage. *Secondary* intertextuality applies to texts that intentionally refer to the primary text, as in sports promos or Sports Center highlights. *Tertiary* intertextuality is the rapidly expanding world of texts produced by the viewers themselves either online or in conversation. In the age of the Internet, tertiary texts are widely circulated and form a collective form of response and feedback, often taken seriously by producers of the primary text.

Here again, in the concepts of gap-filling polysemy and first, second, and third degree intertextuality, we find television theory vividly illustrated in the experience of televised sports viewers. What critics – and sometimes family members – describe as over-developed knowledge and concern by the sports fan creates what television theory identifies as polysemy and intertextuality, a rich contextual embedding which greatly enhances the television sport experience, in a self-reinforcing cycle.

The politics of "representation"

Television representation evokes controversy because of the complex relationship between the television program and the real world outside of television. Does television representation provide an accurate picture of women, children, ethnic groups, political factions, occupations, or regions of the nation and the world? Jonathan Bignell (2004) asks three questions of television representation.

- Who makes the representation?
- Who and what is represented and in what ways?
- How do audiences respond?

Sports pose a special challenge because the usual journalistic rules of balance and fairness are often in abeyance. Sports fans and their journalists are permitted to be "homers." The astute fan, for example, may listen to the local radio broadcast while watching the only-available television feed from a national network precisely because the local broadcaster can express bias and will interpret the sports text in the partisan local version.

"Codes and conventions" of representation

"Codes and conventions" organize the sign systems of television and are constituents of television's politics of representation (Fiske, 1987). A *code* is the system of signs agreed upon by the members of a culture – the English language, highway signs, law enforcement and courts. A *convention* is a widely accepted social or textual practice that employs coding in a customary way. The sequencing of commercials, station breaks, the sporting event itself, breaks in the game, cross-promotions, and other materials is a convention completely familiar to the sports fan. In fact, the regular breaks in sports action conveniently enable placement of commercials and promotional materials. In this context, is it possible that the failure of soccer to capture the American public, alone in the world, is that its continuous 45 minutes of action in each period are irreconcilable with the financially mandatory American commercial breaks? The codes and conventions of television translate the external world into the television world, blending reality, representation, and ideology, in the view of Fiske (1987). American television viewing operates within the ideo-logical conventions of individualism, competition, patriarchy, consumerism, capital-ism, materialism, militarism, and other consensus deep-structure American ideologies and values. These ideological sets are not antithetical to sports, although sports can operate within quite different ideologies. But these seven ideological values and other related ones are provocatively activated by and celebrated within the American version of what David Rowe, in this book, calls the media sports cultural complex.

Representation and "absence"

Theorists of the politics of television representation find gaps, inconsistencies, errors, and distortions in the picture that television proposes. Television reality is not actual reality, as Gerbner's cultivation theory (Morgan, 2002) has spelled out. Crime and violence occur much less often in American reality than they do in American television, but the heavy viewer comes to accept the simpler, clearer, and more dramatic "mean world" as that of society as well as television. Television may, representa-tionally, "over-determine" reality; that is, it may make of a complex, subtle social world a black–and–white world of obvious rights and wrongs. The sports viewer a thousand miles away can believe his or her reading of a controversial call is more accurate than that of the referee or umpire within feet of the event. Stuart Hall notes that representation is constitutive, not reflective, and the challenge is to unpack the codes and conventions, get inside them, interrogate them. The British authors of *Television Studies: The Key Concepts* (Casey et al., 2002, p. 200) note the socio-political origins of television's representational practices:

> This issue of point of view and identification also links back to questions of power and therefore ideology. It raises the question: who has the right to speak? And who is silenced in these representations? The important point here is that representations are produced and circulate within a context of meanings (such as "common sense") but this is governed by a system of power, offering legitimacy to some meanings and marginalizing others.

The world of television sports, as large as it is, is not necessarily comprehensive or balanced relative to the actual world of sports or, most notably, to the society in which both reside. It took years for NCAA women's basketball to receive even minor coverage while the men's game basked in television glory. Sports like lacrosse, rugby, curling, and darts, had to await the arrival of 100-channel systems before they found even the slightest representation on television. Their followings may be small compared to major sports, but in the world of television representation they did not exist at all.

(Mis)representing sex, race, and class

Gender and race raise especially complex questions in terms of television representation, specifically in terms of "absence." British television theorist Nick Couldry (2003, p. 143) zeroes in on this in warning: "Media studies must face up to the long-term consequences of an entrenched politics of absence, the absence of most people from the process of representing whatever worlds we share." What does it suggest about America and its television system when the number one spectacle of the country is an all-male event? Women do not play in the Super Bowl or even in the sport it celebrates, with only tiny exceptions. Feminists may respond in varied ways to this, as Marie Hardin explains in her chapter in this book, but female absences are as troubling as stereotypes within the media sports cultural complex. Both television and sports are complicit in representing and celebrating a world in which there are many noteworthy absences.

Questions raised decades ago about the Super Bowl's gender and racial bias (Real, 1975) remain significant within the politics of television representation. African-American males are very over-represented in college and NFL football, NBA and college basketball, and boxing, as well as some other sports. Does this mean real-world across-the-board minority opportunity has won the day in the world outside sports? Against that, recall that the same demographic group is hugely over-represented in America's prison populations and in overall unemployment. The exaggerated presence of African-American males in specific social categories and television representations points more to a pathology of limited opportunities than a success story. Just as the "politics of representation" confronts television theorists with profound questions, so it also challenges sports sociologists and theorists.

Once again, but this time more sadly, the maps of television theory and sports match up with striking similarities.

Absences in television globally

"Information gap" theory applies to television as well as other media in distinguishing between the information rich (who have access to newer technologies and know how to benefit from them), and the information poor (who lack technologies and the know-how associated with them). This information/knowledge/media gap exists within countries but also between different countries and regions of the world. Straubhaar (2007, p. 16) calls this "assymetrical interdependence" in which countries have variable but unequal degrees of power and initiative.

Because of this gap, one finds major absences in even the most international sports events. The Olympics, with notable exceptions, celebrate the success of rich nations and the absence of poor nations. For every Nepalese or Kenyan medal there are dozens of golds for nations affluent enough to provide advanced sports facilities, world class coaching, athlete subsidies, travel to international competitions, and all the other expensive prerequisites to Olympic success. Much of the developing world has never heard of the Winter Olympics, much less participated in them.[1] Largely absent from the Olympics and most of the media sport cultural complex are the majority on the African continent, most of the Muslim world, large urban and rural under-classes in Latin America, sections of Asia, and many other major population segments around the world. Group viewing of World Cup matches and increasing affluence in China and India soften somewhat the global gap between haves and have nots, but even the universality of soccer cannot alone mend the gap or overcome the absences. The one-way flow of television and information from privileged centers to marginalized peripheries (Nordenstreng & Varis, 1974; Guback & Varis, 1986) provides a wide range of televised sport choices in the center but far fewer on the periphery. A spiral of silence about these gaps, absences, and inequalities reflects McChesney's thesis on the absence of media self-criticism in *Rich Media, Poor Democracy* (1999). Given the many absences, television theories of the politics of representation point to numerous inequalities in the media sport cultural complex.

Narrative structure and the pleasure of the text in television

"Narrativity" in television

Narrative lies at the heart of history and cultural identity. Narrative is as universal as human language. Fiske (1987) notes that it comes as no surprise that television is predominantly narrative in content. As Roland Barthes (1977, p. 79) wrote:

> The narratives of the world are numberless. Narrative is first and foremost a prodigious variety of genres. ... Narrative is present in every age, in every

place, in every society; it begins with the very history of mankind and there nowhere is nor has been a people without narrative. All classes, all human groups, have their narratives. … Narrative is international, transhistorical, transcultural; it is simply there, like life itself.

Because the structure of a sporting event is essentially narrative, with a beginning, plot complications, and resolution, it feeds television's insatiable hunger for narratives.

"Plot" versus "narration"

Narrative theory distinguishes plot, which is the content of a story, from narration, which is the manner of telling the story. In this sense, the sports event is the plot and the television presentation is the narration. Studies by Zillman, Bryant, and various co-authors on the importance of television commentary illustrate how television's narration takes us well beyond the plot within the sports event. Arledge's innovations in sports television sought to maximize the power of narration without ignoring the plot, the competition itself. A sports television fan may experience frustration attending a live event because it lacks the television narration of announcers, statistics, replays, multiple viewpoints, and more. Taking portable electronic devices to the game is an effort to compensate for this, as is the addition of jumbotrons in stadiums.

"Enigma, delay, and resolution" in narrative

The structure of sporting competition follows the three stages of the narrative hermeneutic code identified by Barthes (1974): enigma, delay, resolution. The "enigma" prompts us to ask a question. What athlete or team will win today? What individuals will perform best or disappoint? The "delay" works to sustain our interest through plot complications and suspense-building narration. Can this team come back from this far behind? Will the star return to the game after an injury? What strategy and tactics do specific situations call for? The delay plays with our fears and hopes and offers frustrating detours and dilemmas, but all are essential to enjoying narrative. The "resolution" completes the narrative by bringing dramatic closure. The resolution resolves the curiosity aroused by the enigma and satisfies the complications from the delay. Casey et al. (2002, p. 141) note "television coverage of sporting events relies a great deal" upon this sequence of enigma, delay, and resolution.

But there is not only one sequence of enigma, delay, and resolution in a narrative; there are also many small narratives within each larger narrative. Each inning, each at-bat is a dramatic narrative as well, with enigmas, delays, and resolutions. The television series extends narratives across an entire season, and sports do the same. One can also find in the sporting event all seven of Butler's (2007) expanded list of television's narrative components: protagonist, exposition, motivation, problematic, cause–effect chain, climax, and resolution/denouement. Because sports events come with a dramatic plot structure built into them, they perfectly fulfill television's demand for narrative content.

"Reassurance, identification, and agency" in television narrative

Television narratives offer three rewards to the viewer. There is "reassurance" in the sense-making that the story provides in making the links between events appear meaningful and understandable (Fiske, 1987, p. 129). Narrative sequencing affirms that people, places, and actions are not random or anarchic but make sense. Characters and activities are placed in a cause-and-effect relationship that propels the story and ends in closure. The actions within athletic competition carry the same structural elements. If your favored athlete or team plays better than the opponent and does not suffer bad luck, you will experience vicarious victory. The victory comes in a meaningful sequence in which actions lead to results and finally to closure. The gratification of reassurance that patterned television narrative offers is already present in the sporting competition.

The second reward is psychological "identification" with television's characters and narratives (Fiske, 1987, p. 169). On the engagement side, we project ourselves into what we are viewing and, on the distancing side, we know that we are distinct from it; it is the vicarious participation that narratives draw us into. This is what Horton and Wohl (1956) famously explained as the parasocial interaction that media can provide. In the process of psychological identification, an individual merges aspects of his or her own identity with those of the characters in the story. Once again, we see in sports a dynamic exactly parallel to that of television. The spectator in sports, whether fanatic or casual, merges his or her personal hopes and fears with those of the competitors. This accounts for the affective reaction studied by social psychologists, including the noxious reaction described by Zillman (1996, p. 208) as "fearful apprehension about deplorable events that threaten."

The third reward for the active reader of television is "agency" (Staiger, 2005, p. 7), which is not automatic but rather achieved by taking control of the viewing experience. The viewer goes beyond the content of the program and reads the text in distinctive, even resistant, ways, as described above in reference to reception theory. In the process of active viewing, one achieves agency through reading beyond the given text. The viewer recalls the actual historical context of a docudrama or connects a comedian's routine to current politics, accurately or not. The sports spectator has always been inclined this way, long before television. Sport fan agency is achieved by going beyond passive absorption of the event and engaging in active interpretations, emotions, and responses. The reassurance of sense-making structures, the psychological identification with actors and action, and the agency achieved by active viewing all serve to unite effectively the television viewer and the sports spectator into a single doubly participating subject. The sport and television narrative – each operating on the same principles – interact to enhance each other.

"The pleasure of the text"

Bypassing debates over audience media effects and viewer gratifications, it was once again Roland Barthes (1975) who coined the memorable motivational phrase "the pleasure of the text." Fiske (1987) employed this concept in labeling television a "producerly" medium because the viewer produces meaning from the text, completing the process begun by the producer (in contrast to film where the director is dominant) in making the program. Producerly activity is stimulating and rewarding. Pleasure arises in the power to make meanings, especially meanings which do not come obviously from the program. The viewer achieves agency and experiences power, control, and satisfaction in the viewing experience, in short, the pleasure of the text.

Here, as in so many dimensions of television theory, the experience of televised sport exactly matches what television itself does. The fan finds pleasure in the text or he or she would not keep coming back. The Arledge slogan for *Wide World of Sports*, written on a plane flight, "the thrill of victory – the agony of defeat" summarizes the emotional power of combining sports and television. Sports fans come in all varieties – masochists, ecstatics, belligerents, technicians, gripers, delusionals – but all somehow find pleasure in the text.

"Commodification" and television

Political economy, by examining the economics, structures, and decision-making within the television industry (McChesney, 2008), has indirectly contributed to theories of television's formal elements as well. Because television in America has been primarily a commercial industry, television's form is employed to generate audiences, ratings, and profit. This means that, in addition to ensuring the frequent insertion of commercials, television's imagery and narratives are suffused with promotional and self-promotional qualities. The intrusive omnipresence of logos, brands, products, and pitches marks the commodification of television. Commodification restricts the purpose of an object or act to its monetary exchange value, shorn of any historical, artistic, or relational value. At the same time, inducements to purchase add a fetishistic quality to the goods or services, extending their attraction with magical, compelling associations. As commercial television has extended its presence around the world, it has become a fundamental contributor to and expression of what Jameson (1992) calls the postmodern condition of late capitalism.

As sports have become more integrated with television, sports have also proven to be fertile ground for commodification. Naming rights for stadiums, exclusive athletic shoe or sponsor contracts for athletes and teams, brand names for college football bowl games, the selling of every component of major events from coin toss to background signage, and many other commercial extensions distinguish sport in the age of television as a site of entertainment, consumption, commodification, and ideological legitimization (see, for example, Butterworth & Moskal, 2009). The history of the modern Olympic Games illustrates this. In the 1960s, television became the vehicle through which the world public accessed the Olympics; by the 1980s, television rights fees had become the single largest source of funding for the Games; also in the 1980s, the IOC created the TOP program to sell sponsorships of the Games, a program which soon matched television rights for Olympic income. The Olympics became a financial bonanza of sponsorship and commodification (Real, 1996a, 1996b). Before television, an Olympic star might make the cover of a Wheaties cereal box. Today, a Michael Phelps becomes a virtual brand and industry in his own right.

Television commodifies every aspect of itself, but sports bring added value. The athletes and competitions exist on their own before and outside of television, unlike drama or comedy with stars whose success and fame occur only within entertainment media. The athletic achievements of a Derek Jeter or Tiger Woods give added weight to their role as celebrity endorsers. The fact that most young people play a number of sports and identify with them gives added impact to the product or brand that associates itself with sports. Sports also serve very conveniently to meet the demographic audience targets of television. The demographics of viewers of curling contrast with those of the Ultimate Fighting Championship or World Wrestling Entertainment, and advertisers can target commercials to either to make their purchase of time more efficient.

The changing aesthetics of television in the digital era

Digital technology has the potential to change television in ways more profound than we can possibly identify at this time. David Rowe, in his chapter in this book, examines this. The conversion to digital television in America in 2009 seems already to have affected sports. Dick Ebersol, chairman of NBC Universal Sports & Olympics, credits high definition (HD) television with increasing the ratings of televised football. With HD in roughly half of U.S. households, average NFL audiences were 13% higher in 2009 than 2008, and college ratings also climbed. Ebersol says, "In football HD is just so much more effective, particularly in [visually] setting up the play before it starts" (Friedman, 2009). The 2010 Super Bowl drew the largest audience ever, 106.5 million, for an American television program (Nielsenwire, 2010). But the changing place of television within the digital multi-media mix will inexorably affect where we watch it, what we watch, from where we obtain it, with whom we watch, how we mix television with other media, and what we create with television beyond watching.

Television has been a dominant and stand-alone medium until now. It has been the classic "lean back" technology, often viewed from a couch or even recliner, in contrast to the "lean forward" technology of the computer. At the end of the first decade of this century, Nielsen (Petterle, 2009) reminded us that almost 99% of video content watched in America is still done on traditional television, even with steady increases in online and mobile video watching. Sports fans may supplement the televised game by tracking live information online, but they still follow the televised version. Television's original functions and role are shifting as the medium becomes a more integrated piece within a larger system. But, as David Thorburn and Henry Jenkins (2003, p. 12) remind us, "The process of media transition is always a mix of tradition and innovation, always declaring for evolution, not revolution."

Television "aesthetics"

Aesthetic theories of television remind us of its basis in light and movement but also its social function of providing access to the world, access that is motivated by our instinctive drive to seek information in order to survive as a species. Echoing Lasswell's famous designation (1960) of communication as surveillance of the environment, Julianne Newton (2005) notes that television extends our view and our awareness. Even the mundane and trivial are part of the environment that television lets us scan. Newton proposes an "ecology of the visual" to identify television's role in our integrated psychological and cultural system that enables us to survive and evolve. She employs a vivid metaphor for this (p. 117).

> It is as if the aesthetic of television is both creating and showing us our entrails. By addressing our deepest fears, anxieties, and desires through the experiences of real people (however constructed their video presentations may be) and fictional personae, we cut open the raw innards of the human psyche for mass view. ... It offers a touch of the experience of feeling, seeing, and hearing that may otherwise be absent in our lives. In this way the aesthetic of television draws and repels us, informs, fools, reforms us.

In this context, sports as television content offer some of the entrails of the human race, but not all. The fundamental human experiences of birth, death, and marriage do not often occur within sports, though violence, aggression, and strong emotions are evident. There is the possibility of death, especially in auto racing or bullfighting, but sport generally offers only analogies and metaphors for primordial human experiences. News and fictional drama incorporate more readily these parts of the raw innards of the human psyche for mass view.

"Control" and "reality" in television aesthetics

Sports in other ways are imperfect matches for the television medium. For example, they do not enable the complete control of sequence that television prefers. The unpopular team wins; two minor-market teams play for the championship; a much-awaited game turns dull. But this is also a strength of television. The outside world intrudes and has its say, lending to the televised sports event a wildness, an unknownness, an open-endedness that makes its suspense more real.

Yet, on a deeper level, sports lack any larger purpose and consequence They are, underneath all the money, time, organizations, hype, and hoopla, just a game. The televised sporting event is not directly connected to solving political problems, manufacturing tangible goods, curing cancer, or eradicating poverty and hunger. This lack of consequence is essential to the attraction of sports. Your team loses, so what? Except for news and documentary programming, television content similarly lacks consequence. It is far more than escape and diversion, but fundamental to its attraction is its ease of access and lack of demands. Of course, both sports and television are often touted for teaching many worthwhile lessons of life, but they do so through stories, characters, and analogies and they stand a bit apart from actual life and personally experienced truth. The entrails look prettier on television and the raw innards of sport are kept largely out of sight.

Another imperfection of sports for television is that they are subject to external forces. Bad weather can ruin televised skiing and snowboarding, rendering them invisible or inaccessible. Tasteless or pathological personal behavior of athletes off the field can drag down the reputation of teams, leagues, and sports. Owner lock-outs or player strikes can cancel an NHL or NFL season. Television can turn imperfections into enticements, as it savors every detail of such problems, but scripted and acted television content is much less subject to victimage by forces outside its control.

A marriage in transition

Television, as we know it, is a set of both technologies and social institutions. As these change, so does the very definition of what television is and does. Newton (2005) has described the aesthetic innards of television; she also explains how television's aesthetics are challenged and perhaps liberated by current shifts in technology. She writes of television's aesthetic of movement and how the Internet may challenge that and open new possibilities (p. 105):

> Until the Internet began to command significant attention as the technology of the moment, television epitomized that moving aesthetic through its ability to reinvent itself at will – and quickly. As the Internet gathers steam as the carrier of our increasingly global conversation – and debate – television enters a new era of aesthetic exploration … as art did when photography came along, as photography did when movies came along, as radio, movies and print publications did when television came along. It is the way of growing, dynamic entities.

What may become of engagement with sports when television becomes thoroughly enmeshed with other Internet-based media, databases, and fan communities defies facile projections, but the possibilities further excite already enthusiastic sports fans.

"Real virtuality" in the "network society"

One of the most comprehensive theories of society and media today is that of Manuel Castells. In his view, following World War II, television was at the heart of the transition away from the old order of what – following McLuhan – Castells calls the Gutenberg Galaxy. Other media were re-organized around it in the television-centric McLuhan Galaxy, positioning television as the epicenter of modern societies, most of all the United States. But these galaxies have now been replaced by "the network society." Networks are sets of interconnected nodes – from stock market exchanges to drug trafficking systems. Communication within networks is easy but between networks is difficult. The new global media network brings together television systems with computers, news, and mobile devices to generate and receive signals that are at the heart of cultural expression and public opinion. Unlike the television era, the emerging network society is inherently interactive rather than one-way. Castells writes (2000, p. 365):

> The fact that the audience is not a passive object but an interactive subject opened the way to its differentiation, and to the subsequent transformation of the media from mass communication to segmentation, customization and individualization, from the moment technology, corporations, and institutions allowed such moves.

Castells objects to today's concept of "virtual reality" as a specific category of media activity because it implies other communication is not virtual. To Castells, *all* forms of communication are based in the production and consumption of signs – language, conceptual knowledge, media. In the constructivist sense, he insists that there is no prior real world directly known that precedes signs. Reality cannot be separated from symbolic representation in human experience. The reality known to humans is always "virtual" because it is perceived through signs. Instead of virtual vs. direct reality, Castells suggests that the new electronic integration of communication modes constitutes "real virtuality." They are as "real" as anything humans know but their open-ended complexity and diverse interpretations make them "virtual" rather than exact and absolute. He charges (2000, p. 404): "When critics of electronic media argue that the new symbolic environment does not represent 'reality,' they implicitly refer to an absurdly primitive notion of 'uncoded' real experience that never existed."

The real virtuality of life in the new network society incorporates multiple discourses. For example, Castells cites how it blends political and fictional discourses in the strange 1992 debate on unwed mothers between Vice-President Dan Quayle and TV character Murphy Brown. He could cite how the receiver formerly known as Chad Johnson changed his legal name to an (incorrect) Spanish version of his jersey number, Ochocinco. Previous distinctions of real vs. imagined seem no longer to apply. What Castells calls for is ensuring that the new network society be correctly configured. The system can transform time, space, and identity. Participants will adapt to the system's logic, its language, its encoding and decoding, its points of entry. Because of this, maximizing the system's potential is the fundamental struggle in the emerging network society. Castells (2000, p. 405) cautions, "This is why it is so critical for different kinds of social effects that there be the development of a multinodal, horizontal network of communication, of Internet type, instead of a centrally dispatched multimedia system, as in the video-on-demand configuration." Sports have been used by media moguls such as Rupert Murdoch to propel television into a dominant, centrally controlled, satellite delivery system. Can sports also serve to diversify and decentralize this medium within the new integrated system anticipated by Castells?

The "sublime" in television

Nick Hornby (1992, p. 240) has written vividly of sport's ability to deliver "unanticipated delirium." Television theorists have occasionally rhapsodized on the potential of television to transcend, to offer the sublime. The words of DiTomasso (cited in Newton, 2005, p. 112) help to answer Paddy Scannell's question about what happens when we turn on the TV, and they offer an inspiring climax to our considerations of what the holy union of television and sports suggests:

> To witness the incomprehensible possibility of the play of light and movement in a "life-less" object is to witness the sublime event of life being created. We simply need to switch on our set to encounter and appreciate this continual event of becoming and creation. Indeed, it is precisely at the moment of instantiation that we become confronted with our aesthetic experience of television as sublime. ... We are in awe, if only for a moment, enraptured by the sublime and unthinkable movement of life in an inorganic object.

Note

1 In 1999, I addressed a group of 30 sports journalists in Ethiopia. This is the home country of historic marathoner Abibi Bikila and other Olympic distance runners. At the conclusion of my remarks about television and the Olympics, one of the sportswriters asked, with affirmative nods from others, "What are the Winter Olympics?"

References

Abelman, R. & Atkin, D. (2002). *The televiewing audience: The art and science of watching TV.* Cresskill, NJ: Hampton Press.

Appadurai, A. (1996). *Modernity at large.* Minneapolis: University of Minnesota Press.

Arledge, R. (2003). *Roone.* New York: HarperCollins.

Barthes, R. (1974). *S/Z: An essay* (R. Miller, Trans.). New York: Hill & Wang.

Barthes, R. (1975). *The pleasure of the text.* (R. Miller, Trans.). New York: Hill & Wang.

Barthes, R. (1977). *Image-music-text* (S. Heath, Trans.). London: Fontana.

Bignell, J. (2004). *An introduction to television studies.* New York: Routledge.

Billings, A. (2008). *Olympic media: Inside the biggest show on television.* New York: Routledge.

Bryant, J., Zillmann, D., & Raney, A.A. (1998). Violence and the enjoyment of media sports. In L. Wenner (Ed.), *MediaSport* (pp. 252–65). New York: Routledge.

Bryant, J., & Raney, A.A. (2000). Sports on the screen. In D. Zillmann & P. Vorderer (Eds.), *Media entertainment: The pyschology of its appeal* (pp. 153–74). Mahwah, NJ: Erlbaum.

Butler, J. (2007). *Television: Critical methods and applications* (3rd Ed.). Mahwah, NJ: Lawrence Erlbaum Associates.

Butterworth, M.L. & Moskal, S.D. (2009, December). American football, flags, and "fun": The Bell Helicopter Armed Forces Bowl and the rhetorical production of militarism. *Communication, Culture & Critique, 2*(4), 411–33).

Casey, B., Casey, N., Calvert, B., French, L., & Lewis, J. (2002). *Television studies: The key concepts.* New York: Routledge.

Castells, M. (2000). *The rise of the network society. The information age: Economy, society and culture Vol. I.* Malden, MA: Blackwell.

Corner, J. (1999). *Critical ideas in television studies.* New York: Oxford University Press.

Couldry, N. (2003). *Media rituals: A critical approach.* New York: Routledge.

Eco, U. (1970, January). Articulations of the cinematic code. *Cinemantics,* no. 1, London.

Fish, S. (1980). *Is there a text in this class? The authority of interpretive communities.* Cambridge, MA: Harvard University Press.

Fiske, John. (1987). *Television culture.* New York: Methuen.

Friedman, D. (2009, December 21). Ratings hike. *Sports Illustrated, 111*(25), 68.

Gray, J., Sandvoss, C., & Harrington, L. (2007). *Fandom: Identities and communities in a mediated world.* New York: New York University Press.

Guback, T. & Varis, T. (1986). Transnational communication and cultural industries. *Reports and Papers on Mass Communication,* no. 92. Paris: UNESCO.

Hall, S. (1980). Encoding and decoding. In S. Hall, D. Hobson, A. Lowe, and P. Willis (Eds.), *Culture, media, language* (pp. 128–39). London: Hutchinson.

Harris, C. & Alexander, A. (1998). *Theorizing fandom: Fans, subculture and identity.* Cresskill, NJ: Hampton Press.

Hollander, D. (2008, May 28). Sports on TV better with the sound off. *Huffington Post.* Retrieved from www.huffingtonpost.com/dave-hollander/sports-on-tv-better-with_b_103959.html

Hornby, Nick. (1992). *Fever pitch.* London: Gollancz.

Horton, D. & Wohl, R. (1956). Mass communication and para-social interaction: Observations on intimacy at a distance. *Psychiatry, 19*(3), 215–29.

Jameson, F. (1992). *Postmodernism or the cultural logic of late capitalism.* Durham, NC: Duke University Press.

Kristeva, J. (1973, October 12). The system and the speaking subject. *Times Literary Supplement,* p. 1249.

Kristeva, J. (1980). *Desire in language: A semiotic approach to literature and art.* New York: Columbia University Press.

Lasswell, H. (1960). The structure and function of communication in society. In W. Schramm (Ed.), *Mass communication.* Urbana: University of Illinois Press.

Lotz, A.D. (2007). *The television will be revolutionized.* New York: New York University Press.

McChesney, R.W. (1999). *Rich media, poor democracy.* Urbana: University of Illinois Press.

McChesney, R.W. (2008). *The political economy of media: Enduring issues, emerging dilemmas.* New York: Monthly Review Press.

Metz, C. (1974). *Film language: A semiotics of cinema* (Michael Taylor, Trans.). New York: Oxford University Press.

Meyrowitz, J. (1985). *No sense of place: The impact of electronic media on social behavior.* New York: Oxford University Press.

Morgan, M. (Ed.). (2002). *Against the mainstream: The selected works of George Gerbner.* New York: Peter Lang Publishing.

Morley, D. (2004). Audience research: Reception analysis. In H. Newcomb (Ed.), *Encyclopedia of television (2nd Ed.)* (pp. 170–71). New York: Fitzroy Dearborn.

Nielsenwire (Feb. 8, 2010). Super Bowl XLIV most watched Super Bowl of all time. Retrieved from http://blog.nielsen.com/nielsenwire/media_entertainment/super-bowl-xliv-most-watched-super-bowl-of-all-time/

Newcomb, H. (1974). *TV: The most popular art*. Garden City, NY: Anchor Press/Doubleday.

Newton, J.H. (2005). Television as a moving aesthetic: In search of the ultimate aesthetic – the self. In J. Wasko (Ed.), *A companion to television* (pp. 103–25). Malden. MA: Blackwell.

Nordenstreng, K. & Varis, T. (1974). *Television traffic – a one-way street*. Norwood, NJ: Ablex.

Petterle, A. (2009, Dec. 7). Nielsen: DVR, online viewing on the rise. *Adweek*. Retrieved from www.adweek.com/aw/content_display/news/media/e3ibbd28f12604b55314393e 9ea722ee8ce

PRWeb. (2008). Fantasy sports industry grows to a $800 million industry with 29.9 million players. Retrieved from www.prweb.com/releases/2008/07/prweb1084994.htm

Raney, A.A. (2003). Enjoyment of sports spectatorship. In J. Bryant, De. Roskos-Ewoldsen, & J. Cantor (Eds.), *Communication and emotion: Essays in honor of Dolf Zillman* (pp. 397–416). Mahwah, NJ: Erlbaum.

Real, M.R. (1975). Super Bowl: Mythic spectacle. *Journal of Communication, 25*(1), 31–43. See also M. Real, 1977. *Mass-mediated culture*, Chapter 3, (pp. 90–117). Englewood Cliffs, NJ: Prentice-Hall. (This chapter is the full version of this study.)

Real, M.R. (1996a). Is television corrupting the Olympics? Media and the (post)modern games at age 100. *Television Quarterly, 28*(2), 2–12.

Real, M.R. (1996b). The postmodern Olympics: Technology and the commodification of the Olympic movement. *Quest, 48*(1), 9–24.

Real, M.R. (2005). Television and sports. In J. Wasko (Ed.), *A companion to television* (pp. 337–60). Malden, MA: Blackwell.

Reiter, B. (December 21, 2009). Smooth transition. *Sports Illustrated, 111*(25), 67–68.

Sandvoss, C. (2005). *Fans: The mirror of consumption*. Malden, MA: Polity Press.

Scannell, P. (2009, February). An introduction to the phenomenology of television: What happens when I turn on the TV set? Lecture presented at the Annenberg School for Communication, Philadelphia, PA.

Staiger, J. (2005). *Media reception studies*. New York: New York University Press.

Straubhaar, J.D. (2007). *World television: From global to local*. Thousand Oaks, CA: Sage.

Thorburn, D. & Jenkins, H. (2003). *Rethinking media change: The aesthetics of transition*. Cambridge, MA: MIT Press.

Westerwick, S.W., David, P., Eastin, M.S., Tamborini, R., & Greenwood, D. (2009, December). Sports spectators' suspense. *Journal of Communication, 59*(4), 750–67.

Wilson, T. (2004). *The playful audience: From talk show viewers to Internet users*. Cresskill, NJ: Hampton Press.

Zillman, D. (1996). The psychology of suspense in dramatic exposition. In P. Vorderer, H.J. Wulff, & M. Friedrickson (Eds.), *Suspense: conceptualization, theoretical analyses, and empirical explorations* (pp. 199–231). Mahwah, NJ: Erlbaum.

3

THE POWER OF A FRAGMENTED COLLECTIVE

Radical pluralist feminism and technologies of the self in the sports blogosphere

Marie Hardin

PENNSYLVANIA STATE UNIVERSITY

With the rise of the Internet in the early 1990s as a site free from institutional control of mass communication arose optimism among feminists about its transformative potential in the lives of women (Worthington, 2005). Women's participation in online communities was seen as allowing for feminist political resistance to institutional/mainstream media messages, which have long been criticized as reinforcing women's oppression (van Zoonen, 1994; Vavrus, 2007). "Cyberfeminism" was coined for work on the ways the Internet could be used to empower women (Shade, 2002).

The possibilities of the Internet for female athletes and the promotion of women's sport have been part of this work. Advocates have envisioned it as a space of possibilities for moving women's sports from the cultural margins to a position similar to the hallowed place for men's sports (Favorito, 2007; Maxwell, 2009; Messner, 2002). There is no disputing the lowly place of women's sports in relationship to men's in U.S. culture; the research demonstrating this reality across time and space, in every medium and across every sport, is voluminous and easily accessible. (See the Appendix in this book for a list of key articles.) The dominant discourse in relation to women's sport is one that devalues female athletes through a paucity of coverage and presents them in ways that often emphasize their femininity and (hetero)sexuality (Duncan, 2006).

Although the "jury is still out" on the transformative potential of the Internet for girls and women in sport, research indicates that, thus far, the overall trend does not look promising (Hardin, 2009). Sites such as *Deadspin* and *The Big Lead*, where sexist discourse is run-of-the-mill fare, dominate the sports blogosphere. For instance, *Deadspin* introduced the new Nike World Cup home jersey for the U.S. women's team by showing the uniform on a Playboy model; a *Big Lead* entry on the attractiveness and attire of ESPN commentator Hannah Storm drew comments by readers such as "I'd bang her" and "I'd just buy her shot after shot and then (allegedly) rape her in a bathroom" (Duffy, 2010; Petchesky, 2010).

New-media discourse, it seems, is simply replicating the old. From a Gramscian perspective, the landscape can still be summarized as reinforcing traditionally masculine, patriarchal hegemony, where women generally remain powerless in relationship to the sport/media complex.

There are pockets of progress. Women's professional sports leagues often communicate with fans in an unfiltered manner. Athletes such as tennis champion Serena Williams, WNBA star Candace Parker and Olympic hockey player Angela Ruggiero use Web sites and Twitter feeds to build a fan base. And a tiny – but growing – number of bloggers are amassing around women's sports.

How can and should sports feminists assess these developments? What theoretical lens best situates the potential for the Internet – specifically, the blogosphere – to transform the dominant discourse around women's and men's sports? As a sports feminist who has also been a participant in the sports blogosphere (albeit sporadically), I have been intrigued by the women and men who gather there on behalf of the women's sports enterprise. Thus, I have aimed to consider the transformative power of the blogosphere through a project with a much narrower aspiration: to discover how a handful of bloggers, connected through a network of blogs, relate to dominant discourses and see their missions.

In doing so, I chose a Foucauldian perspective for reasons I will explain as this chapter unfolds. I do not try to present the totality of Foucauldian thought – only key features, through a feminist lens, as they apply to this work. I present Foucauldian concepts through a selected group of key feminist scholars, some identified directly with scholarship on sport.

Promise and peril: the relationship between Foucault and feminism

The work of philosopher Michel Foucault (1926–84), especially his suggestions about how *power* works in modern culture, have been useful for scholars in a number of fields – from criminology to social work – and have justified judgment of Foucault as one of the most influential philosophers of the last century. Foucault's ideas about power provide a material contrast to Gramscian notions about domination and hegemony – which have also been highly influential for scholars in pursuit of how and why cultural hierarchies are created and maintained (Gramsci, 1996; Pringle, 2005). Although the majority of sports feminists and critical sports scholars have worked from the Gramscian perspective, a growing number have found Foucault a useful impetus to "ask new questions, think differently and allow for the creation of new understandings and possibilities" (Pringle, 2005, p. 273).

Foucault argued through his voluminous work that the nature of power had evolved from a "sovereign" model to one where power is dispersed and works discursively (Cole, Giardina, & Andrews, 2004). A Foucauldian understanding of power rejects the identification of a handful of groups or a class of individuals as wielding power over another (powerless) group or class (Foucault, 1994; Markula, 2003). The idea that power is possessed, with those at the top of a socio-political hierarchy using it to repress those below, is rejected for a vision of power as constantly deployed among individuals at all levels of society through discourse. Discourse legitimates and circulates those ideas we understand as "truth" (knowledge); thus, power and knowledge are constantly at work (Markula, 2003). The daily discursive relations between people produce social realities and subjectivities, and the effects of the "network of historical power relations" among individuals are dominations such as sexism or racism (Markula, 2003, p. 94; Markula & Pringle, 2006). Power relations at the *micro-level* enable domination at the *macro-level* (Sawicki, 1991).

Perhaps Foucault's most famous metaphor for explaining his conceptualization of power relations is his use of the prison panopticon – a tower located centrally to create the illusion that prisoners are always being watched. The effect is the belief of inmates that they are under watch for certain behaviors understood as morally acceptable (or not). The prisoners, then, become their own surveillance, extending the knowledge/understanding of certain behaviors to their lives and disciplining their bodies in accordance with that understanding (Cole et al., 2004). This concept is useful for scholars – including sports feminists – exploring the relationship between media, women, and rituals of body maintenance (Cole et al., 2004; Duncan, 1994; Germov & Williams, 1999).

Ultimately, scholars with a Foucauldian focus understand all as participants in the power-knowledge process, as "both victims and agents within systems of domination" (Sawicki, 1991, p. 10). They consider *how* power is used at all levels, with special attention paid to everyday uses of discourse and how knowledge is created and circulated within power relations (Markula, 2003). It is in these everyday power relations where resistance to dominant discourse also takes place (Ramazanoglu, 1993). Foucault's strategies for cultural transformation do not advocate organized, revolutionary tactics aimed at institutions, but instead "more localized and less coordinated approaches focused on the connections between discourses and subjectivity" (Pringle, 2005, p. 271).

In looking at micro-level discourse and practice, Foucault also rejected binary/ essentialist judgments – clear categorizations of the "liberatory" and "repressive." Thus, a Foucauldian perspective requires careful consideration of the cultural conditions of given practices because a discourse/practice designed in one context to be liberating can be – and often is – repressive in another, and vice-versa (Raby, 2005; Ramazanoglu, 1993; Sawicki, 1991; Thorpe, 2008). Even those social movements designed to fight oppression – the feminist movement, for instance – amass power and then, in turn, can become guilty of their own forms of repression (Ramazanoglu, 1993).

Foucault's concept of *reverse discourse* is also useful. He suggests that a group aiming to free itself from oppression may employ the same discourse used against it for a different result (Foucault, 1990). Ultimately, though, the truths/knowledge that underpin the discourse remain intact (Fairclough, 1992; Soper, 1993). An example of reverse discourse related to the focus of this chapter – discourse related to women's sports – might be the argument by women's sports advocates that a reason to resist the "second-class status" of female athletes is that they are just as athletically capable as are men. This turn in discourse may attract support for initiatives such as Title IX and increase (at least in the short term) interest in consumption of women's sports. Ultimately, this argument does not challenge the taken-for-granted "truths" that govern the way sports are valued, and, instead, reinforces them.

The trouble for feminists

Foucault's work rarely engaged – at least directly – topics of patriarchy or sexism, two key concepts for feminists, including those focused on sport (Birrell, 2000). Furthermore, his conceptualization of power as exercised at all levels, his refusal to divide the universe into an oppressor/oppressed binary and to recognize the need for organized social movements to fight institutions deemed repressive, and his resistance to recognizing essential identities (such as "woman") has made him controversial among feminists. Sawicki (1991) and Ramazanoglu (1993) both present book-length discussions of feminists' objections to Foucault: He is seen as delegitimizing the work of feminism as a collective, macro-level movement with the goal to fight universal injustice in the form of institutional patriarchy and sexism. Thus, according to Ramazanoglu (p. 8), "Feminism is in danger of being shifted from an emancipatory global movement, to a philosophical socialism [that] provides legitimization for political pluralism."

The truth, however, is that feminism has never been a singular movement. Ramazanoglu (1993, p. 5), in her critique of Foucault, also recognized that "feminism is deeply contradictory because women's lives are contradictory." The notion of "sisterhood" based on fixed, collective identities around gender (female or male) is impossible – and a reason feminism has not met its potential (Sawicki, 1991). Colwell (1999) rightly argued that sports feminists also have relied on assumptions about the collective identities of women (and men) that ultimately undermine their arguments.

The contradictions and inconsistencies in feminist thought are evident in its myriad iterations over the decades. Major (second-wave) strands of feminism, which should not be viewed as mutually exclusive, have been grounded in liberal democratic beliefs or the interrogation of structural power relations and have, then, pointed to different remedies for the marginalization or oppression of women (Scraton & Flintoff, 2001). Sawicki (1991), however, points out that a Foucauldian analysis of competing feminisms suggests that they situate power similarly: as being located in institutions, and not with women (who are defined universally). Their proposed remedies are also grounded similarly: as universal and rooted in institutional transformation. No matter the account or the remedy, women are ultimately positioned as powerless, leading to their alienation from one another and from the movement (Sawicki, 1991; hooks, 1984).

As hooks (1984) suggests, shared victimization is a destructive foundation for feminists because, at least in part, it fails to resonate with the mainstream experiences of most women. North's (2009) interviews with female journalists, for instance, found that they resisted association with and were even hostile toward the identity of "feminist" even when some of the movement's recognized goals (such as equal pay for equal work) resonated with them. According to Braithwaite (2002), the perception of second-wave feminism as too rigid, prescriptive and morally universalist has been a reason many young women have turned away from the identity. The same might also be suggested of perceptions of sports feminism (Colwell, 1999).

hooks (1984) suggests that a far more appealing and powerful identity for women to share is built "on the basis of shared strengths and resources" (p. 46). This seems to mesh with Foucauldian notions of power, which are built in socio-cultural contexts and would encourage feminists to abandon the notion of universal unity and instead use difference as a resource (Sawicki, 1991). Post-structuralist feminists, part of feminism's "third wave," have been accessible to many (Scraton & Flintoff, 2001). Post-structuralism's politics of difference resists universal explanations and a binary model (e.g., dominance/oppression or powerful/powerless) and gears judgments to specific contexts and provisional categories (Sawicki). Negotiation and contradiction are part of its discourse; for instance, while it may critique beauty standards in Western culture, it also incorporates an acknowledgment of the pleasure and defining power of this industry in the lives of many women (Braithwaite, 2002). A parallel example of critique for women's sports advocates is in hyperfeminized and sexualized images of female athletes; post-structuralism allows for the acknowledgment that female athletes may (legitimately) feel empowered in posing provocatively for the camera (Carty, 2005; Weaving, 2002).

Integrating Foucault into feminism: the radical pluralist model

Sawicki (1991), Macleod (2006) and other post-structuralist feminists have used Foucault – adapted – to underpin their efforts toward correcting the movement's universalist/prescriptive missteps. Of interest to this research is Sawicki's (1991) proposal of a *radical pluralist feminism* that recognizes *plurality* both within and between subjects and politicizes relationships at the micro-level of society. It resists totalizing pronouncements in practices/discourses as liberatory or oppressive; it links the micro- and macro-levels in the everyday; and it relies on a dynamic model of subjectivity that is situated in power relations (Macleod, 2006).

It is not surprising that radical pluralist feminism has been met with resistance by feminists – including those who study sport – who fear it fails to prompt activism and social change and is simply too relativist. For instance, Edwards and Jones (2009, p. 331) argue that the "ethical relativism" in a post-structuralist approach to understanding sport "undermines critical reflection and political action."

Macleod (2006) suggests that such fears, however, are ground in a perspective that embraces the artificial binary pitting relativism against an absolute (universal) truth. It is not that Foucauldian feminists abandon truth, but they ground it in a socio-historical context. She also suggests that fears about the failure of radical pluralist feminism to spur political activism around a unified category of "woman" are also unfounded; Foucauldian feminists recognize the connections among women as a "chain of equivalence" threading them together via specific experiences that deny them equitable positions as subjects. So, also, do Foucauldian feminists recognize that men generally occupy dominant positions in key institutions; thus, they, too, may be threaded together by a higher stake in maintaining those positions (Macleod). Thus, although radical pluralism advocates multiple, local points of intervention based on social circumstance, the recognition of the chains of equivalence "prevents feminism from slipping into rampant relativism" (p. 379). Furthermore, she suggests, Foucauldian feminists allow critique of patriarchy and sexism. Such critique is not privileged, however, over attention to the micro-level, everyday practices of power among women and men.

Foucault and sports feminism

Increasingly, women's sports activists have recognized the limitations of second-wave feminisms, which tend toward Gramscian understandings of power and resistance, in grappling with the complex issues involving depictions of female athletes (Markula, 2004; Edwards & Jones, 2009). Post-structuralism, which conceives of power and identity in Foucauldian terms, allows for "new understandings and possibilities" in considering old questions (Pringle, 2005, p. 273).

One of the major points of differentiation between Foucauldian and Gramscian notions of power is the way in which they situate the body. For Foucault, the body was central in the mechanisms of discourse and power, and this focus has evoked attention to his work by sports scholars (Pringle, 2005; Markula & Pringle, 2006). Influential sports feminists, including Cole (1993; Cole et al., 2004), Duncan (1994; Eskes, Duncan & Miller, 1998), and Markula (2004; Markula and Pringle, 2006) have incorporated Foucauldian ideas into their work. Generally, (sports) feminists have used Foucault's notion of power to explore the rationales and discourses used by women to discipline "docile" bodies (Gill, 2007). Scholars have also adapted Foucault's (1994, p. 146) notion of "technologies of power," defined as a web of discourse/practice disciplining the body through the terms (knowledge) of domination, to sport and to media (Cole, 1993; Thorpe, 2008). The "discursive web of normalizing practices" for women in relation to their bodies has been considered through these technologies (Markula, 2003, p. 88; Thorpe, 2008).

Technologies of the self

More recently – and, for scholars who seek change in sport, appropriately – attention has turned to Foucault's suggestions for the ways social transformation can take place. In his later writing, Foucault discussed the concept of "technologies of the self" (Foucault, 1994, p. 146), and this concept has been usefully and thoroughly explicated in the sport context by Markula (2003; Markula & Pringle, 2006). Markula suggests technologies of the self as key in considering how individuals might change dominant discourses; thus, this concept is critical to a feminist agenda. She explains the concept by starting with Foucault's explanation that such technologies are those practices allowing individuals to transform themselves in ways that allow them to attain self-fulfillment, wisdom and other positive attributes. As Markula (2003) writes, "Through these technologies an individual begins to recognize her/himself as a subject and in this sense, s/he can be understood to counter the technologies of power" (p. 88). In short, technologies of the self involve the problematizing of codes that govern a person's actions and the development of practices as a result (Markula & Pringle, 2006).

Markula (2003) reviews research by sports feminists and the writings of feminist philosopher Moya Lloyd (1996) to explain what technologies of the self require. Critical to technologies of the self is the concept of "practices of freedom" (Markula, 2003), which essentially means the movement by an individual from critique and self-reflection to strategies and actions to (re)build a self-identity consistent with critical awareness of problematic discourses. To do so, an individual must see her or his life as "material that can be formed and transformed" (Markula & Pringle, 2006, p. 150). Lloyd (1996) suggests concrete ways an individual can attempt self-transformation, one of which is of particular interest to this research: "writing the self" through journals, diaries or memoirs. This idea of self writing was key to Foucault, who believed it was an "essential stage" of the fashioning of discourses that are "recognized as true, into rational principles of action" (Foucault, 1997). Lloyd (p. 246) added that "the point is that they all involve the subject in the active (though not necessarily always independent) production of themselves."

The *motive* behind the individual's transformation is key; it is not shaped by dominant discourses – such as work to maintain one's weight in pursuit of social norms – but is instead driven by the desire to develop as an ethical being. Thus, any self-fashioning itself is not evidence enough to judge whether it is a practice of freedom; the act itself does not determine its function. For instance, an act that might be interpreted by feminists as reinforcing dominant discourses might actually be "allied to critique" (Lloyd, 1996, p. 250) by the person engaged in it, and, thus, is a practice of freedom and an ethical use of power.

In this light, technologies of the self are not a guaranteed formula for the transformation of cultural power relations (Markula & Pringle, 2006). Depending on the individual and the context, there are limits to how freedom is conceptualized and practiced because "the field of choice is already partially constituted" by existing discourse (Lloyd, 1996, p. 246). It is also not surprising that some feminists see the practice as too weak and dispersed to exact any coherent movement from which widespread political change can result (Markula, 2003). One way to view technologies of the self, then, is that they may not lead to social change, but they are essential for real change in one's individual condition.

Markula challenges feminist researchers to recognize how women in sport employ technologies of the self; analysis requires identifying the actions of individuals within discursive power relations and discovering how these actions have influenced their identities (Markula & Pringle, 2006). Furthermore, Markula (2003) challenges feminist sport researchers to explore ways they also can become ethical users of power. A recent example of work in this vein is by Thorpe (2008). Her exploration of the ways technologies of the self are exercised by competitive female snowboarders is especially instructive. Thorpe reviewed evolving patterns of discourse in media representations of snowboarding before moving to an analysis of her conversations with female snowboarders. She sought not to discover the "truth" in discourse surrounding snowboarding culture but instead uncovered the reality: multiple, contradictory and competing discourses in media depictions and, more to the point of her research, among male and female snowboarders. In the discourse of the snowboarders, Thorpe discovered what she described – using Markula's explication – as technologies of the self at work.

Much of Thorpe's inquiry centered on interpretations of sexualized images of female athletes in snowboarding publications. Thorpe recognized a divide among women and men based on their cultural context, which she related to second- and third-wave feminism. Second-wave feminists interpret such images as universally demeaning to female athletes; third-wave feminists (including post-structuralists) are far less likely to read the images in such stark terms, instead embracing the contradiction displayed in an athlete such as racecar driver Danica Patrick or Olympic swimmer Amanda Beard depicted passively. Heterosexual, hyper-feminine displays, then, are not necessarily opposed on the grounds that all such images are demeaning; they are considered in concert with other considerations: Who is the athlete? What is the commercial motive? What is the context? Thorpe suggested that a third-wave reading of sexualized images could see athletes as powerful for their willingness to embrace, rather than cloak, their sexuality.

Accordingly, Thorpe found that some athletes opposed the images, and some did not. Thorpe noted that those who did not may have been practicing technologies of the self, as such practice does not require the rejection of particular discourses as a litmus test. However, failure to oppose the images did not, on its face, mean a technology of the self had been employed. Thorpe wrote that "the ability to develop a critical awareness of the discourses of femininity depends on the individual's experiences and position within the existing power-discourse nexus" (p. 217).

Thorpe pointed to evidence of the "first step of technologies of the self" (p. 218) in the *conscious, active critique* by snowboarders of discursive constructions of sexism, including those in snowboarding films. Thorpe pointed to the involvement of some snowboarders in alternative, all-female snowboarding videos as a "second step," which she defined as practices of freedom (p. 220). It is here, in practices of freedom, where power relations may start to be destabilized and ultimately, over time, transformed (Markula, 2003).

This research: taking Foucault into the blogosphere

As a feminist focused on the ways media depictions of sport intersect with the experience of girls and women in U.S. culture, I have often been frustrated by the underlying thesis of much of the Gramscian-oriented feminist work (including my own) in regard to women and sport: that power is "out of our hands" because we are at the bottom of a sport hierarchy and generally cannot create a more just, equitable situation for ourselves. (Yes, we must fight to be free of oppression, but how? We ponder, without much progress.) Thus, I fear that much of the literature produced by myself and other sports feminists has taken on the effect of a scratched CD: It is a repetitive cacophony of powerlessness, frustration and alienation born from the best of intentions but lacking in any real reason to hope for change.

Perhaps that is why I find the interpretations of Foucault by sports feminists such as Markula so intriguing, especially in light of my recent involvement with a group of women and men who obviously see things differently. As I learned more about this group, it was difficult to view their work and its potential through the same Gramscian lens I had always used. I also struggled with the difference I found among a group of individuals who all seemed to profess the same goal: the promotion of women's sports. I had learned to be skeptical of such claims; after all, a standard defense of sexualized depictions of female athletes has been that somehow these images, on their face, are empowering for women's sports (Carty, 2005; Duffy, 2010). Thus, I sought to understand this fragmented collective and to situate how members understood (and then promoted) women's sports.

That inquiry became the genesis of this project. I grounded it – interviews with members of a blog network devoted to coverage of women's sports – in *radical pluralist feminism* and aimed at recognizing how women and men employ *technologies of the self* to promote women's sports.

Through my interviews, I sought to learn how bloggers, most of whom were women and most of whom were also former or current competitive athletes, related to dominant discourses and how they saw their identities in relationship to their blogging. I believe blogging, which can act as a form of what Foucault would call "self writing" (Foucault, 1997; Lloyd, 1996), can be a concrete practice of self-production/transformation. However, as Lloyd points out, it is the role of critique that determines whether any act is a practice of freedom. Thus, I sought, through conversation, to discover how blogging was situated in the lives of the women and men I interviewed and how their work was changing their lives.

Women Talk Sports: a blog network

I came to this project through my own blog, which I began several years ago as a way to extend my work in feminist sports media studies beyond purely academic venues. In early 2009, I was invited to join a network of blogs devoted to coverage and commentary focused on women's sports. The network, Women Talk Sports (www.womentalksports.com), was launched in February and quickly grew, both in the number of contributors (more than 100 by the end of the year) and in the number of unique visitors (from 550 in February 2009 to about 29,000 a month by the end of 2009). Exactly one year after the network began, in February 2010, Women Talk Sports received an enormous boost in visibility (and a spike in unique visitors) when a member blog, "One Sport Voice," posted a critique of skier Lindsey Vonn's photograph on the cover of *Sports Illustrated*. The blog post received widespread coverage in the mainstream media.

Many of its contributors are sporadic, posting perhaps only once or twice a month, while others post weekly or daily. Many blogs are general in focus; others focus on issues such as Title IX or on media coverage of women's sports or are written for niche sports fans. (One blog focuses on rodeo barrel racing. Others focus on women in auto racing or in boxing.) Most of the contributors are women. Contributors are sometimes recruited by one of the network administrators; they can also request to join. The posts of member blogs are featured on the Women Talk Sports Web site, which also includes an RSS feed of stories about women's sports, a Twitter feed, and other features. Women Talk Sports also maintains a presence on Facebook.

Its mission statement reads:

> With the goal of promoting and empowering female athleticism, Women-TalkSports.com is an online network that connects the best blogs relating to women's sports. The site aims to raise the level of awareness of women in sport by providing comprehensive sport coverage, spotlighting outstanding achievements, and working with sporting associations on advocacy issues and empowering programs.

My goal was not to assess whether Women Talk Sports has been able to meet its goal to raise awareness levels for women's sports – certainly a laudable mission. Instead, I wanted to understand what drew individual contributors to this mission – and how each saw her or himself within it.

This project

I approached the founders of Women Talk Sports and asked for their help in recruiting members of the collective to participate in telephone interviews; I described these interviews as a part of a project to explore the orientation of bloggers toward feminism and women's sports. The founders responded with enthusiasm and sent out a recruitment message, approved by the Institutional Review Board at my university, on the Women Talk Sports mailing list. The invitation stipulated that I would make a $25 donation to the network (made available through funding I had obtained for the project) for each participant, that the identities of individual participants would be confidential in any published work (thus, I use pseudonyms in this article), and that I would summarize my findings and share them with the network.

One of the founders of the network was the first to be interviewed, and afterward, she wrote to network members encouraging them to participate. Several weeks later, she wrote another note to network members, and several who had already been interviewed responded on the listserv, describing their experience as a positive one. A total of 24 members, including three men, volunteered. The bloggers are from a variety of backgrounds, with several in graduate school and a handful with a background in women's studies in their college coursework. A few are professional athletes (track and field) but most are women who played sports competitively when they were younger and have translated their participation to active fandom. Their ages ranged from 21 to 49 years old. In the course of the interview, most participants disclosed their marital status or sexual orientation; I did not ask. Most bloggers are married, and some have children. Two women identified as lesbian.

Before the interviews, I read recent entries on participants' blogs and added their blogs to my Google Reader account so I could easily follow their posts after the interview. (Although I will discuss some participants' blog posts, their posts are not a focus of this chapter.) Understanding their blogs was important for establishing rapport with and the confidence of interviewees as early as possible in the interview (McCracken, 1988); it served as a way to communicate to them that I was interested in their work and saw it as important.

The interviews

Each interview took place by phone and was recorded for transcribing with the participants' permission. Interviews lasted anywhere from 55 to 75 minutes and were focused using a set of guiding, open-ended questions (McCracken, 1988). As McCracken suggests, the interview began with opening, non-directive questions ("grand tour questions") such as "How did you develop an interest in sports?" and "Tell me about how you started your blog." Remaining questions were designed to pursue the relationship between the blogger, women's sports, and "writing the self" (Lloyd, 1996, p. 246) on the blog. Several questions were also aimed at how individuals saw the role of their blog and how they viewed femininity, feminism, and female athletes. Examples of general questions were: "Do you consider yourself a feminist?" "What do you think of mainstream coverage of women's sports?" and "How do think your blog has changed you?" I started with a list of 20 basic questions for all bloggers; my follow-up questions varied based on their responses and on the particular topic of their blog. For instance, discussion of coverage of women's sports often started broadly but then narrowed to sports more directly related to those covered in participants' blogs.

Prompt for discussion

I used a recent sports-related event – publication of *ESPN the Magazine*'s "Body Issue" in early October 2009 – to discuss the display of sexuality by female athletes and the role of debate on the Women Talk Sports network. I believed this topic to be salient because its publication – especially the cover photo of Serena Williams sitting cross-legged and smiling, wearing nothing but bright red lipstick and matching nail polish – had generated a range of blog posts. Opinions varied dramatically. For instance, a 29-year-old track and field athlete wrote about Williams:

> Yes, she looks sexy. Good for her. Serena is workin' with a *whole lotta body*, and in my opinion she works it well. I take issue with people who believe that athletes should be one-dimensional. Being a badass on the court should not diminish your femininity or your ability to put on lip-gloss and heels and pout your lips with the best of them – if that's what you so choose.
>
> *(Glenn, Oct. 19, 2009)*

Another WTS blogger, a man in his 40s who covers a variety of women's sports, wrote that the Body Issue was a disappointment because

> two out of the three women are presented in a sexualized, passive, swimsuit edition type way (including a deliberately unthreatening photo of Serena), whereas none of the men are. Two out of the three men are only photographed from the waist up, for instance. ... In other words, the [men's] sexuality gets to be implied whereas the women's must be on display and available to the viewer.
>
> *(Women's Sports Blog, Oct. 10, 2009)*

Although most of the bloggers I interviewed had not weighed in on the debate, most were aware of the magazine and of the WTS discussion, allowing me to use it as a way to learn about how they viewed sexualized images in a specific context and how they viewed difference as a value for the network.

Analysis

My analysis of the interviews did not take place as a discrete step in this project; it began as I read the blogs and learned about the blog network, and I continued it via note-taking during and immediately after the interviews and again in reading the transcripts after they had been reviewed by participants (Potter, 1996). I read the transcripts through an interpretive lens informed by my study of the Foucauldian concepts of difference, power, discourse and technologies of the self; my reading of the transcripts was thorough yet focused.

By degree: self-awareness and practices of freedom among bloggers

Feminist identity and difference

Most of the bloggers I interviewed – some with more conviction than others – were willing to accept the "feminist" label while articulating the boundaries of their identification. The image of feminists as angry, morally rigid and out-of-touch was evident in the responses of some participants to my question, "Are you a feminist?" Interestingly, this item in my interview protocol seemed to have "made the rounds" among participants; several told me they had done some reading in anticipation of answering. For instance, a 45-year-old woman who blogs about women's college basketball, after looking up the definition of "feminist" online and finding a generic description – "promotion of women's rights, interests and issues," told me:

> I guess I would have to say yes. We're not out there marching on the front lines with picket signs and burning our bras, but if you were to line us up issue-wise, I think we would be more aligned with kind of a feminist point-of-view than not.

Other bloggers were less tentative but aimed to define their feminism more narrowly. Marjorie, one of three founders of the network, recalled a recent Women's Sports Foundation event where she found herself standing next to women's sports icon Billie Jean King and thinking, "She's a feminist of a different generation than mine." She struggled to articulate what she saw as the substance of the difference and declared herself part of a "gray area" in the women's sports movement. "Now that there's more opportunity, the base of women's new support in female sports has grown, and the definition of the female athlete has changed," she added.

Two of the three men I interviewed identified as feminist; one, a women's sports fan who said his goal was to keep "furthering the cause," had written about "amazon feminism" on his blog to describe his view that women were as capable of "athletic prowess" as were men. The male blogger who did not identify as feminist said that although he had researched the term, he was still unsure of its meaning and preferred to see himself as a "supporter and sympathetic observer of feminism."

Sexualization of female athletes

WTS participants were more conflicted and contradictory about the sexualized display of female athletes than they were about feminism. The willingness of participants to be critical of images of Serena Williams and others was aligned with their adherence to second-wave, third-wave, or post-feminist (I use "post" in the sense of "anti") ideals. This alignment was similar to that found by Thorpe (2008) in her discussions with male and female snowboarders.

Those who spoke in the starkest terms about sexualized body displays and their negative impact on women's sports identified most closely with the second-wave ideals. It is also interesting to note that all three men I interviewed registered strong objections to such displays. Jake, a 30-year-old graduate student, said although the photo of Williams was "complicated" because it displayed a body shape often not glamorized, he didn't believe it "moves women's sports forward." Generally, he added, it "demeans the athlete ... every man's going to regard them as sexual fantasy and nothing more." Later in the interview, he spoke of women as in need of "collective advocacy," which, he said, was a primary reason for his objection to sexualized displays of athletes. He added that sexualized displays are "perpetuating things that have been negative to women for so long."

One participant seemed to use "reverse discourse," in Foucauldian terms, to register her displeasure with hyperfeminine images. Ellen, a 50-something blogger who contributes to a women's basketball blog, said sexualized images aren't attracting fans – "it pisses people off" instead. She suggested that women's sport advocates "poke a hole in it. I'm tired of the whiny, 'Oh, stop it.' Does it flip?" She explained what she meant by using a recent article in *ESPN the Magazine* that featured Candace Parker in a passive cover shot and then, in the accompanying article, referred to the size of her breasts in the lead. Men, she said, should be objectified the same way:

> Let me just rewrite the phrase and talk about the size of LeBron's jock strap. Would anybody write that about LeBron James' jock strap? Then, why are they talking about Candace Parker's breasts? I'm just saying: I'm not arguing that you shouldn't write about her breasts, but just also write about his penis.

On the other end of the spectrum, several bloggers I interviewed saw images of Parker, Williams and other athletes as simply part of being a modern, high-profile female athlete or as empowering. Alicia, a 30-year-old track and field athlete who did not identify as feminist and posted a well-trafficked entry on the site about the Body Issue, said those who object to such images offend her:

> I have a hard time understanding where the judgment comes from. ... It's still kind of new, accepting women's sexuality in sports, so people will find a way to kind of find some negativity within it, and it's a shame that it comes from both the feminist perspective, and it comes from men, and it comes from people who are not in the sports realm.

It is important to note that most participants were not as unambiguous regarding the Williams cover and hyper-feminine images of female athletes as Jake, Ellen and Alicia; they fell on a spectrum rife with contradiction as they grappled with this issue. One, a feminist professor of sports studies at a major university, said she was "torn" on the issue; another, a mother of elite-level, adolescent female athletes, spoke on the issue from several perspectives, including from her role as a business owner (describing Danica Patrick's decision to pose suggestively in several magazines as "very smart") to that of a mother (suggesting that Patrick be "a little bit more respectful").

Difference

A feature of Women Talk Sports is its display of blog posts from members that offer competing points of view; members can then post comments in response. The ESPN Body Issue is just one of a number of issues that have drawn a range of opinions and occasionally outright debate among members.

I asked participants how comfortable they were with the range of perspectives displayed on the site; without exception, they saw *difference* as a feature that made Women Talk Sports appealing. A few bloggers referred to online debates they had with others in the network. Some talked in terms of appeal to visitors. (The discussion about the Body Issue "did nothing but help in the traffic" noted one blogger.) Others talked about the value of different perspectives in their own growth, such as a woman who said, "We don't want it to be a site where everybody thinks the exact same thing, because where is our progress going to be?"

Roy, the blogger who identified as an "amazon feminist," said he sometimes rethinks his position after reading what others write. He also believes the conflicting discourse is part of the site's appeal:

> If people come out, and they see that you have a community … that shares a general sense of where we want things to go and in this case the importance of female athletes [and] women's sports – but at the same time is tolerant of discussion and disagreement and that sort of thing – I think that's probably better overall. … as long as it's not complete anarchy.

Technologies of the self: "first steps"

In her study of snowboarders, Thorpe (2008) identified *conscious, active critique* of sexism in media depictions as a "first step" in technologies of the self. Understood on its surface, this assertion might suggest that anyone who blogs about women's sports – who feels a need to provide, through her/his discourse, an alternative to mainstream coverage – would automatically be practicing this first step of technologies of the self. I suggest, however, that such critique cannot be entirely external but must involve self-awareness and critical self-reflection; this is the element of *consciousness* to which Thorpe refers. I also suggest that the second step which Thorpe identified, *concrete practice*, must clearly be connected to the first. Critical self-reflection is required for critical practice to work as Foucault intended it (Lloyd, 1996).

Thus, I could not rely solely on participants' critique of mainstream media coverage of women's sports in my assessment; I went further, asking them to discuss how and why they maintained a blog. How did blogging enhance their lives? Had it led to active, conscious critique of their belief systems?

Here, I heard an array of responses. A few involved very little in the way of self-consciousness and seemed to reinforce the dominant discourse about women's sports. One example was from a participant who, although she positioned her blog as a way to improve her writing, did not see it as a way to address gender issues and generally rejected any critique of gender dynamics in sport.

Most, however, indicated that "first step" to which Thorpe refers. Bloggers talked about transformational power of "writing the self." Jake, for instance, saw the role of his blog as advocating for the "advancement of women," and said he spent time reading other feminist blogs. "I've thought a lot more deeply about what feminism means to people," he said. Kelly, a graduate student who maintains a blog that critiques media coverage of sport, said her blog has made her more aware of gender issues. "Maybe I've become a better or more consistent thinker," she said. Jim, who maintains a blog following his local WNBA team, told me that beyond spending about 15 hours a week researching and writing directly for the blog, he read about feminism and topics related to women's sport and talked to other bloggers about how to better promote women's basketball in light of the discrimination female athletes face. The third male blogger, Roy, said his blogging has "changed me quite a bit," adding that:

> I think it has because in the process of blogging, you have to look at so many different things and so many different viewpoints that it really causes you to reflect on a lot of things that you probably wouldn't have considered so much before and, of course, new things altogether that you just weren't aware of.

"Second steps": practices of freedom

In her study, Thorpe (2008) interpreted the participation of some snowboarders in alternative, all-female snowboarding films as a "second step" – the demonstration of practices of freedom – in technologies of the self. It is critical to remember, however, that it is the *intent*, not the act itself, that determines a practice of freedom; the subject must engage in the act with the purpose of ethical transformation. Such ethical transformation, then, leads to discourses that may counter dominant discourses (Lloyd, 1996). For instance, a snowboarder in Thorpe's study may have participated in the production of an all-female film for purposes that had nothing to do with critique; in that case, the participation was not a practice of freedom. On the other hand, a snowboarder may have chosen to *reject* participation in such a film for reasons allied with self-consciousness; that snowboarder could be viewed as engaging in a practice of freedom.

To consider whether and how bloggers engaged in practices of freedom, I stepped back and viewed the totality of the interview for the ways in which they situated themselves and described their choices in relation to blogging, to activism and to women's sports. What I observed was an array of practices that, together, demonstrate the *power in difference* and the ways these participants are *challenging knowledge/practice* in the ways Markula (2003, p. 88) believes can "counter the technologies of power."

Some participants challenge knowledge/practice in discourses involving women and sports outside the WTS network. Marjorie, who studied the relationship between new media and sports as a graduate student and often blogs about it, said she has been frustrated by the ways women's sports are ignored by sports marketers. When she noticed that conferences on the topic did not include sessions on women's sports, she reached out to organizers with a question: Why aren't you inviting us? She continued:

> And they get all bent out of shape when I do that. "You're taking the wrong approach" – but no, I'm not. You're ignoring us – that's my opinion. And that's actually been very effective at getting our voice heard, and I'm going to continue doing that.

For others, their challenge is more local: on the Women Talk Sports site. An example of this was Jennifer, a 27-year-old graduate student who identifies with what she calls the "body acceptance movement" which postulates: "Be active, eat right, and don't worry about it." Her adherence to that movement has given her reason to challenge others on the network and in the blogosphere in general who focus on ideal-body fitness:

> It's been interesting to me to watch body issues come and go across the women's sports blogosphere. And that's something that I talk about that I'm sure people are pretty sick of at this point because I'm not going to let it go. I try not to be confrontational directly, but I'm just like, well, let's reiterate again: Health at every size – good idea.

Not all practices of freedom appeared as such, judging from the act alone. A good example of this was in the choice by Emily, a 29-year-old blogger who focuses on auto racing, to support Danica Patrick as the driver was criticized for choosing to pose in publications oriented toward men such as *Maxim*, *FHM*, and *SI*'s swimsuit edition. Patrick had been cited by several other participants in negative terms for marketing herself as hyper-feminine and sexually charged. Emily, however, saw her public defense of Patrick as a morally just choice on behalf of female athletes:

> I don't know how much impact just my little blog has, but if enough people are willing to take a stand and get that out there and get their voice heard, then maybe that's what it's going to take. ... I try to make sure that I stay true to the causes that are important to me, which is for women to succeed.

This explanation from Emily – her alliance of critique with action – turns an act that appears to unconsciously comply with dominant discourse into a practice of freedom. It also serves as a reminder of the limits of practices of freedom for transforming cultural power relations – a reason many feminists may ultimately find Foucault so unsatisfying (Markula, 2003; Markula & Pringle, 2006).

Translating individual practice to social transformation

As I launched this project to marry a Foucauldian, post-structuralist approach to my exploration of the Women Talk Sports network, I had to set aside my assumptions about power and reconsider my own feminist orientation. What I discovered is that a radical pluralist lens on these interviews allowed me to see – in a way I would not have otherwise seen – the power that clearly circulates in this network of bloggers and to conceptualize the differences among these bloggers as effective and ultimately working in concert to destabilize – in tiny ways – dominant discourses. I was also able to appreciate the ways these individuals were experiencing freedom (through practice) from those discourses within a social reality that involves contradictions within and between subjects (Sawicki, 1991).

As Macleod (2006) asserted, radical pluralist feminism – at least my understanding of it through this project – does not translate to rampant relativism, fail to consider macro-structures such as sexism or fail to produce meaningful activism. To the contrary and even more importantly, it allows for connections between women that are built on shared strengths and resources, as hooks (1984) advocates.

Along the way, I have positioned this research as similar to Thorpe's (2008) analysis of the discourse of female snowboarders; I have reached the same conclusions in regard to feminist orientations as dividers among women. Unlike Thorpe, however, I found that age was only one divider on issues such as feminism and sexualized displays of athletes. Other characteristics, including whether the blogger was male or female, was a competitive athlete, or had children, were also key to participants' social context and, consequently, their views. Thus, the expectation that all women (and men) can ever share a common feminist orientation is unrealistic. The participants in this research accepted this as common sense; hence, their acceptance – indeed, their embrace – of difference.

My role in this research: ethical use of power?

As Markula (2003) suggests, I was cognizant throughout this project of my use of power. Feminist researchers, as a matter of course, are concerned with the power dynamic between researcher and subject, which makes the relationship fragile and open to misunderstandings and even abuse (Ramazanoglu & Holland, 2002). Because I was involved in the network and I was a speaker in a well-publicized Webcast forum about women's sports and the blogosphere (of interest to WTS members) during the time I was conducting interviews, I was known to WTS members. Furthermore, I was likely the first researcher who had interviewed them about their blogs, and several told me that the attention made them feel important. They wanted to know what I thought of the network and of their work. After the interviews, some bloggers posted about the issues we had discussed and weighed in on the network's listserv about the interviews.

I have occasionally received questions from members of the network about issues related to coverage of women's sports, and I have written blog posts designed primarily as a response to those queries. Through this process, I have aimed to, as Markula (2003, p. 105) suggests, engage in my own "critical self-reflection" within the researcher–subject relationship by being critically self-reflexive and resisting the imposition of my own brand of feminism. I believe my choice of a radical pluralist perspective has helped me avoid discursive strategies that might alienate the subjects of this research.

Conclusions

Research on the Web and on sports-related Web sites, in particular, indicates that it has not been an empowering space for women (Hardin, 2009; Shade, 2002; Worthington, 2005). What this research suggests, however, is that the way power, resistance and transformation are imagined determines our answer to that question. With a more pluralist lens, feminist sport researchers can engage in research and advocacy that will allow us to see the ways women and men in all areas of sport – including in the blogosphere and other forms of entrepreneurial media – are reforming their own identities, engaging in ethical practices, and countering technologies of power. Through these small, even imperceptible steps, perhaps they are moving us toward the social transformation we seek. It is our obligation to assist in this enterprise.

References

Birrell, S. (2000). Feminist theories for sport. In J. Coakley & E. Dunning (Eds.), *Handbook of sports studies* (pp. 61–76). Thousand Oaks, CA: Sage.

Braithwaite, A. (2002). The personal, the political, third-wave, and postfeminisms. *Feminist Theory, 3*(3), 335–44.

Carty, V. (2005). Textual portrayals of female athletes: Liberation or nuanced forms of patriarchy? *Frontiers: A Journal of Women Studies, 26*(2), 132–72.

Cole, C.L. (1993). Resisting the canon: Feminist cultural studies, sport, and technologies of the body. *Journal of Sport and Social Issues, 17*(2), 77–97.

Cole, C.L., Giardina, M.D., & Andrews, D.L. (2004). Michel Foucault: Studies of power and sport. In R. Giulianotti (Ed.), *Sport and modern social theorists* (pp. 227–224). New York: Palgrave Macmillan.

Colwell, S. (1999). Feminisms and figurational sociology: Contributions to understandings of sports, physical education, and sex/gender. *European Physical Education Review, 5*(3), 219–40.

Duffy, T. (2010, Feb. 12). Lindsey Vonn's sexuality is empowering, not exploitative. *The Big Lead.* Retrieved at http://thebiglead.com/index.php/2010/02/12/lindsay-vonns-sexuality-is-empowering-not-exploitative/

Duffy, T. (2010, April 28). Hannah Storm tapes a clue for Jeopardy, looks great. *The Big Lead*. Retrieved at http://thebiglead.com/index.php/2010/04/28/hannah-storm-tapes-a-clue-for-jeopardy-looks-great/#comments

Duncan, M.C. (1994). The politics of women's body images and practices: Foucault, the panopticon, and *Shape* magazine. *Journal of Sport and Social Issues, 18*(1), 48–65.

Duncan, M.C. (2006). Gender warriors in sport: Women and the media. In A.A. Raney & J. Bryant (Eds.), *Handbook of sports and media* (pp. 231–52). Mahwah, NJ: Lawrence Erlbaum Associates.

Edwards, L. & Jones, C. (2009). Postmodernism, queer theory and moral judgment in sport. *International Review for the Sociology of Sport, 44*(4), 331–44.

Eskes, T.B., Duncan, M.C., & Miller, E.M. (1998). The discourse of empowerment: Foucault, Marcuse, and women's fitness texts. *Journal of Sport and Social Issues, 22*(3), 317–44.

Fairclough, N. (1992). *Discourse and social change*. Malden, MA: Polity.

Favorito, J. (2007). *Sports publicity: A practical approach*. St. Louis, MO: Butterworth-Heinemann.

Foucault, M. (1990). *The history of sexuality, Volume 1: An Introduction*. New York: Vintage.

Foucault, M. (1994). *The essential Foucault*. P. Rabinow & N. Rose (Eds.). New York: The New Press.

Foucault, M. (1997). *Ethics: Subjectivity and truth*. P. Rabinow (Ed.). New York: The New Press.

Germov, J. & Williams, L. (1999). Dieting women: Self-surveillance and the body panopticon. In J. Sobal & D. Maurer (Eds.), *Weighty issues: Fatness and thinness as social problems* (pp. 117–32). Piscataway, NJ: Aldine Transaction.

Gill, R. (2007). *Gender and the Media*. Cambridge: Polity Press.

Glenn, B. (2009, Oct. 19). The (HOT) Body Issue. *Women Talk Sports*. Retrieved at www.womentalksports.com/items/read/57/71718

Gramsci, A. (1996). *Prison notebooks, Volume 2*. J.A. Buttigieg (Ed.). New York: Columbia University Press.

Grimshaw, J. (1993). Practices of freedom. In C. Ramazanoglu (Ed.), *Up against Foucault: Explorations of some tensions between Foucault and feminism* (pp. 51–72). New York: Routledge.

Hardin, M. (2009, Sept. 24). Does "new media" bring new attitudes toward women's sports? *Tucker Center for Research on Girls and Women in Sport* Web site. Retrieved at http://tuckercenter.wordpress.com/2009/09/24/does-%E2%80%98new-media%E2%80%99-bring-new-attitudes-toward-women%E2%80%99s-sports/

hooks, b. (1984). *Feminist theory: From margin to center* (2nd Ed.). Cambridge, MA: South End Press.

Lloyd, M. (1996). A feminist mapping of Foucauldian politics. In S.J. Hekman (Ed.), *Feminist interpretations of Michel Foucault* (pp. 241–65). University Park: Pennsylvania State University Press.

Macleod, C. (2006). Radical plural feminisms and emancipatory practice in post-apartheid South Africa. *Theory & Psychology, 16*(3), 367–89.

Markula, P. (2003). The technologies of the self: Sport, feminism, and Foucault. *Sociology of Sport Journal, 20*, 87–107.

Markula, P. (2004). "Tuning into one's self:" Foucault's technologies of the self and mindful fitness. *Sociology of Sport Journal, 21*, 190–210.

Markula, P. & Pringle, R. (2006). *Foucault, sport and exercise: Power, knowledge and transforming the self*. New York: Routledge.

Maxwell, H. (2009). Burden, buzz or both? Reflections on social media and women's sports. *Tucker Center for Research on Girls and Women in Sport*. Retrieved from http://tuckercenter.wordpress.com/2009/10/28/social-media-womens-sports-burden-buzz-or-both/

60 Marie Hardin

McCracken, G. (1988). *The long interview*. Thousand Oaks, CA: Sage.

Messner, M. (2002). *Taking the field: Women, men, and sports*. Minneapolis: University of Minnesota Press.

North, L. (2009). *The gendered newsroom*. Cresskill, NJ: Hampton Press.

Petchesky, B. (2010, April 29). New USA kit looks good on a pretty lady. *Deadspin*. Retrieved at http://deadspin.com/5527375/new-usa-kit-looks-good-on-a-pretty-lady

Potter, J. (1996). Discourse analysis as a way of analyzing naturally occurring talk. In A. Bryman & R.J. Burgess (Eds.), *Qualitative research* (pp. 323–41). Thousand Oaks, CA: Sage.

Pringle, R. (2005). Masculinities, sport, and power: A critical comparison of Gramscian and Foucauldian inspired theoretical tools. *Journal of Sport & Social Issues, 29*(3), 256–78.

Raby, R. (2005). What is resistance? *Journal of Youth Studies, 8*(2), 151–71.

Ramazanoglu, C. (1993). Introduction. In C. Ramazanoglu (Ed.), *Up against Foucault: Explorations of some tensions between Foucault and feminism* (pp. 1–28). New York: Routledge.

Ramazanoglu, C. & Holland, J. (2002). *Feminist methodology: Challenges and choices*. Thousand Oaks, CA: Sage.

Sawicki, J. (1991). *Disciplining Foucault: Feminism, power, and the body*. New York: Routledge.

Scraton, S. & Flintoff, A. (2001). Sport feminism: The contribution of feminist thought to our understandings of gender and sport. In S. Scraton & A. Flintoff (Eds.), *Gender and sport: A reader* (pp. 30–46). New York: Routledge.

Shade, L.R. (2002). *Gender and community in the social construction of the Internet*. New York: Peter Lang.

Soper, K. (1993). Productive contradictions. In C. Ramazanoglu (Ed.), *Up against Foucault: Explorations of some tensions between Foucault and feminism* (pp. 29–50). New York: Routledge.

Thorpe, H. (2008). Foucault, technologies of self, and the media: Discourses of femininity in snowboarding culture. *Journal of Sport & Social Issues, 32*(2), 199–229.

van Zoonen, L. (1994). *Feminist media studies*. Thousand Oaks, CA: Sage.

Vavrus, M.D. (2007). Opting out moms in the news: Selling new traditionalism in the new millennium. *Feminist Media Studies, 7*(1), 47–59.

Weaving, C. (2002). Like beauty, exploitation is in the eye of the beholder: An examination of women Olympic athletes posing nude. In K.B. Wamsley, R.K. Barney, & S.G. Martyn (Eds.), *The global nexus engaged: Past, present, future in interdisciplinary Olympic studies*. Proceedings of the Sixth International Symposium for Olympic Research.

Women's Sports Blog (2009, Oct. 10). ESPN's Body Issue: Poor start. *Women Talk Sports*. Retrieved March 1, 2010, at www.womentalksports.com/items/read/40/68899

Worthington, N. (2005). Women's work on the World Wide Web: How a new medium represents an old problem. *Popular Communication, 3*(1), 43–60.

4

MOCKING THE FAN FOR FUN AND PROFIT

Sports dirt, fanship identity, and commercial narratives

Lawrence A. Wenner

LOYOLA MARYMOUNT UNIVERSITY

Popular characterizations of the sports fan are riddled with images of people who are seemingly bizarre and possessed. In fueling an "imagined community" (Anderson, 1983, p. 6) of sports fans, much media imagery is self-serving, relying on the most animated and colorful of fans, thereby naturalizing what might be seen from a step back, as diehard, unbalanced commitment. So frequently do we encounter those who live and die for their team, rant their viewpoints on sports talk radio and blogs, paint their bodies in team colors, go hoarse chanting and do the wave in stadia, and seemingly know more trivia about sports than they do about more important real world matters that it is not surprising that many see sports fans as morons or idiots who lack meaning in their lives (Are all sports fans morons? 2007; Barrett, 1995; Johnston, 2006; Most sports fans are complete idiots, 2008). Such a casting is rein-forced by even the most straight-laced social-psychological literature on sport fan-ship. Here, renderings feature seemingly quirky compensatory and defensive strategies in the mostly male fan's obsessive tendencies. Ever nimble, sports fans BIRG (bask in reflected glory), CORF (cut off reflected failure), COFF (cut off future failure), and Blast (derogating disliked opponents) in order to maintain what may seem an odd and fragile equilibrium (c.f., Wann, Melnick, Russell, & Pease, 2001). All this fuels a folklore of sports fans and their laughable dysfunctionalities that characterize their undying commitment to sport.

While empirical and ethnographic research may paint a far more tempered – and even rational – picture, narrative constructions of the sports fan, alongside those of other kinds of fans, continue to pathologize fanship as obsessive, hysterical, or as a form of psychological compensation (Jenson, 1992; Sandvoss, 2005). Such narrative castings of the fan are increasingly common in today's Web 2.0 world, where sport specific sites and blogs encourage the fanship story to be seen as one characterized by an "always on" distraction, where obsessive checking of the latest scores, injury reports, or betting odds are just a click away. In investigating such tendencies, there is a need to interrogate what is seemingly an oxymoronic and hegemonic dynamic: the strategic use of the mocked sports fan in advertising narratives to help sell to those being mocked. To frame this effort, the next sections locate key understandings that undergird mocking the male sports fan and outline a reader-centered strategy to critically assess the "dirty logics" and ethical fissures in such tactics.

Locating the mocked sports fan

Understanding narrative sensibilities is necessarily a complex endeavor. Indeed, at least three interlocking forces frame consideration of advertising narratives that rely on the mocked sports fan. Foremost are tendencies to commodify sports fanship. These are followed by understandings of the tendencies and reception of the male sports fan. Finally, reliance on these first two elements interacts with the building social stereotype of men as losers. Brief consideration of each follows.

The commodified sports fan

With the rise of sports marketing and with sports programming having become one of the few remaining "big tents" for broadcasters, the commodification of sport fanship has become a ubiquitous feature of modern life. Indeed, Crawford (2004) builds a cogent case that one must necessarily study sport fanship in the context of consumption. He relies on arguments by Giulianotti (2002, p. 27) that "hypercommodification" characterizes our points of contact with sport and Kellner (2001, p. 38) who poses that the new norm for sport has become "spectacle that sells the values of products, celebrities, and institutions of the media and consumer society." This shift constitutes a broader cultural change that Bauman (1998, p. 26) notes has made for a "primacy of consumption in social relations" such that "one needs to be a consumer first, before one can think of becoming anything in particular." Amplifying Horne's (2005) arguments that the "consumerization" of fanship has been fueled by media strategies that have naturalized the logics of advertising and sponsorship in the sporting context, Crawford (2004, p. 4) concludes that so much relates "directly or indirectly to acts of consumption" that "being a fan is primarily a consumer act and hence fans can been seen first and foremost as consumers."

Clearly, in a variety of media settings, the role of the sports fan is idealized as a consumer. In advertising in particular, we are regularly cast into this role and the role is regularly performed to simulate and stimulate our carrying it into the marketplace. Such a dynamic undergirds the spectacle/performance paradigm of the audience (Abercrombie & Longhurst, 1998). In attempting to mobilize this, television commercials in sports programming work to shape characterizations that imagine fanship communities to strategic advantage. By casting sports fans in consumer roles, advertisers naturalize how sport relates to the consumption of other things. Thus, studying commercial narratives can reveal not only how the fan's role is imagined, but also how the power of sport can be tactically ported to reach the consumer in diverse markets (c.f., Wenner, 2008a).

The male sports fan

That the commodified sports fan has largely been male has been a blessing for advertisers and broadcasters. This floats the boat of sports programming. Here, advertisers have a stable way to reach an elusive and desirable young male demographic with notably discretionary incomes (Horne, 2005). There are further benefits when one examines the underpinnings and character of men's relation to sports. Historically, sport has been a male cultural practice. Today it remains ideologically a male domain (Gosling, 2007). Most importantly, it remains a soothing last bastion of "vestigial hypermasculinity" (Wenner, 1998). In the face of increasing demands to adapt to changes in gender roles and power relations, men continue to largely "own" sport consumption. The trajectory for this starts early. A recent ESPN poll contrasts building sport socialization and increased sports viewing as boys become men to the comparative disinterest on the part of girls, a trend that continues in the 25–34 age group when men's viewing is at its highest (Mulhern, 2009). Such foundational socialization anchors continued commitment. According to a Pew Research Center poll, 57% of men contrasted with 35% of women follow sports "very" or "somewhat" closely, with men pulling further ahead when the most avid are compared (Who's a sports fan? 2006).

This combination of socialization and practice has bred an archetype for the male sports fan as invested, engaged, and committed. The reality of this is good news for advertisers who have worked to encourage and normalize such dispositions and take advantage of weakened sensibilities fueled by fanship obsessions. Such strategies set the stage for making fun of men's complex relationship with sport. Indeed, evidence shows male fanship strongly intertwined with self-esteem and substantial identity investment. Men more avidly follow sports news and wager on game outcomes. When compared to women, male fans more fully prepare for contests, get more aroused and excited, drink and eat more during spectating, and are more likely to brood after a favorite's loss. It is easy to see how such passion and commitment for sport contests, whose outcome is writ small in the course of world events and everyday life, may open the door to ridicule the male fan as moron, idiot, or loser (Dietz-Uhler, Harrick, End, & Jacquemotte, 2000; Gantz & Wenner, 1995; James & Ridinger, 2002; Wann, Melnick, Russell, & Pease, 2001; Wenner & Gantz, 1998).

The commodified male sports fan as loser

Meshing with such proclivity to see men's passion for sports in ludicrous and even demeaning terms has been increased sensitivity to and appreciation of diversity. With this has come some disquiet in poking fun at "protected" identity groups. In this climate, it is often difficult to know who will take offense what most would regard as relatively benign jocular slights. As a result, the boundaries of political correctness have often stopped at the group perhaps least deserving of protection, the White male. In part, this has enabled the institutionalization of "male bashing," some in fun and some not, and the formation of interlocking stereotypes of the male as bumbler, slacker, and "himbo" (Nathanson & Young, 2001; Patterson, 1996; The bumbling man, 2008). In a multi-stage study of psychological schemas underlying categorization of male stereotypes, Edwards (1992) notes that the recently emergent loser subtype has moved to a position of relative primacy, surpassing positive castings as family man and businessman. Further, Edwards finds firm contours to the male loser stereotype (and their synonyms of jerk, nerd, bum, wimp, geek, and the like) with core attributes anchored in not trying, underachieving, bad attitude, pessimism, being a quitter, and low social skills, confidence, motivation, and self-esteem. Unsurprisingly, other psychological studies find that this stereotypical profile contributes to bias against men (Fiebert & Meyer, 1997).

Reinforcing this, Nathanson and Young's (2001) *Spreading Misandry* argues that persistence of these stereotypes in popular culture has taught and legitimized contempt for men. Taking the form of "gender sneer" in advertising, Kane (2005, p. C2) observes that the prevalence of "man as a dope" imagery has made it virtually impossible to "watch commercials or read ads without seeing helpless, hapless men." In advertising directed at the sport audience, Wenner and Jackson (2009, p. 23) note that the male consumer as loser is so often seen being "foiled and flummoxed by beautiful and smarter women" that he has become "a poster child for masculinity lost." Messner and Montez de Oca (2005, p. 1882) see such images as result of a "destabilized hegemonic masculinity" fueled by historic structural changes in social formations. Yet, their study focused on the "white-guy-as-loser trope" (p. 1905) in Super Bowl beer commercials finds a two-pronged danger in routine employment where irony reifies his lowered status and masks building distrust of and anger at women. Recent studies (Duncan & Aycock, 2009; Wenner, 2009a, 2010b) of commercials featured in sports programming show continued reliance on negative themes of males as losers and narrative characterizations emphasizing the male sport fan's relational ineptitude with both women and buddies. Building on these findings, this study melds a broader host of issues that come together – about commodified fanship, the tenor of male fanship, and increased reliance on the male loser stereotype. In doing so, it attempts to unravel the mystery of how strategic mocking of the male sports fan services marketing to that desirable target market.

Approaching the mocked fan narrative

Finding answers to a mystery of this complexity requires a multi-faceted approach. Particularly suited to the task is a far-ranging "dirt theory of narrative ethics" (Wenner, 2007) that has been used extensively to deconstruct commercial narratives and their reading as well as interrogate the ethical nature of that transaction (Hilliard

& Hendley, 2004; Wenner, 1991, 1994, 2004, 2006, 2007, 2008a, 2008b, 2009a, 2009b, 2010a, 2010b, 2011). Brief consideration of the three prongs of the approach and the issues it raises for mocking the male sports fan for fun and profit follow.

Finding dirt

In essence, dirt as "matter out of place" (Douglas, 1966, p. 35) facilitates transferring power and logic from old to new settings (Enzenberger, 1972; Hartley, 1984; Leach, 1976). The communicative power of porting dirt is recognized when we say "sex sells" or celebrity athletes use the "power of sport" to endorse diverse products. By applying old logics to new stories, dirt relies on "cultural borrowing" (Wenner, 1991, p. 392) to bring familiar understandings, impose restraints, and pollute meaning. As these workings and tensions frame dirt theory, it is essential to follow the dirt. In assessing commodified narratives that mock the male fan, one must consider the sensibilities that dirt brings about both sport and gender. What are its origins and character? How is importation negotiated? How do entailments shape meaning in new contexts? With dirt's infiltration, what distortions and fallacies are embraced or masked? Such concerns frame assessments of reading dynamics and the working of dirt in characterizations of the mocked fan.

Constructing readers

In reading, we necessarily soil new texts with old dirt. Anchored in what readers bring to texts, reception theory (c.f., Machor & Goldstein, 2001; Tompkins, 1980) shares necessary preoccupation with dirt. Dirt analysis embraces Iser's (1974, 1978, 2006) concern with the (1) contextualization of implied readers, (2) drawing of readers in and by texts, and (3) nature of the reading act (c.f., Wenner, 2007). To fully reveal narratives that invoke mocking the male sports fan, consideration must be taken of sporting "interpretive communities" (Fish, 1980), characterizations of textual surrogates and strategies (e.g., camera position, direct address) to encourage preferred reading, and how negotiation of redundancies and gaps in texts stimulates readerly disposition. From such interlocking queries about how dirt frames assertions of the commodified male sport fan, the forces that undergird reading an "imagined community" that is somehow worthy of being mocked may be seen. In this course, improprieties taken to naturalize readers' alignment with the merits of mocking the male sports fan can be clarified. Thus, the last step of dirt theory calls for ethical assessment of the transaction between dirt and its reading.

Deconstructing ethics

Once debated (Carroll, 2000), ethical criticism has become inescapable and integral in narrative analysis and cultural critique (Booth, 1998; Eaglestone, 2004; Eagleton,

2003; Gregory, 1998; Kellner, 2000; Zylinska, 2005). With focus on ethical tensions in texts and reading, it raises questions about greater good, minimizing harm, other-respecting care, veracity, fairness, justice, and other issues in order to reveal moral flaws in narratives as both aesthetic defects and culturally problematic. Thus driven, a dirt-centered focus considers what the "matter out of place" (Douglas, 1966, p. 35) really is and does. Consideration is given to whether assumptions about the male sports fan were ethically flawed prior to importation. In assessing new narratives that rely on mocking him, such an approach interrogates not only the propriety of dirt being imported but also the dirtiness encouraged in characterizing both the reader and pathways that reading invites (Wenner, 2007). Fueling ethical assessment are answers to questions about the landing, build-up, movement, and interactive workings of sport, gender, and fanship dirt with other matter. Have liberties been taken with dirt to characterize the "imagined community" of the commodifed male sports fan or push improprietously to control reading of him? Have flawed logics about him been used to mask truth, reinforce prejudice, perpetuate inequities, and forego other-respecting care or greater good? Such queries guide ethical stocktaking of commercial narratives that mock the male fan.

Deconstructing mocked fan narratives

Narrative constructions mocking the male sports fan are plentiful. Key word searches (driven by permutations of fan, stadium, name of sport, etc.) at adcritic.com, the largest advertising industry propriety database of commercials, yielded approximately 150 such narratives. From this, five archetypal categories dominated constructions of the commodifed male sports fan as: (1) nut case, (2) loser, (3) juvenile, (4) relationally deficient, and (5) emasculated. Brief dirt theory analyses introduce illustrative examples and then key on two commercials within each variant (n.b.: accessed in February 2010, all referenced commercials are available for viewing by subscription at adcritic.com by title).

The nut case

Reliant on evidence that male passion for sport is considerable, narratives in this category cast the male sport fan as unhinged "whack jobs." Here, much fun is had by a wide variety of sponsors. Adidas comically medicalizes the malady in their "Footballitis" series, Fox Sports Net in "Feet" shows a father with eyes glued to sport pinning diaper to baby with his toes, Coca-Cola in "Tailgating" shows crazed guys fantasizing action with thrown pork chops and Coke bottles, and in "The Whack" TruTV celebrates clownish but violent fan hyperactivity.

In "Giant Loser," the Los Angeles Dodgers lean on archetypal "certifiably insane" male fan behavior. A "hidden camera" on a grungy city bus filled with riders documents an odd, almost creepy, fan, wearing a Dodger jacket and cap, begin to badger a complete stranger who reacts with trepidation. Bemused passengers, eschewing involvement, look the other way as the Dodger fan, ignoring a "don't bother me" plea, plows ahead mounting a Giants cap on his victim. Pointing at his patsy, the Dodger fan loudly taunts the man as a "Giant bum" with "no chance to get past boo" who "likes to cheer on people who don't win." Having played his scene, the Dodger fan grabs the Giants cap back, catches a breath of relief and nervously thanks the victimized passenger as a "You Have to Be There" superimposition closes the ad.

In "Marty," Bud Light gives a name to and honors the behavior of such uncontrollable fanship. Here, "to help celebrate ESPN's 25th anniversary," an announcer striding forward on a stage set as a gallery of crazed fans "salutes the 25 greatest fans in sports, guys like Marty Silverton." Testimonials are then intercut with nerdy Marty in action. A sportscaster elevates Marty beyond being "a heckler," casting him as "psychological warrior." A referee, victim to Marty's ire, explains he "is the reason I'm in therapy." His mother reflects "he never had many friends at school, but he always liked sports." In a locker room, a player laments "he was just hateful." In closing, the announcer points at the camera, pronouncing "have a Bud Light Marty, you're on the list."

Framing these nut cases relies on porting dirty stereotypes of the male sports fan as so committed that he "should be committed" for such insane behavior. Yet, reading position encourages seeing this as a natural state of affairs, and in "Marty" engages in ironic valorization of this as behaviorally legitimate. Indeed, while characterizations of textual surrogates, cast as passengers on the bus and testimonial givers to Marty, recognize such behavior as notable, its naturalization is not contested. In doing so, the ethical posture is schizophrenic. On one hand, it encourages enjoyment in reading these as routine sagas of men as nut cases. On the other, it encourages looking the other way and, with a nod and a wink, giving men a free pass as "boys will be boys" in explaining that's the way men are. It perpetuates seeing a low bar for men, routinely beyond the pale, but very much expected.

The loser

Less "certifiable" but just as common are sagas of male sports fans as losers who can't get anything right and are constantly assaulted by the world. In "Bad Day," NFL.com seemingly offers fantasy football as salvation for fans prone to losing too many bets on games. The loser in Coors Light's "Baseball" is a clueless fan who gets beaned while reaching for a beer. In Southwest Airlines's "Video Game," excited losers, mimicking game action, dim-wittedly hurl a baseball and fracture their new large screen television.

This "just can't win" pallor follows the loser in Bud Light's "Dude (Stadium)." From taking it in the groin entering the turnstile gate, the loser lamely cries "dude" to those responsible for each mounting humiliating affront. Seemingly so downtrodden that he seems clinically depressed, our loser suffers beer spilt on his lap, embarrassingly stumbles into a sportscast, encounters both foul odors and an occupant in a toilet stall, and is invisible in calling to a beer vendor. In closing, the terminal slacker fights back but is foiled in his attempt to invade a hospitality suite.

Further humiliation awaits another loser fan in Fox Sports Net's "Stadium." Here one young adult brother reflects upon his loser twin, wondering "what happened to Ernie?" Over nostalgic faux family footage of the two growing up, he notes they were "real close," "treated like they were normal," and "liked the same teams." Moving to the present, he laments that Ernie has "become a fair weather fan" whose "elevator doesn't go to the top floor." In shifting alliances from his brother's losing team, Ernie is painted as opportunistic loser, "a lunatic" whose "seat came off his tractor." For this, he is shown being deservedly hassled, beaten, and even thrown into a men's room urinal at the stadium. The narrative closes on an injured, hospitalized Ernie being beaten by his brother over televised game viewing punctuated by the superimposed reminder "Don't Be a Sellout."

Predicated on dirtied importation of broad-based cultural stereotypes of men as helpless and hapless, these narratives embrace aspects of both "laughing at" and "looking down on" men seen in spreading misandry (Nathanson & Young, 2001). Yet, in reading both these losers, encouragement is given to laugh and look down without empathy or pity. It is understood that somehow they deserve it. While this may be "all in good fun," there is homage to what is posed as underlying truth: men today just can't get it right. This assertion functions as both punching bag and punch line. In Bud Light's "Dude" this is a broad claim about the contemporary beleaguered state of everyman. In Fox Sport Net's "Stadium," it pertains not only to Ernie as sorry metaphor for following one's own star, but also to his brother and others who are so preoccupied with fanship identity that they cannot tolerate difference. In each, the moral pathways we are invited to follow are flawed. Taken together, they magnify a double bind. Not only do we look down and laugh at men who accept perpetual subjugation, but also when they, like Ernie, try to take another tack.

The juvenile

Perhaps setting the backdrop to the male sports fan as innate loser is his ready characterization as juvenile and childlike. Archetypal are fans such as Cablevision's "Johnny Bandwagon," a middle-aged man whose ludicrous immersion into accoutrements (athletic jerseys, caps, and gear) and technology reeks of the immaturity of adolescence. In ESPN's "Medical Condition," ostensibly professional men at work are so infantile in their pre-occupation with a jury-rigged shooting contest that participants call childlike fouls and for medical "do-overs." In Holiday Inn Express's "Fans," similarly infantilized men break into stereotypic fanship euphoria for a breakfast buffet.

Such characterization of men as boys underlies XanGo's "Biggest Fans." In direct address, a solemn corporate spokesman, standing in the XanGo corporate lobby, begins "Ever since we sponsored Real Salt Lake, things haven't been the same."

Supportive vignettes show clumsy, portly, and White middle managers, madly enacting boyhood sports fantasies, wreaking havoc in the office. Here they dash downfield kicking and screaming, terrorize an opening elevator with a kick at goal, strip to undershirts in jubilation, streak naked through a shocked company cafeteria, and douse themselves with XanGo juice as celebratory champagne in the men's room. Of this, the unshaken corporate spokesman closes, "XanGo is the proud sponsor of Real Salt Lake, maybe too proud."

A flipside to men's euphoric juvenile nature is shown in Major League Baseball's "Tree" commercial. Here, tuxedo-clad former Dodger manager Tommy Lasorda stares up a tree, asking a woman, "How long has he been up there?" As she replies, "Since his team was eliminated from the post-season," we see her dejected husband wearing a Cubs jersey, childlike, clinging to his perch. As MC, Lasorda commands the couple's daughter at an organ to "hit it kid!" With "Take Me Out to the Ballgame" grinding, Lasorda's pep talk exhorts, "Real fans don't hide in October, Frank," reminding the Cub fan "you're a bigger fan of baseball" and commanding him to "get out of the tree." Jumping down to smiles, neighbors wearing different team jerseys reinforce Lasorda's characterization that "we all live for this" as reason to watch the post-season on Fox.

In these spots, a broader dirty assertion that men are really immature boys is given specificity – sport makes men boys – to aid marketing aims to grow fanship iden-tification. The reading position embraces seeing this as both natural and extending to all men, which in both instances is not the case. Yet, through this, the normalcy of infantilized men sets a baseline for narrative understanding. Even in such mocking jocularity, assertions of the veracity of claims about men's true nature serve the marketing goals of both XanGo and Fox. They give both permission and excuse for men to take juvenile time-outs for sport. While indeed little harm may come from men's periodic escapes through sport, the staying power of broad-based assertions about men's infantile nature is far less ethically benign.

The relationally deficient

The juvenile casting of the male sports fan undergirds his ready painting as deficient in relationships with women (c.f., Messner & Montez de Oca, 2005; Wenner, 2010b). Seen along broad product categories, men's preoccupation with sports illuminates broader relational ineptitude. From Coors Light's "Beer Babe," where a nerdy fan prematurely "ejaculates" beer at the sight of his dream girl (Wenner, 2010b), to Bud Light's "Satin Sheets" where a man can only be bribed to sex from sport with a beer (Duncan & Aycock, 2009), to an antenna-wearing sports addict in TiVo's "Baseball" who is oblivious to his wife's sexual advances, men's relational deficiencies are cast as givens. This is the case even in narratives offering solutions, such as when a wife's help in Viagra's "Sports" make "sports kind of disappear," and Budweiser's "Relationship Counselor" where a chagrined wife with marital problems is flummoxed to see her husband "male-bond" with the counselor over sports.

Throughout, men's disingenuousness and distraction are the orders of the day. In Birra Moretti's Zero's "On the Couch" we see a gorgeous blonde woman, alone watching a romance movie, nod as her disheveled husband with beer bottle stumbles drunkenly to sit beside her. Reacting abhorrently to his guzzling, burping, and clumsy advances, she throws the remote control at him and bolts from the room. Pleased at the results of his faux drunkedness, the man quickly changes channels, "sobers up" with a grin, and enjoys his soccer match. The closing shot superimposes "0% Alcohol, 100% Beer" as reminder of the product's complicity in the man's deception.

Providing portraiture to deficiency, Fox Sports Net's "Pregnancy Test" finds a couple seated on a living room couch watching a game. Attempting to hand over unseen results from a home pregnancy test to her husband, a nervous wife says "if it's blue, we're pregnant." Uncomfortable, the man reluctantly takes the test while his wife anxiously grabs his hand and closes her eyes to hear the results. Distracted by a television reminder of an upcoming Mets vs. Phillies game, his wife's "well?" marks his slowness and her eager anticipation of results. In the end, the husband loses focus, distractedly observing "the Mets will kill 'em," and telling his wife to "take this thing" (the pregnancy test).

In these ads, the cultural stereotype of men's inability to be genuine and engaged in their relational lives with women is imported as dirt and then reinforced by characterizing the hold of sport on men as a key element in that problem. In this, sport becomes metaphor for men's self-absorption. The naturalization of this, and that humor is found in this being an inexorable trait of contemporary manhood, forms the basis for reading. On both points, the narrative assertions are ethically suspect. While posing the disingenuousness to disinterest continuum as delimiters of man's relational capacity may be funny and even beg credulity, its veracity is suspect and its celebration is ultimately self-defeating for both men and women. Yet, in these instances, it serves the goals of these marketing narratives by granting permission for men to once again exercise their privileges.

The emasculated

Making fun of men's insecurity and rising fears of emasculation are regular occurrences in sport-related advertising. On one hand, men are regularly threatened by women. In Michelob Ultra's "Light Beer Just Got a Little Darker," they are taunted and embarrassed by women in touch football, and in Tooheys' "Man vs. Woman vs. Beer," a woman out-toughs men drinking at a bowling alley (Wenner, 2010b). On the other hand, men are threatened by the specter of men breaching compulsory heterosexuality. In Heineken's "Male Bonding Incident" men attracted to each other are threatened by that possibility, and in Amstel's "Offside" men are threatened by their attraction to an attractive cross-dressing male (Wenner, 2009a).

In Budweiser's "Huge" the depths of male fragility become the butt of the joke. We see a young woman, wearing only an oversized sweatshirt, bring beers and join her boyfriend at the game-viewing couch. To his query "Where'd you get that, it's huge" she replies "my old boyfriend." As they cuddle, he reticently observes "he must have been huge" and she acknowledges "he was." Persisting, he asks "why don't you change into one of mine" only to get the disheartening reply "nah, yours are kind of small." Adding insult to injury, she admits "smalls are OK, but these just feel better." A narrative break by Budweiser marks this as "true" prior to the ad's salt-into-wound closing with the girlfriend amorously noting "you have the tiniest little hands" as the man is further broken.

Flo TV's "Spineless" shows a man pushed to further depths of emasculation by his female partner. In an "injury report on Jason Glasby" from a department store lingerie section, CBS football announcer Jim Nantz reports that "his girlfriend has removed his spine, rendering him incapable of watching the game." Accompanying this, we see a laconic, perhaps sedated, 20-ish Jason, seemingly oblivious to a red brassiere that has been strewn over his shoulder, dutifully carrying shopping bags as his girlfriend pulls him away from the television department, where football is on screens, and up an escalator for her further shopping adventures. Seeing this, Nantz reports "that's hard to watch" and counters "how 'bout not" when Jason suggests "how 'bout lavender" for one his girlfriend's purchases. Disgusted, Nantz commands "Jason, get your self a Flo TV personal television" so "live sports goes where you go," closing on a final admonition: "Change out of that skirt, Jason."

"Huge" and "Spineless" get their laughs by bringing dirt of men's broad-based fears to the sacred grounds of male sports fanship. In this, such affronts are made even greater. In both, the reading position naturalizes that in today's relational world, women have the upper hand and often wield it in ways that now routinely demean men. Yet, at the same time, this insensitive and morally suspect posture is given power as permission is granted to make it a joke. Here, the size of masculinity is always at stake. In "Huge," one's sweatshirt, hands, and presumably other things, are never big enough. In "Spineless," men face the ever-prescient prospect of being cut down to size. In each case, size matters, a posture that betrays other-respecting care and encourages other moral fissures in relational life.

Reflections on mocking and privilege

This study has examined the perplexing dynamics at play in commercial narratives that rely on mocking the male sports fan. Indeed, positive portrayals of male sports fans in the commercial context do not seem to exist. In this landscape, the male sports fan is mocked as: (1) nut case (2) loser, (3) juvenile, (4) relationally deficient, and (5) emasculated. Here, the tensions between mocking and privilege are very much hand-in-glove. In differing ways, each speaks to shifting sands and moral fractures in cultural relations. Nut case narratives build on stereotypes of committed male fanship and the privileged position of men to act these out. Loser narratives bring more bite; men here, assaulted by the world, struggle for pleasures, even in their home territory of sport. In juvenile narratives, privilege, as seen in the nut case narratives, is recognized, but rather than being based in men's passions, privilege remains largely vestigial where sport is a last playground for those diminished by their own infantilism. In narratives of men as relationally deficient, themes of diminished capacity layer on those of juvenility and are used in strategic ways to explain men's disingenuousness as a foundational moral flaw that undergirds their pragmatism. Narratives of men as emasculated seemingly draw a moral line where tolerance for such tendencies end as men are called on their game and put in their place by women. Yet, in each narrative strain, set as they are in sporting reminders of men's once greater power, humor and irony enable men to maintain some sense of dignity. This is true whether privilege is granted to be juvenile or loony over sports, or whether these narratives justify why in today's world men are losers, relationally deficient, or increasingly emasculated. Nonetheless, it isn't a funny state of affairs and it isn't just about sports.

We know that in a culture that has increased sensitivity to political correctness that one of the final resting stops for poking fun is the privileged White male. This requires some speaking to. Admittedly, White male privilege can still fuel substantial benefits. Yet, these have been tempered in recent times by both righteous and less so forces. One of the downsides of political correctness is a cultural loss of humor that comes with the sensitivities magnified by such a knee-jerk approach to manners, however materialized. As a result, one of the few targets of what might be called "characteristics" humor, perhaps better stated as humor coming from stereotype, is the White male, and one might add heterosexual White male. Indeed, one can understand the notion of his time having come.

Nonetheless, the systemacity of the assault on straight White males as clueless clods wreaking havoc and incompetent in their personal lives and the world seen here is a remarkable archetype that is both a shrine to and unfortunate artifact of post-feminist times. This observation is spoken as a committed feminist. Such diminution of males, reliant on a broad swatch stereotype such as those that continue to affect women everyday, should not receive a welcome home in feminism. Such attacks, even those couched in jest or caricature, can bring quiet venom. In considering the cultural spread of misandry, Nathanson and Young (2001) speak to the lasting power that comes in making men the last and lasting butt of jokes. Still, in our times, most would plead to the beleaguered White male to "lighten up" as once might have been said to an African-American, Latina/Latino, gay or lesbian for deriding a playful stereotype. But just as harm felt by these groups would be real, it can be real here also, but is likely overlooked by straight White males conditioned not to express weakness. In recessionary times, when men have been hit particularly hard, such assaults merely add insult to injury. Still it seems somehow improprietous for the straight White male to lodge a complaint. Admittedly, there are more pressing problems. But based on the analyses here, his time is due.

In tackling something so complex as the oxymoronic tensions of using the mocked male fan in selling to that target demographic, there is no doubt a nod to the naturalization of our immersion into the postmodern pastiche. Humor, too, needed here to soften the artifice of assault on the male sport fan as loser, can work in complex and often hegemonic ways, where the target of derision gains pleasure in being the butt of the joke. Still, once a dynamic such as this one can be coherently revealed as an intentional and strategic social construction, this opens the door to the mobilization of resistance. This possibility, and the merits of it, is the main contribution of a study of this sort. It remains possible of course that being thusly mocked is a vestigial affirmation of historical White male privilege. Perhaps these narrative strategies merely valorize that the White male today still doesn't have to try so hard to achieve dominance. Yet, evidence suggests that such claims increasingly rely on crumbling myths about the male condition. In today's world, men are losing ground on many fronts (Tyre et al., 2006). Their trajectory in education has fallen while continuing to rise in criminal justice punishment. Increasingly, the destabilization of their roles in the work force has caused concomitant fissures in their family lives. While in socialization "real men" learn to have thick skins, one wonders, under such conditions, whether mocking men as losers is something to continue to joke about.

References

Abercrombie, N. & Longhurst, B. (1998). *Audiences*. London: Sage.

Anderson, B. (1983). *Imagined communities*. London: Verso.

Are all sports fans morons? (2007, January 27). Retrieved February 1, 2010 from the Word Matter blog at http://findingwords.blogspot.com/2007/01/are-all-sports-fans-morons.html

Barrett, W.M. (1995, March). Fools for fans. *USA Today*, 77.

Bauman, Z. (1998). *Work, consumerism, and the new poor*. Buckingham, UK: Open University Press.

Booth, W.C. (1998). Why ethical criticism can never be simple. *Style, 32*, 351–64.

Carroll, N. (2000). Art and ethical criticism: An overview of recent directions of research. *Ethics, 110*, 350–87.

Crawford, G. (2004). *Consuming sport: Fans, sport, and culture*. London: Routledge.

Dietz-Uhler, B., Harrick, E., End, C., & Jacquemotte, L. (2000). Sex differences in sport fan behavior and reasons for being a sport fan. *Journal of Sport Behavior, 23*, 219–31.

Douglas, M. (1966). *Purity and danger: An analysis of the concepts of pollution and taboo*. London: Routledge & Kegan Paul.

Duncan, M.C. & Aycock, A. (2009). "I laughed until it hurt": Negative humor in Super Bowl ads. In L.A. Wenner & S.J. Jackson (Eds.), *Sport, beer, and gender: Promotional culture and contemporary social life* (pp. 245–59). New York: Peter Lang.

Eaglestone, R. (2004). Postmodernism and ethics against the metaphysics of comprehension. In S. Connor (Ed.), *The Cambridge companion to postmodernism* (pp. 182–95). Cambridge: Cambridge University Press.

Eagleton, T. (2003). *After theory*. New York: Basic Books.

Edwards, G.H. (1992). The structure and content of the male gender role stereotype: An exploration of subtypes. *Sex Roles, 27*, 533–51.

Enzenberger, H. (1972). Constituents of a theory of the media. In D. McQuail (Ed.), *Sociology of mass communication* (pp. 99–112). Harmondsworth, UK: Penguin.

Fiebert, M.S. & Meyer, M.W. (1997). Gender stereotypes: A bias against men. *Journal of Psychology, 131*, 407–10.

Fish, S. (1980). *Is there a text in this class? The authority of interpretive communities*. Cambridge, MA: Harvard University Press.

Gantz, W. & Wenner, L.A. (1991). Men, women, and sports: Audience experiences and effects. *Journal of Broadcasting and Electronic Media, 35,* 233–43.

Gantz, W. & Wenner, L.A. (1995). Fanship and the television sports viewing experience. *Sociology of Sport Journal, 12,* 56–74.

Gantz, W., Wenner, L.A., Carrico, C., & Knorr, M. (1995a). Assessing the football widow hypothesis: A coorientation study of the role of televised sports in long-standing relationships. *Journal of Sport and Social Issues, 19,* 352–76.

Gantz, W., Wenner, L.A., Carrico, C., & Knorr, M. (1995b). Televised sports and marital relationships. *Sociology of Sport Journal, 12,* 306–23.

Giulianotti, R. (2002). Supporters, followers, fans, and flaneurs: A taxonomy of spectator identities in football. *Journal of Sport and Social Issues, 26,* 25–46.

Gosling, V.K. (2007). Girls allowed? The marginalization of female sport fans. In J. Gray, C. Sandvoss, & C.L. Harrington (Eds.), *Fandom: Identities and communities in a mediated world* (pp. 251–60). New York: NYU Press.

Gregory, M. (1998). Ethical criticism: What it is and why it matters. *Style, 32,* 194–220.

Grossberg, L. (1992). Is there a fan in the house? The affective sensibility of fandom. In L.A. Lewis (Ed.), *The adoring audience: Fan culture and popular media* (pp. 50–65). London: Routledge.

Harris, J. (2003, September-October). Male bashing. *Off Our Backs,* 58–59.

Hartley, J. (1984). Encouraging signs: TV and the power of dirt, speech, and scandalous categories. In W. Rowland & B. Watkins (Eds.), *Interpreting television: Current research perspectives* (pp. 119–41). Beverly Hills, CA: Sage.

Hilliard, D.C. & Hendley, A.O. (2004, November). Celebrity athletes and sports imagery in advertising during the NFL telecasts. Paper presented at the annual meeting of the North American Society for the Sociology of Sport, Tucson, AZ.

Horne, J. (2005). *Sport in consumer culture.* New York: Palgrave Macmillan.

Iser, W. (1974). *The implied reader: Patterns of reading in prose fiction from Bunyan to Beckett.* Baltimore, MD: Johns Hopkins University Press.

Iser, W. (1978). *The act of reading: A theory of aesthetic response.* Baltimore, MD: Johns Hopkins University Press.

Iser, W. (2006). Reception theory: Iser. In *How to do theory* (pp. 57–69). Oxford: Blackwell.

James, J. & Ridinger, L.L. (2002). Female and male sport fans: A comparison of sport consumption motives. *Journal of Sport Behavior, 25,* 260–78.

Jenson, J. (1992). Fandom as pathology: The consequences of characterization. In L.A. Lewis (Ed.), *The adoring audience: Fan culture and popular media* (pp. 9–29). London: Routledge.

Johnston, B. (2006, February 3). Memo to rabid Hawks fans: Get a life. Retrieved February 1, 2010 from the Seattle Post-Intelligencer Web site at www.seattlepi.com/opinion/258105_sports03.html

Kane, C. (2005, January 28). As spots belittling women fade out, men become the target of the seemingly inevitable gender sneer. *New York Times,* p. C2.

Kellner, D. (2000). Cultural studies and philosophy: An intervention. In T. Miller (Ed.), *A companion to cultural studies* (pp. 139–53). Oxford: Blackwell.

Kellner, D. (2001). The sports spectacle, Michael Jordan, and Nike: Unholy alliance? In D.L. Andrews (Ed.), *Michael Jordan, inc.: Corporate sport, media culture and late modern America.* New York: SUNY Press.

Leach, E. (1976). *Culture and communication.* Cambridge: Cambridge University Press.

Machor, J.L. & Goldstein, P. (Eds.). (2001). *Reception study: From literary theory to cultural studies.* London: Routledge.

Messner, M.A. & Montez de Oca, J. (2005). The male consumer as loser: Beer and liquor ads in mega sports media events. *Signs, 30,* 1879–1909.

Most sports fans are complete idiots (2008, March 21). Retrieved February 1, 2010 from the Special Kind of Stupid Web site at www.seattlepi.com/opinion/258105_sports03.html

Mulhern, M. (2009, August 28). ESPN studies sports demographics, and finds some interesting results. Retrieved December 10, 2009, from MikeMulhern.net Web site: www.mikemulhern.net/index.php?q=breakingnow/espn-studies-sports-demographics-and-finds-some-interesting-results

Nathanson, P. & Young, K.K. (2001). *Spreading misandry: The teaching of contempt for men in popular culture.* Montreal: McGill-Queen's University Press.

Patterson, P. (1996). Rambos and himbos: Stereotypical images of men in advertising. In P.M. Lester (Ed.), *Images that injure: Pictorial stereotypes in the media* (pp. 93–96). Westport, CT: Praeger.

Sandvoss, C. (2005). *Fans: The mirror of consumption.* Cambridge: Polity Press.

The bumbling man. (2009, April 27). Reinforcing male stereotypes. Retrieved February 1, 2010 on the community.feministing.com Web site at http://community.feministing.com/2009/04/the-bumbling-man-reinforcing-m.html

Tompkins, J.P. (Ed.). (1980). *Reader-response criticism: From formalism to post-structuralism.* Baltimore, MD: Johns Hopkins University Press.

Tyre, P., Murr, A., Juarez, V., Underwood, A., Springen, K., & Wingert, P. (2006, January 30). The trouble with boys. *Newsweek,* 44–52.

Wann, D.L., Melnick, M.M., Russell, G.W., & Pease, D.G. (2001). *Sport fans: The psychology and social impact of spectators.* New York: Routledge.

Wenner, L.A. (1991). One part alcohol, one part sport, one part dirt, stir gently: Beer commercials and television sports. In L.R. Vande Berg & L.A. Wenner (Eds.), *Television criticism: Approaches and applications* (pp. 388–407). New York: Longman.

Wenner, L.A. (1994). The dream team, communicative dirt, and the marketing of synergy: USA basketball and cross-merchandising in television commercials. *Journal of Sport and Social Issues, 18,* 27–47.

Wenner, L.A. (1998). In search of the sports bar: Masculinity, alcohol, sports, and the mediation of public space. In G. Rail (Ed.), *Sport and postmodern times: Culture, gender, sexuality, the body and sport* (pp. 301–32). Albany, NY: SUNY Press.

Wenner, L.A. (2004). Recovering (from) Janet Jackson's breast: Ethics and the nexus of media, sports, and management. *Journal of Sport Management, 18,* 315–34.

Wenner, L.A. (2006). Sports and media through the super glass mirror: Placing blame, breast-beating, and a gaze to the future. In A.A. Raney & J. Bryant (Eds.), *Handbook of sports media* (pp. 45–60). Hillsdale, NJ: Erlbaum.

Wenner, L.A. (2007). Towards a dirty theory of narrative ethics. Prolegomenon on media, sport and commodity value. *International Journal of Media and Cultural Politics, 3,* 111–29.

Wenner, L.A. (2008a). Playing dirty: On reading media texts and the sports fan in commercialized settings. In L.W. Hugenberg, P.M. Haridakis, & A.C. Earnheardt (Eds.), *Sports mania: Essays on fandom and the media in the 21st century* (pp. 13–32). Jefferson, NC: McFarland & Company.

Wenner, L.A. (2008b). Super-cooled sports dirt: Moral contagion and Super Bowl commercials in the shadows of Janet Jackson. *Television and New Media, 9,* 131–54.

Wenner, L.A. (2009a). Brewing consumption: Sports dirt, mythic masculinity, and the ethos of beer commercials. In L.A. Wenner & S.J. Jackson (Eds.), *Sport, beer, and gender: Promotional culture and contemporary social life* (pp. 121–42). New York: Peter Lang.

Wenner, L.A. (2009b). The unbearable dirtiness of being: On the commodification of mediasport and the need for ethical criticism. *Journal of Sports Media, 4*(1), 85–94.

Wenner, L.A. (2010a). From football widow to fan: Web narratives of women and sports spectatorship. In A.C. Earnhardt, P.M. Haridakis, & B. Hugenberg (Eds.), *Fandemonium: Explorations of fan power, identity, and socialization* (pp. 188–200). Lanham, MD: Lexington Books.

Wenner, L.A. (2010b). Gendered sports dirt: Interrogating sex and the single beer commercial. In H. Hundley & A. Billings (Eds.), *Examining identity in sports media* (pp. 87–107). Thousand Oaks, CA: Sage.

Wenner, L.A. (2011). Reading the commodified female sports fan: Interrogating strategic dirt and characterization in commercial narratives. In K. Toffoletti & P. Mewett (Eds.), *Sport and its women fans*. London: Routledge.

Wenner, L.A. & Gantz, W. (1989). The audience experience with sport on television. In L.A. Wenner (Ed.), *Media, sports, and society* (pp. 241–69). Newbury Park, CA: Sage.

Wenner, L.A. & Gantz, W. (1998). Watching sports on television: Audience experience, gender, fanship, and marriage. In L.A. Wenner (Ed.), *MediaSport* (pp. 233–51). London: Routledge.

Wenner, L.A. & Jackson, S.J. (2009). Sport, beer, and gender in promotional culture: On the dynamic of a holy trinity. In L.A. Wenner & S.J. Jackson (Eds.), *Sport, beer, and gender: Promotional culture and contemporary social life* (pp. 1–32). New York: Peter Lang.

Who's a sports fan? (2006, June 14). Retrieved December 10, 2009, from Pew Research Center Social and Demographic Trends Web site: http://pewsocialtrends.org/pubs/?chartid=135

Zylinska, J. (2005). *The ethics of cultural studies*. London: Continuum.

5

FAIR BALL?

Exploring the relationship between media sports and viewer morality

Arthur A. Raney

FLORIDA STATE UNIVERSITY

Musings about the relationship between sports and morality are not new. In the Academy, Plato insisted on the ultimate importance of both physical and moral education; in Greek mythology, victory and virtue were inextricably linked. The current International Olympic Charter celebrates "the joy of effort, the educational value of good example and respect for universal fundamental ethical principles" (International Olympic Committee, 2007, p. 11). Coaches and managers from Little League to Major League stress the parallels between sport and life, arguing that developing physical and moral excellence – most often in the form of sportsmanship – on the field nurtures the same off the field. But by and large these discussions have traditionally centered on the role of sports *participation* in the moral lives of individuals. The purpose of this chapter is to move the discussion beyond participation to spectatorship. More specifically, taking cues from entertainment scholarship on fictional narratives, I will explore the role that subjective morality plays in the consumption of and reaction to live televised sports. The ultimate goal of the chapter is to offer a framework from which scholars can begin examining the intersection between media sports and viewer morality.

As highly dramatic events, sports share much in common with fictional narratives. Perhaps most importantly, the two share the centrality of characters and the ultimate importance of outcomes. For instance, two teams trading baskets in the waning seconds of a WNBA game is perfectly analogous to the back-and-forth, nonstop action in your typical adventure film, or even romantic comedy for that matter. Of course, characters and outcomes alone mean little unless viewers are emotionally invested in them. Media enjoyment scholarship, as well as the daily lived experiences for nearly everyone, clearly demonstrates that viewers willingly make such investments – from *Avatar* to *Zombieland*, the Oakland A's to the New Orleans Zephyrs – and that those emotional affiliations, in conjunction with hoped-for outcomes, are key to the enjoyment of media entertainment.

Disposition-based theories as lens

The similarities between sports and fictional narratives give us justification to examine the former in a manner similar to the latter. But to do so, an evaluative lens that highlights those similarities, while acknowledging the differences, is needed. So-called disposition-based theories of media enjoyment provide such a lens (see Raney, 2006a, for a recent overview). In the broadest terms, disposition-based theories explain how individuals evaluate and form affiliations with media characters, with enjoyment subsequently impacted by what happens with and to those characters. The first such theory described the process through which enjoyment is experienced with jokes involving the disparagement of a person or group (Zillmann & Cantor, 1972). The principals of the so-called disposition theory of humor were later applied to the enjoyment of other content, yielding the disposition theories of drama (Zillmann & Cantor, 1976) and sports spectatorship (Zillmann, Bryant, & Sapolsky, 1989; Zillmann & Paulus, 1993).

Although this chapter will deal with additional media consumption issues, a quick word about the term *enjoyment* is needed at this point. Entertainment theorists (e.g., Bosshart & Macconi, 1998; Raney, 2004; Vorderer, 2001; Vorderer, Klimmt, & Ritterfeld, 2004) have been examining the process of enjoyment for decades and generally agree on several operational issues. First, we primarily experience enjoyment as an *emotional* response, through activation of neurotransmitters in the limbic and sympathetic nervous systems. In other words, enjoyment is primarily experienced as a *feeling*. However, enjoyment also involves the cognitive processing of information presented, requiring attention, working and extended memory, comprehension, schema activation, and mental-models development. Because of this, enjoyment is conceptualized as a *judgment* based on the interaction of user-, content-, and environmental variables. So, enjoyment (as a judgment or evaluation) is also seen as a cognitive process. The necessity for this brief introduction to conceptualizations of enjoyment will hopefully become clearer shortly.

The enjoyment of mediated sports events is the central focus of the disposition theory of sports spectatorship (for a recent summary, see Raney, 2006b). The theory describes the process of enjoyment as a function of the intense emotional attachments (i.e., affective dispositions) formed by fans toward athletes and teams and the outcomes of contests involving those athletes and teams.[1] More specifically, bonds are formed toward teams along a continuum of affect, from intense disliking through indifference to intense liking. More often than not within the sports context, these bonds are referred to in terms of *fanship*. Thus, those holding intense positive feelings toward a team are ardent fans or true fanatics, while others might be called casual (or even fair-weather) fans.

At any rate, the love that ardent fans have for their favorite teams is typically only rivaled in intensity by the hatred they hold toward the bitter rivals of those favorite teams. According to the disposition theory of sports spectatorship, these passions hold the key to the enjoyment of sporting contests. The theory states that enjoyment of a mediated sports event should increase in proportion to the positive feelings held toward the winning team and/or the negative feelings held toward the losing team. Conversely, enjoyment of a mediated sports event should decrease in proportion to the negative feelings held toward the winning team and/or the positive feelings held toward the losing team. The basic formula for the disposition theory of sports spectatorship has widespread empirical support, from studies of professional and intercollegiate American football to Olympic and intercollegiate basketball, tennis, even professional wrestling (e.g., Peterson & Raney, 2008; Raney & Kinnally, 2006, 2009; Tamborini & Lachlan, 2008; Tüzünkan, 2007).

Over the past several decades, entertainment scholars have also examined how those affective dispositions are formed in the first place. This is where morality enters our picture, at least in the case of fiction. With fictional narratives, dispositions have been observed to be a function of the viewer's careful moral evaluation and judgment of character actions and motives (Zillmann & Cantor, 1976). That is, as fiction viewers, we come to like more those characters whom we judge – presumably based on our real-world senses of morality – to be morally acceptable; in contrast, we grow to disdain those characters who exhibit immoral actions or motivations. As a result, we cheer for the heroine to defeat the villain because we like her. But our liking is not capricious: We like her because she is moral, because she is good. Therefore, we want her to defeat the villain because we think she *should* win, because good *should* defeat evil. Heroes, as the instruments of justice, are right and moral. And we, as viewers, are thus morally justified to love them, to empathize with their hardships, to fear their defeat, and to enthusiastically celebrate their victory; we are morally justified to do so because the hero's actions and motivations are virtuous.

Thus, moral judgment and moral considerations are at the very heart of the enjoyment of fictional drama. In fact, a review of the disposition literature suggests three phases in the entertainment experience during which moral concerns and judgments can be examined: before (i.e., how morality influences selective exposure to narratives), during (i.e., how morality influences interpretation of characters and enjoyment of narratives), and after (i.e., how morality is influenced by narratives) reception. With this framework as a backdrop, the remainder of the chapter will probe how morality might likewise operate during each of these three phases of sports media consumption. To be clear: Few definitive statements about morality's role in the sports reception process will be offered, primarily because few empirical studies have examined these issues. However, what I hope to offer is a framework upon which those studies might be conducted in the future.

Morality influencing what sports we watch

Of course, when it comes to media sports we tend to tune in to see teams that we love win (or even teams that we hate, with the hope that they lose). It is true: Some sports fanatics will sit down to watch a game no matter who is playing. But for most of us, our viewing is dictated to some degree by the affiliations we have toward the combatants. As noted above, the dispositions we form toward characters in fictional narratives are mediated by moral considerations. But what about sports? To what extent are the dispositions that we hold toward sports teams similar to those held toward dramatic characters, especially with regard to moral concerns? That is, do the affiliations we form toward sports teams carry the same moral tags or weights as our heroes from fiction?

To be honest, the research record reveals little here. But what little it does say leads me to initially suggest that the way we form emotional connections with fictional characters is, in fact, different from the way that we become fans of sports teams. A rich tradition of sports scholarship has explored how people form allegiances toward specific sports teams for various reasons (for an excellent summary, see Wann, Melnick, Russell, & Pease, 2001). The literature suggests that sports fanship is dependent upon many factors such as geography, allegiances held by respected family members and friends, team colors, specific players, styles and strategies of play, and perceived popularity by the masses (or so-called bandwagon effects). Nowhere in this scholarship – at least to my reading – do moral considerations come into play. I suppose that one could argue that evaluations of players as "good guys and gals" (i.e., a moral consideration) might possibly influence fanship, as could evaluations of a team's playing style as "dirty" or "the *right* way." These possible exceptions aside, the role of moral considerations in the formation of sports team dispositions seems to be quite limited, and markedly less important than with fictional characters. But just because moral concerns may play no (or at most, a highly idiosyncratic) role in the *formation* of these dispositions, it does not necessarily follow that sports fanship is an amoral phenomenon.

Balance (Heider, 1958) and cognitive dissonance theories (Festinger, 1957) explain how we generally seek out information consistent with and avoid information contradictory to our attitudes, beliefs, and thoughts. Stimuli incongruent with our existing beliefs lead to psychological and cognitive distress that we then seek to alleviate and avoid in the future. This process explains how and why we selectively expose ourselves to certain media contents while steering clear of others (for a complete summary, see Zillmann & Bryant, 1985). Support for selective exposure to media is widespread (e.g., Klapper, 1960; Sweeny & Gruber, 1984; Vidmar & Rokeach, 1974). For entertainment theorists, media content is generally selected that not only is congruous with prevailing attitudes, but that presumably brings pleasure to the viewer. Thus, it follows that fans of certain genres of programming seek out those contents because of their presumed cognitive and affective benefits. Sports fans are surely no different (e.g., Gantz, 1981; Gantz & Wenner, 1991, 1995). And television ratings continue to confirm that those who find pleasure in consuming sports seek them out in heavy doses; for instance, no program in U.S. television history drew more than the 106.5 million viewers who watched the New Orleans Saints defeat the Indianapolis Colts in Super Bowl XLIV (Brauder, 2010). But beyond pleasure-seeking expectations, can other attitudes and concerns – namely, moral beliefs and perspectives – predict selective exposure?

From research regarding fictional narratives, we have some evidence that moral perspectives can predict exposure to certain media. McCarty and Shrum (1993) found that women who valued idealism (e.g., equality, peace, beauty) consumed more news programs. Some moral attitudes have also been linked specifically to the enjoyment of certain fictional narratives. For instance, Oliver (1996) found that authoritarianism was associated with greater liking of reality-based crime dramas; I have isolated attitudes about vigilantism and punitive punishment as predictors of crime-based drama enjoyment (Raney, 2002, 2005; Raney & Bryant, 2002). Unfortunately, to date, this line of research has not been extended to sports.

Perhaps the closest corollary is the work concerning gender differences in sports viewing. According to Sargent, Zillmann, and Weaver (1998), females tend to report greater enjoyment for stylistic sports (e.g., gymnastics, figure skating, and tennis), while males report greater enjoyment of combative sports (e.g., football, soccer, boxing). Additionally, women tend to enjoy sports that they see as elegant more than those seen as violent or dangerous. For men, enjoyment tends to increase the more violent, active, and dangerous they perceive the sport to be. Zillmann (1995) and Bryant and colleagues (1981) reported similar findings. Of course, gender does not equal morality, but some gender-based differences along the moral orientations of *justice* and *care* have been noted (cf. Gilligan & Attanucci, 1988), though not without controversy. To what extent are gender differences in the appeal of sports viewing motivated by differences in moral perspectives? The research record is silent on the issue. But given the work in selective exposure, it is reasonable to expect that some aspects of an individual's moral makeup – whether tied to gender or not – might influence the forms and even amounts of sports viewing. Sports media scholars might consider examining these and related issues.

Finally, with the explosion of sports news outlets and the inclusion of athletes in celebrity news reports, fans (and nonfans alike, for that matter) know more than ever before about the off-the-field lives of sports personalities. More often than not it seems the news we hear and read about athletes off the court places them in a morally questionable light: positive drug tests, DUIs, domestic abuse, marital infidelities, weapons charges, homophobic rants, and the list goes on and on. What we don't know is how this information affects the ways that fans view those athletes. Undoubtedly, sponsors assume that such negative press about athletes can injure their own image; for instance, AT&T, Gatorade, and Accenture pulled their million-dollar endorsements of Tiger Woods in the wake of his infidelity scandal. But do the moral failings of athletes in their personal lives lead fans to think of them differently in their professional lives? The answer to this question is surely complex.

Consider Pete Rose, MLB's all-time hits leader, who admitted to gambling on baseball games that he managed. A would-be shoo-in for the Hall of Fame, Rose is ineligible for election because of his past sins. Most former players, managers, sports writers, and announcers, and many fans support his continued ban; a quick Google search of "I Hate Pete Rose" yielded nearly 10,000 hits. Yet when announced as a member of the All-Century Team in 1999 (which was voted on by fans), Rose received one of the loudest ovations from those in attendance (Sandomir, 1999); "I Love Pete Rose" yields more than 24,000 hits on Google! Of course, Pete Rose is just one example of an athlete whose moral failings continue to be adjudicated in the court of public opinion, without a unanimous verdict. But how does knowledge about an athlete's flaws impact our willingness to watch and cheer for her? For instance, will viewers despise Tiger's extramarital affairs and still hope that he wins golf tournaments? Will long-time Steelers fans question their loyalty to the team if it chooses to not trade Ben Roethlisberger?

Back to diposition theory, it would seem that our emotional ties to athletes would certainty moderate our reactions to revelations about personal failings and our subsequent willingness to view them perform. On the one hand, we might be more willing to forgive the sins of our favorite players so that we can continue liking them; this possibility is addressed at length below. In contrast, being associated with moral failure is potentially damaging to one's self concept and public image. As with team losses, some sports fans might seek to cut off the reflected (moral) failure (or CORF; see Wann & Branscombe, 1990) of a once adored athlete, distancing themselves from the publicly shamed. In many ways, this issue points to a much larger discussion about the way that audiences view athletes in general. Charles Barkely famously argued "I am not a role model." Some responded, "Well, you should be." And others claimed, "Yes, you are whether you like it or not." How athletes, as moral agents, can influence fans' willingness to view and cheer for them is surely an area for sports media scholars to further explore.

Morality influencing how we watch sports

Zillmann (2000) argued that viewers of fictional drama must serve as untiring moral monitors of the actions and motivations of characters, rendering moral judgments that impact dispositional valence and intensity. Or stated another way, fictional narratives require us to continually view and interpret them (at least in part) through a moral lens. In the current section, I'd like to apply that same argument to *in situ* viewing of sports. Specifically, I argue that during viewing fans imbue their favorite teams with moral superiority, they interpret the rule-breaking behaviors of their favorite teams as morally acceptable, and they experience emotional responses to the action that carry moral weight.

Favored team as morally superior As I noted above, fiction viewers generally like characters who are morally superior and grow to detest those characters who exhibit immoral actions or motivations. Thus, heroes are the embodiment of good, serving as forces for good, and therefore – given our existential hope in justice winning out over evil – heroes should prevail. How about with our sports "heroes"? I contend that we project the same *ought-ness* to our favored team winning as we do to the hero's success. That is, I argue that we think that our beloved teams *ought* to win, that their winning is the just and proper thing to happen, that it is the morally appropriate outcome, that it is what *should* happen in a rational and righteous universe. And please note: *Should* here refers not to an expected probability based on likelihood of winning, but rather on the moral presumption of what is right and proper. The affiliations that we hold toward the ones we love – our children, our partners, our favorite television and movie heroes – lead us to expect as much in other situations; why should our thoughts about our favorite sports teams be any different?

The language that we use to describe sports suggests that we see our fanship through such moral lenses. For example, after the long program of U.S. figure skater Johnny Weir at the 2010 Winter Olympics, many fans thought that his performance was undervalued by the judges. One comment posted to ESPN.com's coverage summed up the outrage: "I feel Johnny was robbed!!!! Did he deserve the gold? I don't know, but he should have gotten a medal" (Caple, 2010b). Similarly, after the U.S. hockey team's upset of Canada in the preliminary rounds of the 2010 Olympic tournament, many fans of the losing team echoed one poster's comment on ESPN.com: "Canada deserved to win" (Caple, 2010a). These reactions are similar to what you hear in sports bars and living rooms across the nation every day: "We lost but we got what we deserved." "We should have destroyed them." "Hey, that's not fair!"

Of course, sports contests are intended to be the arenas where fairness and justice reign. The impartial referee, umpire, or panel of judges is intended to ensure that both teams have the same opportunity (or right) to win. Fans have accepted changes to traditional playoff structures – the 1994 addition of a wild card team in Major League Baseball, the 2003 move from best-of-five to best-of-seven-game series in the first round of the NBA playoffs, the 2010 expansion of the NCAA men's basketball tournament from 65 to 68 teams – because the new systems allow for a fairer outcome (never mind the millions of more dollars earned for networks and leagues). Justice and fairness are central to sports. It seems reasonable then to expect that the experience of fanship – as an expression of partiality in an otherwise impartial universe – brings with it questions of how just and morally sound a specific sporting event truly is. This tension between the presumed level-playing field and the hopes for one slightly tilted in favor of our team is fundamentally a moral issue. Sports media scholars should further investigate the nature and the cognitive resolution of this tension in the minds of viewers.

Moral disengagement with (some) rule breaking   Moral considerations are also raised when viewers witness acts within sports that violate the established rules of the game. More often than not this rule breaking comes through sports violence or aggression. The research record clearly demonstrates that violence contributes to the appeal and enjoyment of televised sports contests. Several studies have reported that enjoyment within a specific sporting contest increases with the degree of violence, with the relationship being stronger for male viewers (see Gunter, 2006, for a recent summary). Additionally, past studies indicate that enjoyment may increase when viewers merely *perceive* contests to be violent or aggressive, despite any variation in the actual content itself. For instance, Bryant, Brown, Comisky, and Zillmann (1982) created three versions of a tennis match in which the players were described either as best friends, bitter enemies, or neither friends nor enemies. Viewers of the players-as-enemies version described the action as significantly more enjoyable, exciting, involving, and interesting than participants viewing the other two versions. Further, a colleague and I observed how enjoyment of a win by a favored team in a hotly contested rivalry game was strongly predicted by how violent the fans perceived the game to be (Raney & Kinnally, 2009). That is, the more violent the game was *thought to be* by the fans, the more enjoyable it was for them (as long as their team won). Surely, sports commentary helps to create these perceptions; as sportscaster Tom Hammond stated, "We have to create heroes and villains and all of those things by telling individual stories" (Billings, 2008, p. 61).

However, because violence or aggression is permissible and even expected within certain sporting contests, the role of moral judgment in the enjoyment of that violence is complex. Many have experienced the way that viewers cheer loudly when a blitzing linebacker blindsides an unsuspecting quarterback, or eagerly awaited the replay of a brutal foul on a drive to the basket, or tuned in to Sports-Center to see the NASCAR wreck that their friends texted them about. The cheer "Hit 'em a lick, hit 'em a lick, harder, harder" has traditionally been heard at many college football stadiums. And without a doubt the likelihood that the viewer will participate in such behaviors increases in proportion to their emotional investment in the participants. But, *if*, or better yet *when*, that violent act leads to an advantage for the other team, the cry of "Foul!" is deafening. In such cases, the calls to "hit 'em back" or the angry reassurances that "two can play at that game" are sure to follow.

The point I am attempting to make is this: Sports fans seem to selectively perceive the moral propriety of sports violence. Our beloved team can play as rough, intimidating, physical, and fierce as is necessary to ensure victory, while our rivals are held to a much stricter standard of conduct. These expressions of side taking and biased processing constitute statements about what is just, fair, and morally appropriate within sports events.

The same, of course, takes place with fictional narratives. Viewers permit all sorts of violent acts to take place for the sake of enjoyment. We don't mind it when the hero gets a little physical with the villain; for instance, viewers find it perfectly acceptable for *24*'s Jack Bauer to rough up a terrorist to save the country. In fact, some evidence suggests that we like it more when this happens (Raney, 2005). But the same latitude is not granted the evil villain. Because we in general love seeing justice restored (Goldstein, 1998), this reality should come as no shock: Viewers of fictional drama allow (and, in fact, hope for) displays of severe retribution in response to injustice. I have previously argued that we as viewers extend moral propriety to fictional characters – that is, we stretch our sense of what is morally acceptable to cover the immoral-but-well-intended actions of a beloved hero – because we like them a great deal, and we desperately want to see them succeed (cf. Raney, 2004). In other words, because we like characters and we know from past media experiences that enjoyment comes from seeing them prosper, we will interpret their morally questionable actions in a way that helps us view them as virtuous. We interpret their actions as morally appropriate and rightly motivated, even if they must break the rules we usually demand be followed.

Scholars in various disciplines have examined this tendency to give moral amnesty to others (whether mediated or real) under certain circumstances. Bandura (1986, 1991) refers to this process by which otherwise unacceptable behaviors are permitted, accepted, and defended as *moral disengagement*. As individual moral agents, we each control how we enforce the moral codes that we carry around in our heads; we can apply our subjectively-held codes more strenuously or leniently depending on the situation. By selectively activating and disengaging the sanctions that are typically used to evaluate and regulate conduct, we can permit and accept behaviors that would otherwise be judged as inappropriate. To alleviate the cognitive distress that should arise during such situations, we rely on a variety of cognitive strategies such as minimizing the consequences of the behavior ("no harm, no foul"), offering an exonerating social comparison ("it wasn't nearly as bad as what they just got away with"), sanitizing the action through euphemistic labeling ("that was a touch foul"), or blaming the victim ("she had it coming"). Bandura has offered eight such strategies in his writings on the subject.

We use these strategies in our daily lives to justify our own behavior, like when we intentionally drive over the speed limit, jaywalk, or otherwise break rules. Likewise, we use the strategies to smooth over the sins of our friends and family. And, as alluded to above, media scholars suggest that we use these strategies to overlook and justify the rule-breaking actions of fictional heroes. Occasional use of these attitude-defensive strategies seems perfectly logical. We generally want to maintain positive dispositions toward those whom we favor. So, when our friends and other loved ones (real or fictional) say or do things we dislike, we pardon them, we "cut them some slack," we blame something or someone else for the behavior, we justify their behavior in our minds. It follows: The more we like them, the more willing we are to utilize these attitude-maintenance strategies.

How does this apply to media sports? I would argue that we often morally disengage when it comes to our favorite team, especially for the sake of enjoyment. We readily permit borderline or even crossing-the-line behaviors – hard fouls, hits just after the whistle, theatrical reactions to non-fouls, arguments with the officials, to name a few – by our favorite team, claiming that these actions fall within the limits of the game or are justly motivated and therefore permissible. In fact, the more we like the team, the more we would presumably be able and willing to do so. Of course, this is not the case when it comes to our favorite team's opponents. Sports fans greatly scrutinize similar or even more benign action when performed by the opponents; in these cases, the actions are wrongfully motivated, overly rough, and clearly deserving of severe penalties.

Are there limites to this tendency to morally disengage with our favored teams? Absolutely. When our favorite players inexplicably act in a reprehensible manner, most fans do not immediately justify the act. For example, when France's Zinadine Zidane head butted Italy's Marco Materazzi during the final match of World Cup 2006, nearly every fan, including those of *Les Bleus*, was outraged (at least in the most immediate aftermath). Similarly, Indiana Pacers fans found it incredibly difficult to justify Ron Artest's charging into the stands to fight a Detroit Piston fan who had thrown a soda at him in 2004. In such cases, the players violated the standards and expectations that we hold for members of our team, for "our" representatives. The athletes are no longer seen as a member of our in-group; therefore, our partiality no longer applies and our moral amnesty for their actions cannot be granted. With that stated, both Zidane and Artest (and the countless other examples you might think of) had their supporters, those who "understood" and could excuse their actions. But extreme cases aside, it seems reasonable to argue that media sports fanship offers similar opportunities to morally disengage as fictional drama. Surely, we would do well as scholars to further explore these similarities.

Sports viewing and moral emotions   Sports media scholars have, for decades, noted the emotional appeal of sports. Something as seemingly innocuous as viewing a photograph of a beloved sports team can shorten startle probe-P3 reflexes, increase positive slow cortical potentials, and increase skin conductance responses (Hillmann, Cuthbert, Bradley, & Lang, 2004). Watching a televised World Cup soccer match led to increased testosterone levels in fans' saliva immediately after the game ended (Bernhardt, Dabbs, Fielden, & Lutter, 1998). Moreover, enjoyment, as the primary reason people tune in to sports, is largely experienced as an emotional reaction closely associated with pleasure, happiness, liking, and elation. Sports and emotions go hand-in-hand.

Borrowing from the field of moral psychology, many of the emotions associated with media enjoyment can be characterized as *moral emotions* since they are experienced in relation to social events not directly affecting the self (Haidt, 2003). Thus, the happiness and sadness that we experience when we watch a fictional hero defeat his evil nemesis, or when we witness our favorite team lose in the final minutes of a heated rivalry contest, are classified as moral emotional responses because they are experienced in relation to events outside our own selves. But not all moral emotions are created equal. Haidt (2003) argues that the moral aspect of an emotion is a matter of degree; some emotions are more prototypically moral than others. Further, he argued moral emotions are distinguished from others along two dimensions: the nature of the elicitor and the resulting action tendency.

Thus, an event (e.g., a home fire) occurring to family members triggers an emotional reaction (e.g., sadness, empathy, distress); a similar event occurring to a complete stranger may also trigger an emotional reaction (e.g., compassion). Because the latter was experienced by a party to whom we are not directly connected (i.e., a disinterested elicitor), then the emotional response experienced should be considered more prototypically moral than the one experienced in the case of the family fire. So, according to Haidt, compassion is classified as a more moral emotion than sadness because it is elicited without an existing connection between the self and the eliciting event. Further, the emotions we experience naturally trigger an action in response to the event causing the emotion. Induced action tendencies that are prosocial in nature (rather than merely self-serving) are likewise said to be more prototypically moral. In the previous example, sadness and compassion might both induce similar action tendencies to intervene, but compassion is considered the more moral emotion because the triggered reaction is directed toward a disinterested party.

Based on this rationale and these criteria, the emotional responses to media entertainment – happiness, sadness, distress at the distress of others, fear – are indeed moral, though they fall within the most minimal classification of moral emotions. That is, the emotions that we experience while watching movies and television programs, reading a novel, playing a video game, or viewing a sports contest can be thought of as moral emotions, but just barely. Why? Because they are emotions experienced in reaction to beloved others, motivating (nonetheless impotent) actions borne of self-interest. But this is not unexpected, nor problematic. As noted above, emotional involvement with fiction and sports teams *requires* partiality; when viewers are disinterested in the portrayed events, they generally do not experience emotional response. Indifference toward characters does not generate the empathy necessary to prompt emotional reactions.

But prototypical moral emotions do exist. Specifically, Haidt (2003) argued that (righteous) anger, elevation, guilt, and compassion are emotional reactions unbound to self-interest and that trigger prosocial action tendencies when experienced. But can entertainment, particularly sporting events, elicit prototypical moral emotions? The simple response is "Yes." For instance, we can all think of films (e.g., *Hotel Rwanda*, *Life is Beautiful*) that lead us to feelings of compassion, guilt, anger, and elevation. At the same time, films like this seem to be the exception rather than the rule. But sports offer more of an opportunity for us to experience such emotions. Extraordinary human effort, like U.S. gymnast Kerri Strug sticking a dismount on a seriously injured ankle during the 1996 Olympic Gold Medal team performance. Inexplicable displays of sportsmanship, like Central Washington softball players carrying an opposing Western Oregon player around the bases to ensure her homerun counted. Near-perfect consistency at one's craft, like New York Yankee reliever Mariano Rivera's playoff performances throughout his career. Athletes overcoming what most would consider debilitating disabilities, like any event in the Paralympics. Heart-wrenching tragedy, like Dale Earnhardt's fatal crash at the Daytona 500 in 2001. Each of these examples – and countless others we could recall – allow the sports viewer to experience those prototypically moral emotions, to feel for fellow humans in (unfortunately too) uncommon ways.

Prototypical moral emotion-evoking incidents in sports media are distinguished from others in that they lead us to ponder things beyond ourselves. They lead us to contemplate our existence, to ruminate on the human condition. Yes, we *feel* prototypical moral emotions, but it seems reasonable to argue that we also *think* them. Entertainment scholar Mary Beth Oliver (2009; Oliver & Bartsch, 2010) has been chief among a group arguing for a better conceptual distinction between media viewing motivated by a desire for pleasure-centered *enjoyment* and that driven by eudaimonic or "truth seeking" *appreciation*. This distinction seems to be relevant in discussions of sports consumption as well. Yes, sports fans primarily seek to experience pleasurable enjoyment when they tune in to a game or match. However, along the way, those purely pleasurable experiences can at times force us to experience a complex combination of affect and cognition, and in so doing to ponder life's purpose, to appreciate what it means to be human. These experiences would seemingly offer sports media scholars quite a bit of fodder for research.

Further, the enjoyment–appreciation distinction may point to important individual differences among viewers. Because sports events focus on human achievement and performance, it seems reasonable that any sporting event could in theory lead to the experience of prototypical moral emotions (not just the remarkable ones mentioned above). This claim leads to some interesting questions for media sports scholars to consider: Are some people more naturally inclined to view sports from a disinterested perspective, such that prototypical moral emotions are more often experienced? If so, what individual differences or variables would predict such? Can these desires, this lens, be cultivated? Alternatively, what sports might encourage this way-of-looking more than others? Do some events lend themselves more to the experience of prototypical moral emotions? It would seemingly be beneficial for sports media scholars to attempt to answer some of these and other related questions.

Morality influenced(?) by the sports we watch

For centuries, philosophers, religious leaders, parents, child advocates, lawyers, policy-makers, and scholars have voiced moral concerns about the influence of entertainment. Such concerns remain today, with many commentators arguing that the "crumbling moral foundation" or "unraveling of the moral fabric" of society coincides with the increased availability and popularity of media entertainment (especially television). One might argue that traditional media effects scholarship constitutes a grand investigation into morality, for example, as the deleterious impacts of consuming violent, sexually explicit, and stereotypical entertainment have been measured as morally wrong (or at least, morally questionable) audience thoughts and behaviors. Sports, of course, are not immune to such criticism. Once Constantine declared Christianity the religion of Rome, the Holy Roman Empire's official attitudes toward sporting contests (and many other entertainment activities) turned markedly negative. Theodosius I put an end to the Olympic Games in the last decade of the 4th Century because of their pagan connections (International Olympic Committee, 2009). And countless other athletic competitions were banned out of fear that they steered participants and spectators away from the church. The athletic teams at the church-affiliated Brigham Young University still refuse to participate in Sunday games for similar religious reasons.

But, of course, these controversies fly in the face of what sports profess to develop in athletes: integrity, honor, loyalty, compassion, respect, humility. The remaining pages in this chapter should not be the place where one perspective is promoted or the seeming paradox is explained away. But, rather, we should consider the role that media sports *can* play in the moral development or moral devolution of its spectators.

First, consider one example of how media sports might deter moral development, or more appropriately, foster a form of morality that most would argue is less than beneficial. In the previous section, I argued that sports give us an opportunity – which we viewers willingly accept – to extend moral propriety to favored teams and athletes. In so doing, we differentially apply our subjective moral lenses to questionable play, justifying it for favored teams while condemning the same from opponents. Ultimately, we morally disengage for the sake of rooting for and ultimately enjoying victories by our favored teams. But one must ask the question: If we readily sanction our team to "hit 'em a lick, hit 'em a lick, harder, harder" or celebrate a victory with a post-game song like the University of Alabama – "Hey Tigers! We just beat the hell out of you!" – then it is hard to deny the possibility of real-world violence erupting in such a climate. If we can interpret the rule-breaking play of our favorite team as justifiable, then is it too much to think that we might do the same to justify our own rule-breaking behavior?

By now, the scene is sadly commonplace: Rioting fans "celebrating" a championship victory by burning cars, looting stores, defacing buildings, fighting one another, and flooding streets with opened fire hydrants. Sports psychologists offer many reasons for this behavior: the volatile mix of excitement, physiological arousal, misplaced importance on the game, fanatic devotion to the team, alcohol, hooliganism, and a mob mentality to name a few. And as mentioned earlier, one could add to this the possibility that a viewer's *perceptions* of the actual games can activate aggressive thoughts. If a viewer perceives an already-exciting contest as more violent than a typical game (as in Raney & Kinnally, 2009), then concepts and behaviors related to violence might become activated, increasing the likelihood of real-world violence. Mix in the sense of moral superiority that is granted the favored team, and you have a formula leading to a reasonable justification for real-world violence.

To be clear, the direct and unique contribution of live sports viewing to personal aggression is extremely difficult to measure, especially as it may operate through the moral disengagement process. However, we as media sports researchers must take seriously the relationship between highly favored teams in highly emotional settings and potential effects, like moral disengagement. If sports fans think that they are morally justified in defending the honor of their favored team, then it is reasonable to expect that in some instances real-world violence might result. Media sports scholars should consider trying to isolate the specific influence of strong team affiliation on the disengagement of one's typical moral code that likely comes along with it.

On a more positive note, sports do seemingly offer the opportunity for viewers to look beyond their own circumstances and to appreciate the rapturous thrills and heart-wrenching agonies of the human condition. They provide for us an opportunity to experience and exercise those prototypical moral emotions of compassion and elevation. In theory, doing so should make those responses more salient, that we would begin seeing all of life more often through non-partial lenses. Of course, at odds with these opportunities for moral-emotional reactions to sports is exactly that element leading us to them in the first place: the powerful affiliations that we form toward specific teams and athletes. Those affective dispositions and the partiality that comes with them work against our selfish disinterest. The desire to see our team win pushes us to primarily view the events through prejudicial eyes and to react to them with biased hearts. The pervasive "win at any cost" narrative that permeates our current sports culture doesn't help either.

Can sports help viewers to develop their moral sense, to train their moral eyes, to seek out the experience of prototypical moral emotions? The answer would theoretically appear to be "Yes." When an athlete is injured in a contest – regardless of how bitter the rivals – the crowd goes silent out of respect. Cheers of concern and supportive applause are offered by friends and enemies. As long as this, and myriad similar responses continue to be modeled for young people, then sports can support the moral development of viewers. But the nature of competition also pushes back against this. We can all long for the day when the ideals preached to athletes – integrity, honor, loyalty, compassion, respect, humility – are universally adopted by their fans. Until then, scholars must train their investigative eye on the role that morality can (and does) play before, during, and after the consumption of live sports.

Concluding thought

The purpose of this chapter was to investigate the role that morality might play in the consumption of media sports. To that end, I have offered more questions than I have answered. Nonetheless, media sport casts an impressive and imposing shadow across the entertainment landscape. As this shadow continues to grow, it is incumbent upon us as media scholars to wrestle with the complexity of the various relationships existing between viewers and content. My hope is that this chapter can be useful to media scholars in unraveling the complexity that surrounds morality and the enjoyment of media sports.

Note

1 For the sake of simplicity, hereafter I will simply use the term "team" to refer to sports participants. The reader, though, should understand that (unless specifically noted) the same principles should apply to individual sports.

References

Bandura, A. (1986). *Social foundations of thought and action: A social cognitive theory*. Englewood Cliffs, NJ: Prentice-Hall.

Bandura, A. (1991). Social cognitive theory of moral thought and action. In W.M. Kurtines & J.L. Gewirtz (Eds.), *Handbook of moral behavior and development: Theory, research and applications* (Vol. 1, pp. 71–129). Hillsdale, NJ: Lawrence Erlbaum Associates.

Bernhardt, P.C., Dabbs, J.M., Fielden, J.A., & Lutter, C.D. (1998). Testosterone changes during vicarious experiences of winning and losing among fans at sporting events. *Physiology and Behaviors, 18*, 263–68.

Billings, A.C. (2008). *Olympic media: Inside the biggest show on television*. London: Routledge.

Bosshart, L. & Macconi, I. (1998). Media entertainment. *Communication Research Trends, 18* (3), 3–38.

Brauder, D. (2010, February 8). Super Bowl is most watched TV show ever. *ABC News*. Retrieved April 26, 2010, from http://abcnews.go.com/Sports/wireStory?id=9776945

Bryant, J., Brown, D., Comisky, P.W., & Zillmann, D. (1982). Sports and spectators: Commentary and appreciation. *Journal of Communication, 32*, 109–19.

Bryant, J., Comisky, P.W., & Zillmann, D. (1981). The appeal of rough-and-tumble play in televised professional football. *Communication Quarterly, 29*, 256–62.

Caple, J. (2010a). US hockey win silences Canada. *ESPN.com*. Retrieved February 28, 2010, from http://espn.go.com/olympics/blog/_/name/winterolympics/id/4934936/us-hockey-win-silences-canada

Caple, J. (2010b). Weir: "Audience reaction was my gold medal." *ESPN.com*. Retrieved February 28, 2010, from http://espn.go.com/olympics/blog/_/name/winterolympics/id/4927147/audience-reaction-was-my-gold-medal

Festinger, L. (1957). *A theory of cognitive dissonance*. Stanford, CA: Stanford University Press.

Gantz, W. (1981). An exploration of viewing motives and behaviors associated with television sports. *Journal of Broadcasting, 25*, 263–75.

Gantz, W. & Wenner, L.A. (1991). Men, women, and sports: Audience experiences and effects. *Journal of Broadcasting & Electronic Media, 35*, 233–43.

Gantz, W. & Wenner, L.A. (1995). Fanship and the television sports viewing experience. *Sociology of Sport Journal, 12*, 56–74.

Gilligan, C. & Attanucci, L. (1988). Two moral orientations: Gender differences and similarities. *Merrill-Palmer Quarterly, 34*, 223–37.

Goldstein, J.H. (Ed.). (1998). *Why we watch: The attractions of violent programming*. New York: Oxford University Press.

Gunter, B. (2006). Sport, violence, and the media. In A.A. Raney & J. Bryant (Eds.), *Handbook of sports and media* (pp. 353–64). Mahwah, NJ: Lawrence Erlbaum Associates.

Haidt, J. (2003). The moral emotions. In R.J. Davidson, K.R. Scherer, & H.H. Goldsmith (Eds.), *Handbook of affective sciences* (pp. 852–70). Oxford: Oxford University Press.

Heider, F. (1958). *The psychology of interpersonal relations*. New York: Wiley.

Hillmann, C., Cuthbert, B., Bradley, M., & Lang, P. (2004). Motivated engagement to appetitive and aversive fanship cues: Psychophysiological responses of rival sports fans. *Journal of Sports & Exercise Psychology, 26*, 338–51.

International Olympic Committee (2007). *Olympic Charter: In Force as from 7 July 2007*. Lausanne, Switzerland: International Olympic Committee. Retrieved February 28, 2010, from http://multimedia.olympic.org/pdf/en_report_122.pdf

International Olympic Committee (2009). *Ancient Olympic Games*. Retrieved April 26, 2010, from www.olympic.org/en/content/Olympic-Games/Ancient-Olympic-Games/

King, C.M. (2000). Effects of humorous heroes and villains in violent action films. *Journal of Communication, 50*, 5–24.

Klapper, J.T. (1960). *The effects of mass communication*. New York: Free Press.

McCarty, J.A. & Shrum, L.J. (1993). The role of personal values and demographics in predicting television viewing behavior: Implications for theory and application. *Journal of Advertising, 22,* 77–101.

Oliver, M.B. (1996). Influences of authoritarianism and portrayals of race on Caucasian viewers' responses to reality-based crime dramas. *Communication Reports, 9,* 141–50.

Oliver, M.B. (2009). Affect as a predictor of entertainment choice: The utility of looking beyond pleasure. In T. Hartman (Ed.), *Media choice: A theoretical and empirical overview* (pp. 167–84). New York: Routledge.

Oliver, M.B. & Bartsch, A. (2010). Appreciation as audience response: Exploring entertainment gratifications beyond hedonism. *Human Communication Research, 36,* 53–81.

Peterson, E. & Raney, A.A. (2008). Exploring the complexity of suspense as a predictor of mediated sports enjoyment. *Journal of Broadcasting & Electronic Media, 52,* 544–62.

Raney, A.A. (2002). Moral judgment as a predictor of enjoyment of crime drama. *Media Psychology, 4,* 305–22.

Raney, A.A. (2004). Expanding disposition theory: Reconsidering character liking, moral evaluation, and enjoyment. *Communication Theory, 14*(4), 348–68.

Raney, A.A. (2005). Punishing media criminals and moral judgment: The impact on enjoyment. *Media Psychology, 7*(2), 145–63.

Raney, A.A. (2006a). The psychology of disposition-based theories of media enjoyment. In J. Bryant & P. Vorderer (Eds.), *The psychology of entertainment* (pp. 137–50). Mahwah, NJ: Lawrence Erlbaum Associates.

Raney, A.A. (2006b). Why we watch and enjoy mediated sports. In A.A. Raney & J. Bryant (Eds.), *Handbook of sports and media* (pp. 313–29). Mahwah, NJ: Erlbaum.

Raney, A.A. & Bryant, J. (2002). Moral judgment in crime drama: An integrated theory of enjoyment. *Journal of Communication, 52,* 402–15.

Raney, A.A. & Kinnally, W. (2006, June). The thrill of victory and the agony of defeat? The complexity of enjoyment in rivalry game wins and losses. Presentation at the annual meeting of the International Communication Conference, Dresden, Germany.

Raney, A.A. & Kinnally, W. (2009). Examining perceived violence in and enjoyment of televised rivalry sports contests. *Mass Communication and Society, 12,* 311–31.

Sandomir, R. (1999, October 31). TV sports: All-Century became all about Rose and Gray. *New York Times.* Retrieved April 26, 2010, from www.nytimes.com/1999/10/31/sports/tv-sports-all-century-became-all-about-rose-and-gray.html

Sargent, S.L., Zillmann, D., & Weaver, J.B. (1998). The gender gap in the enjoyment of televised sports. *Journal of Sport & Social Issues, 22,* 46–64.

Sweeny, P.D. & Gruber, K.L. (1984). Selective exposure: Voter information preferences and the Watergate affair. *Journal of Personality and Social Psychology, 46,* 1208–21.

Tamborini, R. & Lachlan, K. (2008). The effect of perpetrator motive and dispositional attributes on enjoyment of television violence and attitudes toward victims. *Journal of Broadcasting & Electronic Media, 52,* 136–52.

Tüzünkan, F. (2007). The role of morality and physical attractiveness of athletes on disposition formation. Unpublished doctoral dissertation, Florida State University.

Vidmar, N. & Rokeach, M. (1974). Archie Bunker's bigotry: A study in selective perception and exposure. *Journal of Communication, 24,* 36–47.

Vorderer, P. (2001). It's all entertainment – sure. But what exactly is entertainment? Communication research, media psychology, and the explanation of entertainment experiences. *Poetics, 29,* 247–61.

Vorderer, P., Klimmt, C., & Ritterfeld, U. (2004). Enjoyment: At the heart of media entertainment. *Communication Theory, 14,* 388–408.

Wann, D.L. & Branscombe, N.R. (1990). Die-hard and fair-weather fans: Effects of identification on BIRGing and CORFing tendencies. *Journal of Sport & Social Issues, 14,* 103–17.

Wann, D.L., Melnick, M.J., Russell, G.W., & Pease, D.G. (2001). *Sports fans: The psychology and social impact of spectators.* New York: Routledge.

Zillmann, D. (1995). Sports and the media. In J. Mester (Ed.), *Images of sport in the world* (pp. 423–44). Cologne: German Sports University.

Zillmann, D. (2000). Basal morality in drama appreciation. In I. Bondebjerg (Ed.), *Moving images, culture, and the mind* (pp. 53–63). Luton, UK: University of Luton Press.

Zillmann, D. & Bryant, J. (Eds.). (1985). *Selective exposure to communication.* Hillsdale, NJ: Erlbaum.

Zillmann, D., Bryant, J., & Sapolsky, B. (1989). Enjoyment from sports spectatorship. In J. H. Goldstein (Ed.), *Sports, games, and play: Social and psychological viewpoints* (2nd Ed., pp. 241–78). Hillsdale, NJ: Lawrence Erlbaum Associates.

Zillmann, D. & Cantor, J. (1972). Directionality of transitory dominance as a communication variable affecting humor appreciation. *Journal of Personality and Social Psychology, 24,* 191–98.

Zillmann, D. & Cantor, J. (1976). A disposition theory of humor and mirth. In T. Chapman & H. Foot (Eds.), *Humor and laughter: Theory, research, and application* (pp. 93–115). London: Wiley.

Zillmann, D. & Paulus, P.B. (1993). Spectators: Reactions to sports events and effects on athletic performance. In R.N. Singer, M. Murphey, & L.K. Tennant (Eds.), *Handbook of research on sports psychology* (pp. 600–619). New York: Macmillan.

6

SPORTS MEDIA

Beyond broadcasting, beyond sports, beyond societies?

David Rowe

UNIVERSITY OF WESTERN SYDNEY

Introduction: changing technologies, cultures and places[1]

Media is both an umbrella and a plural term. It brings together a range of communicative technologies, institutions, audiences, practices and texts while reaffirming that the constituents of this implied singular entity are, instead, multiple, different and irreducible. So, when discussing sports media, we should take into account the full extent of the "media sports cultural complex" (Rowe, 2004) as it ranges across newspapers and magazines, videos and films, books and blogs, radio stations and websites. Each of these forms of media sports inter-relates in constructing the vast cultural edifice that shadows the image horizon of all the world's citizens, whether by consent or through sheer cultural ubiquity. But one medium, television (Real, this volume, Chapter 2), towers above all others when imagining media sports.

Broadcast television has been the most powerful force in sports economics and culture for over a half a century. As a result, scholars have devoted considerable attention to television's underwriting of sports, influence on its forms and reception contexts, and carriage of social ideologies. However, despite the spectacular (though intermittent instances of) global-scale audiences at events such as the World Cup of association football and the Olympics, the spread of new technologies, cultural arrangements, and societal flows suggests that broadcast television is now under challenge and, at the very least, undergoing a major transitional, if not transformative phase. Broadcast television's once unrivalled capacity to monopolize "live action" for dispersed audiences, the primacy of the physical contest in media representations of sports, and the place of sports TV's imagery within recognizable socio-cultural formations are all to some degree in question (Leonard, 2009; Boyle & Whannel, 2010). But if the era of TV sports hegemony is passing into history, the regime that will replace it – if any – is by no means yet installed.

In this chapter. I will explore the trajectory of sports television, and propose necessary research avenues for media sports scholars. In so doing, it is important to avoid being too sports media centric and absorbed by its internal commercial concerns. Sports media of necessity operate within wider cultural and social environments that are themselves undergoing substantial change. In this respect there is nothing exceptional about sports media in an epoch in which, among sundry disturbances, globalization, regional conflict and often intricate local relations, are in dynamic interplay, and in which the everyday working and domestic lives of people around the world are increasingly uncertain and fluid (Appadurai, 2001; Bauman, 2000). It is for this reason that I will pose some critically skeptical questions about the state of television broadcasting, the cultural status of sports, and the relationships between sports, television and nation. This task entails interrogating the position of sports media within a socio-cultural environment in which the received conceptualization of society itself has been problematical, and even undermined by the instabilities that accompany diffused, intensified mobilities. First, though, there will be a consideration of a sports medium that is still pre-eminent, has now been installed substantially across the world, and yet is troubled by intimations of technological mortality – broadcast television.

Broadcast sports television and its end(s)

Although it is not uncommon to describe "old media" such as television as passé and in terminal decline (see, for example, various contributions, both supportive and skeptical towards this proposition, in Katz and Scannell, 2009), broadcast sports retains considerable potency as witnessed by the size of its audiences and the value of its rights. It is easy to point to gargantuan sports television viewerships as measures of its persistent strength (both regarding television in general and sports in particular). For example, it has been estimated that the largest global television audience ever, 4.7 billion viewers or 70% of the world's population, watched at least some of the 2008 Beijing Olympic Games during its two weeks in August (not including the ensuing Paralympics – Rowe, 2009). However, the "occupation" of mediated cultural space by sports events varies between countries, and the political economy of television sports is shaped not just by the size of its audience, but by its consumer purchasing power. Thus, it is especially significant that in the US, which is home both to the principal Olympic broadcaster (NBC) and to its most important audience in economic terms, the Beijing Games became the country's most-viewed televised event, with a total audience of 211 million and an average daily audience of 27 million people (Nielsen, 2008), and an estimated over 98% of Americans at least "sampling" television coverage of Beijing 2008.

Given that the cost to the NBC network of acquiring the broadcast rights to the Beijing Olympics from the International Olympic Committee (IOC) was US$894 million, there is clearly an expectation that large sums can be recouped from advertisers, sponsors, and through on-selling rights to other media companies. Prior to the 2010 Vancouver Winter Olympics, NBC claims to have made a profit on every summer and winter Games since 1992, accumulating a surplus of US$375 million in that period, including US$100 million from Beijing Olympics broadcasting (Mickle & Ourand, 2010). While such profit results are often disputed in strict accounting terms (Rowe, 2004), there are also less tangible benefits of acquiring premium sports rights, such as the additional advantage of showcasing the network's other sports and non-sports programs without additional cost, and the "spillover" audience momentum of successful broadcasts.

The capacity of sports television, whether on a free-to-air, subscription or pay-per-view basis, both to attract viewers to itself and expose them to supplementary media services, has created vigorous competition for broadcast rights across the globe. NBC, for example, whose parent company is General Electric, is engaged in an expensive contest with other media corporations such as (Rupert Murdoch's) News Corporation and Disney for television and other electronic and online media sports properties. In a recent company report, News Corporation (2009, p. 70) stated that its "commitments, borrowings and contractual obligations" regarding sports programming rights were US$16,866 million. This investment mostly pertains to television, and there is little current evidence, despite aforementioned pronouncements of the decline of broadcasting, that rights revenues are currently in decline. Indeed, the reverse is the case, with NBC's predicted (though at time of writing unconfirmed) loss of US$200 million on the 2010 Vancouver Olympics caused by the rising cost of rights (Mickle & Ourand, 2010) and, in Australia, the prospect of a substantial rise in the value of rights for both Australian rules football and rugby league (Chessell, 2010).

It is not only multi-national, multi-sports events that can attract vast television audiences and so demand substantial broadcast rights. In February 2010, for example, an estimated 106.5 million people in the United States watched the Super Bowl, making this football contest the most-watched broadcast in the history of that nation's television (Fixmer & Pulley, 2010). This nation-based event was simultaneously taken to the screens of many other nations across the world for the benefit of expatriate Americans, the relatively small number of viewers in other countries who are aficionados of gridiron, and, importantly, to a casual viewership drawn in by the spectacle, including the half-time entertainment by such well-known acts as the Who in 2010, and Michael Jackson, Diana Ross, U2, Bruce Springsteen, Prince, the Rolling Stones, Britney Spears, and Paul McCartney in earlier years. This "event" nature of the television broadcast, in which the sports may be of peripheral interest for many viewers who simply "dip into" it, is a powerful aspect of its appeal. The Super Bowl half-time entertainment, which was formerly dominated by non-celebrity college marching bands, even produced its own confected controversy in 2004, with the infamous "wardrobe malfunction" involving Janet Jackson and Justin Timberlake. This incident ensured that the event moved from the sports to the news pages for several days after the sports action had concluded, prompting debates about "decency" and broadcast regulation, and feeding off a potent combination of scandal, sports and international pop music celebrity (Lane, 2006; Wenner, 2004, 2008).

It is this collective, co-present "event" quality of "live" sports television (and, as will be argued in greater detail below, *sports-like* television), that has given it enduring cultural and economic power well into the 21st Century. Indeed, while aggregate broadcast television viewing may be declining in some mature markets with other, freely available media technologies, and viewers per program (either actual or as a proportion of total audience) falling even for many programs deemed to be a success,[2] television events involving a determinate result and an opportunity for focused co-presence are experiencing a high degree of success. In early 2010, when the Australian minister for broadband, communications and the digital economy, Senator Stephen Conroy, stated that the free-to-air sector was in "terminal long-term structural decline" (World News Australia, 2010, n.p.), major sports television like the Super Bowl was flourishing:

> The huge viewership for the game comes after a string of televised events that have seen their ratings pop. In recent months, the Grammy Awards, the Golden Globe Awards and baseball's World Series have all seen ratings increases from prior years.
>
> The ability to reach a mass audience has made big events like championship sports or TV season finales of shows such as "American Idol" must buys for marketers. This year 30 seconds of Super Bowl ad time fetched between $2.5 million to $2.9 million, according to ad buyers.
>
> *(Schechner & Ovide, 2010, n.p.)*

Senator Conroy, as is common, attributed the cause of the posited terminal decline of free-to-air television to a "tidal wave of cost and technological change." Yet, significantly for the contention of this chapter, some analysts have argued that new media and technology can actually help build broadcast television audiences rather than detract from them. For example, in the case of Super Bowl, and by extension other major sports events, social network media might discharge a similar function to that of paid advertising and promotion:

> CBS [the Super Bowl Broadcast Network in 2010] Chief Executive Leslie Moonves said social-networking tools such as Twitter have encouraged TV viewing as Americans exchange opinions on what they're watching.
>
> "I think we've returned a little bit to the water cooler mentality," Mr. Moonves said. "This goes back to watching people walk on the moon; Americans like shared experiences." ...
>
> ... "They've bucked the trend," said Andy Donchin, director of media investments at Carat, a media-buying unit of Aegis Group PLC. "As much as we're pulling away and watching different things, there are some things that we want to watch together."
>
> *(Schechner & Ovide, 2010, n.p.)*

Social network, mobile and online media, therefore, may be encouraged by broadcast television for their contribution to "buzz," but resisted where they provide or support alternative attractions, and especially where they infringe broadcast and other image rights (see various contributions to special issue of *Sociology of Sport Journal*, 2009 [Leonard, 2009]). It is for this reason, as the policing of intellectual property rights has been made more difficult by media convergence, that the Parliament of Australia held an inquiry in 2009 into "The Reporting of Sports News and the Emergence of Digital Media" (Hutchins & Rowe, 2009a). Disputes between sports and media organizations about what constitutes news, how much sports action can be shown by non-rights holders, and so on, are in the current uncertain media sports environment anticipatory rather than entrenched, with little solid evidence presented at the inquiry of actual losses borne by broadcast rights holders as a result of infringements by other parties such as telecommunications companies (Parliament of Australia, 2009). Indeed, as noted earlier, the strength of television audiences suggests that the communal aspects of viewing as a social activity remain paramount, and that the "social" in "social media" means that, by priming interest in sports events, the "Internet can be TV's friend" (Stelter, 2010, n.p.).

Current circumstances, as noted above, are characterized by the proliferation of media, the emergence of digital networked media sports (Hutchins & Rowe, 2009b), and, as the development economist Charles Kenny (2009; see also Tay & Turner, 2010) has recently argued, the spread of television across the world in a manner that, for the foreseeable future, cements its position as the dominant global medium (and, indeed, popular educational forum).[3] As Kenny notes, sports is an integral element of the global appeal of television, alongside programming with a proto-sporting structure of competition and outcome uncertainty:

> As choices in what to watch expand, people will have access both to a wider range of voices and to a growing number of channels keen to give the audience what it really wants. And what it wants seems to be pretty much the same everywhere – sports, reality shows, and, yes, soap operas. Some 715 million people worldwide watched the finals of the 2006 soccer World Cup, for example. More than a third of Afghanistan's population tunes into that country's version of *American Idol – Afghan Star*.
>
> *(Kenny, 2009, n.p)*

Broadcasting, especially in televisual form, is clearly in a state of flux, but there is little substance to the claim that it will be swept aside by new media. It is clear that sports remains a "killer application" for the medium, but the impact of digitization is such that it is a cultural form that must be shared with other media. As Jinna Tay and Graeme Turner (2010, p. 32) argue, under a regime of digitization the "social practice of television" is mutable but also resilient. Following Ellis (2002) they note that the sense of "co-presence" that television provides is crucial to the experience of watching a "high profile sporting event," but that other senses of co-presence might be constructed through, for example, compiling and sharing YouTube clips (Tay & Turner, 2010, p. 45). Little is yet known about these relatively new forms of sociality and, they argue, it cannot be assumed that "watching a football match on broadcast television and downloading a *Saturday Night Live* sketch from YouTube are mutually exclusive activities" (p. 46). However, what is clear is that, in retrospect, live broadcast sports television, which was regarded as a "de-spatializing" force when it took the action to fans outside the stadium, instead "re-spatialized" them in front of screens that, as they became larger and more accessible in private and public space, created new opportunities for physical co-presence and real-time cultural ritual (Rowe & Stevenson, 2006).

There is, of course, much more to sports television than the live event. Preceding, following, attached to, running alongside and detached from the live moment, there are many televisual forms and experiences that range from quiz shows and recorded highlights packages to documentaries and sports-related drama (Rowe, 2004). In broader terms, as Lotz (2007, p. 2) has argued of the world's most important television nation, "Television as we knew it – understood as a mass medium capable of reaching a broad, heterogeneous audience and speaking to the culture as a whole – is no longer the norm in the United States." She concludes (like Tay & Turner, 2010) that, while changes in the uses and expectations of television "have not been hastening the demise of the medium," they are having a clear impact on its capacity to act as "an electronic public sphere ... except for a few remaining events such as the Super Bowl." It is for this reason that access to live major televised sports available free-to-air through broadcast networks to whole populations – by their nature forms of television that break with the usual routines of viewing and everyday life – is the subject of fierce debates over social inclusion and cultural citizenship in many countries (Rowe, 2009). For example, in Australia in 2009 there was a review of the so-called anti-siphoning laws that quarantine key sports broadcasts from exclusive capture by pay television, with similar actions and debates in Europe and Canada (Australian Government, 2009; Scherer & Whitson, 2009). The passionate disputation by media companies, governments and viewers on this matter emphasizes the importance of televised broadcast sports.

Mobile and computer-based technologies are still largely enhancements of the "ultimate" live sports viewing experience, or compensations for an inability to simulate plausibly, in smaller or larger scale (for example, at home in company in the case of the former, or in live sites in urban public space in the case of the latter), the embodied collective experience of the crowd. Thus, for example, during the 2010 Vancouver Olympics non-traditional media produced 20,000 hours of coverage, more than equalling that of broadcast television, but NBC's online audience of 33 million was far smaller than that for traditional television, which approached 3.5 billion (Reuters, 2010). If, though, broadcast sports television is surviving despite new modes of delivery, such as IPTV and mobile telephony, making initial incursions into its space within culture, what might be said of the cultural form on which it is focused? It might be premature to talk of a "post-broadcast" or "post-television" era, but is there a movement, perhaps, towards "post-sports"?

Sports and cultural cannibalism

In earlier discussion in this chapter, I raised the question of the status of sports as a distinctive cultural form in societies infused with an increasing range of "sports-like" genres and practices. Echoes of sports can be found across the cultural spectrum – for example, in the "prize culture" of literature and other arts, with bets taken on the Man Booker and Nobel literary prizes as if they were sports contests (Street, 2005), and substantial television coverage of deliberations and outcomes. Indeed, the Nobel Prize for literature was established in 1901, only five years after Baron Pierre de Coubertin revived the modern Olympics, and included a competitive Cultural Olympiad, in fields such as poetry, alongside the sports (English, 2005). In over a century since, as television became ubiquitous, sports can be said to have cannibalized much of media culture, or to have been consumed by it.

It is a matter of debate, then, as to whether the resemblance of formal sports contests to, say, franchised "reality" television shows such as *Survivor*, *Big Brother* and *I'm a Celebrity, Get Me Out of Here*, cooking contest formats such as *Iron Chef* and *Masterchef*, competitive "song and dance" shows like *Idol, Dancing with the Stars* and *So You Think You Can Dance*, and career-based and self-improvement contests such as *The Apprentice* and *The Biggest Loser*, represent the cultural ascendancy of sports, or its cultural incorporation, subordination and dilution. For example, in the case of programs like the British version of the internationally franchised German game show *Beat the Star (Schlag den Star)*, "ordinary" contestants compete with celebrities, often athletes, such as the tennis players Martina Navratilova, Martina Hingis and Greg Rusedski, in a range of physical and other contest forms. These might be described as the genre of television *as* sports, rather than the more conventional way of seeing television as the *representation of* sports (Brookes, 2002). In this respect, there is a well-established tradition of quasi-sports television that embraces programs, past and present, such as *Gladiator*, *It's a Knockout* (the British program based on the French show *Intervilles*, with various spin-offs like the US's *Almost Anything Goes* in the 1970s), and the Europe-wide *Jeux Sans Frontières* ("Games Without Borders"). When the staple programming of the quiz show is taken into account, especially those with large prizes such as *Who Wants to Be a Millionaire?* and the "gladiatorial" talk show contests embedded in the likes of *The Jerry Springer Show*, it can be proposed that television in general, especially in an era of threat to networked free-to-air broadcast delivery modes, is deeply reliant both on conventional sports contests, and on selected elements of them in other programming types in order to give them the "feel" of competitive uncertainty that is central to sports.

It is becoming increasingly difficult, then, to separate and classify the sporting from other constituents of culture – indeed, the very "mediatization" of sports has accentuated this development, with an hybridic (perhaps postmodern) impulse impeding attempts to isolate and define sports as cultural practice. The mediated treatment of sports has also seen the importation of representational conventions familiar in other popular televisual genres, such as the melodramatic register of soap opera, and the scandalized tone of current affairs. As with quasi-sports television, this development is not new, especially for male aficionados (Rose & Friedman, 1997), but it has accelerated and intensified. The greater use of close-ups (often extreme) of athletes in a manner redolent of daytime TV soap opera's searching of the face for expressive emotion, the setting up of narrativized, binary conflicts between "good" and "evil" that suggest a deeper moral resonance than the sports contest itself, and the attention to the lifestyle of sports stars within the ambit of programs such as *Entertainment Tonight*, are techniques that infuse and surround sports with multiple cultural reference points (Rowe, 2004).

Nowhere is this tendency more pronounced than when a sports-related scandal erupts. Ethical transgressions related to sports performance, such as champion Olympic sprinter Marion Jones's taking of performance-enhancing drugs, or the (late) South African cricket captain Hansie Cronje's involvement in match fixing, are highly newsworthy and attract massive media coverage. But it is off-field scandal involving a sports celebrity, especially of a salacious kind, that most conspicuously spreads and integrates sports across and into a range of cultural sites. The most striking recent example of this phenomenon concerns Tiger Woods, the world's best (and perhaps best ever) golfer, whose marital tribulations and seemingly compulsive infidelities obliterated the coverage of many more orthodox "hard news" stories in late 2009 and early 2010. For example, the BBC received hundreds of complaints in February 2010 when it led its main television news bulletin with Woods's scheduled public apology on a day when a major steel plant closed, British Gas reported a major increase in profit, and a British soldier was killed in Afghanistan. In its defence, the BBC stated:

> As the first sports personality to become a billionaire, Tiger Woods is a colossal figure in the sporting world and therefore of huge interest to many people.
>
> His highly unusual apology after his very public fall from grace is therefore, in our opinion, a big news story that warrants a prominent place in our bulletins.
>
> On that particular day we did not feel there was another story with bigger news impact.
>
> *(quoted in Thomas, 2010, n.p.)*

Thus there is a two-way movement whereby sports, having permeated much television content, is in turn represented in ways that enhance it as dramaturgy, while integrating sports into the more diffuse realm of "broad spectrum" news and entertainment. Brian Pronger (1998, p. 281) has proposed the concept of "post-sport" to describe the division between "modern sport [as] a project of differentiation and socio-cultural boundary maintenance" and "postmodern sport (post-sport) [as] a wild event of de-differentiation and boundary pollution." He is particularly concerned with resisting the constraints imposed by institutionalized sports on the body, but the idea of post-sports could also be seen as a more general breaking down of the boundaries between the sporting and the non-sporting. This development is what David Andrews and Michael Giardina, drawing on Stuart Hall's (1986) revision of the Marxist project, describe as "sport without guarantees":

> In short, we would contend that there is no guaranteed or essential manifestation, experience, or indeed definition of sport. Although physically based competitive activities are a feature of virtually all human civilizations, the popular myth of sport as a fixed and immutable category is little more than a pervasive, if compelling, fiction. Sports should instead be used as a necessarily malleable collective noun suggesting the diversity and complexity of what are temporally and spatially contingent expressions of physical culture ... So rather than seeking to develop some universal definition of sports, a more productive interpretive strategy is to locate particular sports forms and physical cultural experiences in the sociohistorical context within which they came to exist.
>
> *(Andrews & Giardina, 2008)*

It is possible, though, to go beyond even this relativist position on the many variations of physical culture to question the necessary connection between "sports" and the "physical" in a mediatized, culturally dynamic environment. What Arnd Krüger (1989) calls the "sportification of the world" could be read also as the colonization of sports. It was argued above that the live premium televised sports event constitutes the apex of the sporting in contemporary culture, providing the scarcity and time dependency that generates particular cultural and economic value. The sporting action, though, may be incidental for many viewers watching or present for other reasons – to be sociable, for example, or, as in the case of the Olympics, to take in its myth-soaked rituals, or to watch a sports celebrity for reasons of curiosity or sex appeal. For example, it is possible to watch the association footballer David Beckham playing on television for several reasons not directly involving his sporting prowess (Cashmore, 2002), including his sexual attractiveness; reputation as a masculine style leader with regard to haircuts, tattoos and so on; the curiosity provoked by his marriage to former Spice Girls singer Victoria; the notoriety of his reported affair with Rebecca Loos, and so on. When professional sports, then, is taken out of its immediate closed environment of the stadium, it is available for many cultural uses, but of more significance here is the potential confusion over sports as it is conventionally conceived and other contest-based televisual forms.

The use of familiar sports media techniques such as action-related close-ups (mentioned above), slow motion, freeze frames, tactical analysis and commentary on performance (none of which are exclusive to television sports, but which comprise its presentation in combination) in other types of programming erode familiar conceptions of sports as the prime site where symbolic, regulated competition takes place for viewer pleasure and identification. So, too, does the practice of psychological profiling, style display (Coad, 2008) and lifestyle tracking that is now an essential aspect of mediated sports culture. These trends signal a further shift of sports away from its localized, bounded community foundation in early modernity to the more diffuse, multiply-constituted sports entities of the present day "teams" and individuals who invite support.

One audacious instance of this trend is the case of MyFootballClub (MFC), formed in 2007 as the "world's first and only web-community owned football club," under the motto "Own the club, pick the team," and presented as "the ultimate football fantasy" (MyFootballClub, 2010). On the basis of the capital provided by annual membership fees of those who joined, MFC purchased a controlling interest in an English football team, Ebbsfleet United, which at the time of purchase played in the Blue Square Premier League, four levels below the renowned English Premier League (EPL) that is discussed below. The idea of MFC is that fan-members can vote on all relevant club decisions, including team lineups, tactics, player transfers, shirt designs and budgets. Sponsored by EA Sports, the world's largest sports video gaming company, MFC was freed by its web-based nature from the constraints of distance, and so established a substantial international membership. It could be seen, as I and colleagues have previously argued (Hutchins & Rowe, 2009a; Hutchins, Rowe, & Ruddock, 2009; Ruddock, Hutchins, & Rowe, 2010), as a fantasy or football manager game (such as FIFA Manager and Championship Manager) "made real," with actual material consequences for a functioning sports team. A less ambitious but parallel case is that of the Seattle Sounders FC in the US, where part-owner comedian Drew Carey has, in following elements of FC Barcelona's governance in the Spanish context, engineered enhanced rights for fan members, including the right to vote on retention or removal of the general manager (Romero, 2008).

Sports as conventionally conceived is certainly important in such cases, but is part of a more general cultural scenario of a gaming world where the relationship between the material and the non-material is conventionally fluid and "provisional." The innovative nature of the MFC venture has attracted interest from the world's media, and its changing fortunes (so far a trajectory from "boom" to "bust") deployed as something of a litmus test for the state of sports, fandom, community and commerce. Indeed, one of the key areas of tension is between those who live near, and are historically connected to, the football club and its ground (who may or may not be members of MFC), and those whose link to the club is predominantly or exclusively in the realm of cyberspace, and for whom MFC/Ebbsfleet United is an "elective," perhaps amusing leisure option involving little in the way of deep, affective fan commitment. "Beyond sports" in this case means a certain displacement of traditional, locally based sports organization and fandom to the "abstract" spaces and relations of the online world.

But, again, assuming that sports were to remain the most important focus of collective identification for symbolic contests, what would be its terrain? The historical hierarchy of neighbourhood, city, region and nation represents the ascending spatial locus of sports identification as it developed in industrial and representation terms. Even if sports remains recognizable and distinctive as a cultural form – a questionable assumption, as indicated above – where can the "society" be found that mediates action and identification?

Sports deraciné

Sports media scholars, like those in other areas of research in the social sciences and humanities, have tended to adopt a fairly unreflective approach to the sociohistorical context – or, more commonly, "society" – as an object of study and analysis, to which sports is intimately related. John Urry (2000) has criticized the tendency of sociologists (and, presumably, other social scientists) to construct a notion of society as a securely bounded, self-reproducing set of structures and social relations in a way that has tended to bracket out what they don't know or understand, and to imagine the conditions with which they are most familiar as the template for social organization[4]. It is notable that Urry (2000, p. 36), one of the leading proponents of the idea of "post-society" (though not of postmodernism), cites media sports instances as illustrations of the "mobilities" (physical, technological and cultural) that he argues now characterize social existence:

> globalization allows people new opportunities and new activities to develop. These include: ... the possibility to participate in global cultural events such as the World Cup ...

Urry also notes novelist Arundhati Roy's observation in *The God of Small Things* of an elderly female character's extraordinary access to the world through satellite television reception in her home, so that "Blondes, wars, famines, football, sex, music, coups d'etat – they all arrived on the same train" (Roy, 1997, p. 27, cited in Urry, 2000, p. 89).[5] Sports media texts are only part of this cultural cornucopia, but they are important to it, not least because for some audiences they provide the "driver" to access television in the first instance, especially when the sports programming is a highly marketed, glamorous Western sports spectacle that can signify acquisition of an attractive cosmopolitan identity for aspiring consumers in the developing world (Rowe & Gilmour, 2009).

Of course, many sociologists of sports and media sports scholars have analyzed the possibilities and limits of globalization and its inherent mobilities (for example, Bairner, 2001; Bernstein & Blain, 2003; Maguire 1999, 2005; Miller et al., 2001, 2010), but the mere recognition of globalization is not, in itself, necessarily accompanied by a critical rethinking of the idea of "society." Instead, conceptions of globalization may resemble earlier theories of internationalization and imperialism that retain a "billiard ball" model of colliding discrete entities, or conceive of a "global society" as if it were a magnification or simple aggregation of the individual societies out of which it has been created:

These flows [thus] produce the hollowing out of existing societies, especially as a plethora of "sociations" have developed, concerned to reflect upon, to argue against, to retreat from, to provide alternatives to, to campaign for, these various flows, often going beyond the limits of the societal "region." This generates within any existing "society," a complex, overlapping, disjunctive order, of off-centredness, as these multiple flows are chronically combined and recombined across times and spaces often unrelated to the regions of existing societies, often following a kind of hypertextual patterning.

(Urry, 2000, p. 36)

In drawing on the work of Maurice Roche (2000) through the prism of complexity theory, Urry conventionally refers to mega media sports events as illustrative of the "strange attractor of 'glocalization,'" whereby the connections of locally based actions and global consequences have been so reconfigured since Marx's brilliant insights from the middle of the century below last" (Urry, 2003, p. 82). The co-existence, sometimes the result of "customization" of global and local characteristics in the same socio-cultural phenomenon in the concept of "glocalization," is one of the factors that problematizes received notions of societies as bounded entities. It can be argued that it is also possible to exaggerate the extent of these mobilities, and to observe that the capacity for mobility is unevenly distributed across and between populations (Bauman, 2002; Urry, 2007). I have also argued previously – and pro-vocatively – that sports represents in some ways a paradoxical "repudiation" of the project of cultural globalization in its fullest sense (Rowe, 2003), an intervention that prompted a (sympathetic) critique by Andrews and Ritzer (2007, p. 136) as they judge that my analysis "falsely polarizes globalization and localization in a manner that implicitly privileges, perhaps even romanticizes, the local." In this way they broadly reflect Urry and Bauman's typification – and questioning – of the societal, in the light of the:

declining, or even disappearing, relevance of the local and the need to reconceptualise virtually everything we think of as local as glocal. Rather than viewing the core tension as existing being between the global and the local, and certainly as evidenced within the sporting realm, our contention is that the *local* has been so effected [sic] by the *global*, that it has become, at all intents and purposes, *glocal* (Ritzer 2004, p. xiii, xi). Thus, the processual and empirical continuum through which we conceptualize globalization is bounded by *grobalization* ("the imperialistic ambitions of nations, corporations, organi-zations, and the like and their desire, indeed need, to impose themselves on various geographic areas") and *glocalization* ("the interpenetration of the global and the local, resulting in unique outcomes in different geographic areas"): the *grobal* and the *glocal* …

(Andrews & Ritzer, 2007, p. 137)

This is a wide-ranging and difficult debate, being conducted in many fields other than media sports studies. But in the context of this chapter, it has an especially important bearing on analyses of the experiences of media sports, the constituencies that might mobilize around it, and the various contests for power and modes of collective identification that pivot on the relationship between sports and cultural citizenship (Miller, 2006; Rowe, 2009).

It is not, then, easy to find a secure vantage point from which to make critical-analytical interventions in contemporary sports media on such shifting ground. There are powerful analytical approaches available: political economic critiques, for example, that highlight the commercial exploitation of athletes and spectators (especially from disadvantaged communities and developing countries), or inter-pretive readings of ideologies of prejudice and exclusion within sports media texts that give sustenance to class oppression (Whannel, 2008), racism and ethnocentrism (Carrington & McDonald, 2001, 2009), sexism and homophobia (Birrell & McDonald, 2000; Caudwell, 2006), "ableism" (DePauw & Gavron, 2005), and so on. But the sheer scale and complexity of the "media sports cultural complex" (the "complex complex"), and of the positive and negative dimensions of the same phenomena at different times (for example, resistive community solidarity that can also manifest as in-group chauvinism), makes it difficult to advance the kind of comprehensive, authoritative analyses that once seemed achievable through theoretical plausibility, conceptual innovation, and empirical evidence.

To take a brief example – here from a quasi-academic context – David Andrews (2009), one of the more perceptive figures in media sports studies, recently propounded an argument that support for the EPL among Americans signifies substantial disillusionment with corporatized American sports. Drawing on the seminal work *The Uses of Literacy*, whose author Richard Hoggart (1957) sought to understand and criticize the influence of modern American popular culture on the working-class culture of northern England, Andrews asserts:

> In general, today's market savvy sport consumers are contentedly resigned to their role within the domineering sport-media-entertainment industrial complex, and indeed the nature of its spectacularized entertainment and profit-oriented products. However, some are not. The sporting turn to the EPL catalyzes a growing disenchantment felt by some toward corporatized sports forms driven primarily by commercial rationalities and logics as opposed to sporting contingencies. The allure of the EPL to this constituency is simple. To many disillusioned American sports fans, it encapsulates everything that the National Football League, Major League Baseball, the National Basketball Association, and the National Hockey League are not: It is considered to be a historically-grounded, and thereby authentic, sports league rooted in the fervour and commitment of team supporters, and facilitated by a [sic] immediate and organic link between team and the communities in which they are located.
>
> *(Andrews, 2009, n.p.)*

In advancing this self-confessed "brazenly un-scientific analysis," Andrews[6] sees the same resistance to orchestrated consumption that Hoggart detected in 1950s England, despite simultaneously recognizing "the success of the EPL in globalizing the brand (and its sub-brands, i.e. individual teams and players), through its dissemination as a globally ubiquitous material commodity and mediated spectacle." Thus, the branded-logo-wearing bearers of this mediated resistive struggle, he argues, are engaging in a nostalgic fantasy of what sports was like before corporations imposed an order of "hyper commercialism" on sports. These fans, it is posited, are searching for sporting community authenticity, but can do so only by repressing the obvious corporatism of the EPL, by romanticizing some negative aspects of this sports culture, such as hooliganism, and, given their geographical distance from the "grass roots" communities artfully presented to them in ESPN's advertisements for its EPL television coverage, by being almost entirely dependent on the corporate commercial media that they are held by Andrews to condemn.

The idea of sports beyond nation here is salient, with its strong emphasis on a fantasized "real" in another country (and, indeed, time), and the necessary repression of inconvenient "facts" – for example, that the EPL (whose naming rights sponsor is Barclays Bank) is by far the most commercialized of all football leagues in Europe, and carries an estimated half of the total debt for the game in that continent, not least because of "leveraged" purchases of leading EPL teams (such as Liverpool and Manchester United) by U.S. capital (Conn, 2010). Andrews (2009, n.p) is keenly aware of this irony, seeing in it "the dominant figure of the football *flâneur* [who] displays a relatively detached relationship with specific clubs, and indeed leagues, as they promiscuously share their attention across the football marketplace." Such mobile cosmopolitan sports fandom, a striking feature of popular support for U.K. association football and U.S. basketball clubs in the Asia-Pacific (Rowe & Gilmour, 2009), does not necessarily erode the potency of the national, which is still prominent – indeed, to the point of xenophobia on occasion – in much international sports competition. For example, during the 2010 Vancouver Winter Olympics, one journalist was moved to ask and answer a question entirely organized around the nation:

> Where are you now? In Canada. Beyond that, at least for tonight, the fine distinctions of geography and language and distance didn't really matter.
>
> *(Brunt, 2010, n.p.)*

Here the capacity of sports temporarily to override divisions within nations is emphasized – although it is one that can be expected to diminish as the mobility of world populations – not least of athletes – increases. The concepts of society, nation and nation-state, though, are not coterminous, and there are many points of contestation over, for example, representative international sports teams that may be based on nation-states but resisted by elements of the population with different, competing identities (for example, the Scots in the UK, and Catalans – the principal

support base of the aforementioned FC Barcelona – in Spain), or where independent
nations are temporarily constructed for the sake of sports (such as the UK's "home"
nations in football, and, more dramatically, the collection of independent nation-
states that becomes the West Indies "nation" when playing cricket). All of these
forms of national and societal assemblage through sports (see Bairner, 2001) are
deeply reliant on the full panoply of available media, combining, dividing and
recombining peoples and identities in ways that may not place them within securely
defined societies (at least as conceived during the brief, modern-era heyday of the
Western nation-state – see Held & McGrew, 2007). What is clear is that the sports
media are unavoidably dedicated to the promotion of sociality – positive, neutral
and negative – through sports in its myriad forms.

Conclusion: the perils and imperatives of critical analytical intervention in sports media

In this chapter I have engaged with three influential and linked propositions – that
broadcast sports television, the cultural distinctiveness of sports, and the relationship
between individual societies and sports, are all in serious decline. In considering
these questions with due analytical skepticism, I have sought to show that elements
of each trend can be detected, but that current conditions and trajectories are more
complex and uncertain than such heuristically useful but theoretically/empirically
questionable arguments, with their totalizing logics, can legitimately accommodate.
Above all, my argument is that media sports compulsively constitutes and reconstitutes
audiences in relation to sports in ways that are inevitably implicated in interacting
social, cultural and economic forces.

Sports television broadcasts, for example, are revenue sources for sports organizations, avenues to audiences for rights holders, and sources of communal pleasure
for sports fans. Broadcast networks claiming to be the "homes" of nominated popular
sports (if only for the duration of their rights contracts) are also well positioned to
connect viewers with other types of programming to which they will be inevitably
exposed through judicious cross-promotion. Scholars in this field must be constantly
alert to the dynamism of its object and appropriately wary of the claims made
by vested interests and moral entrepreneurs that inhabit it. For example, the decline
of television may be welcome for new media companies, while rights holders feel
compelled to patrol their expensively acquired broadcast intellectual property
(Hutchins & Rowe, 2009a). Some social commentators may welcome the new
choices presented by mobile sports media, while others see them as signs of an
"individualization" of society and the erosion of communal life. Such disputes and
debates are unsurprising and, in various ways, instructive – but they reinforce rather
than challenge the extraordinary capability of sports to stimulate social exchange by
all available means.

It is this quality that has carried elements of sports into diverse cultural spaces, and
in turn, seen sports culture permeated by cultural qualities and practices that have far

exceeded its predominantly Western, heterosexual, male-dominated origins. This is not to argue that there has been a wholesale transformation in the structures of power of sports (a premature and implausible conclusion, as the discussion here has revealed), but rather that it is now much more difficult to contain and seal off sports from other socio-cultural spheres. While this cultural portability and permeability of sports is contentious, another facet of its extraordinary qualities is revealed here – a potent adaptive appeal, borne by emergent media technologies, practices and uses, across the entire cultural landscape. This constitutive characteristic of sports means that it can also move freely across national cultural formations, both standing for global culture and exposing its fissures during mega media sports events (see, for example, Luo & Richeri, 2009), and more routinely marking out national identities and boundaries while in other respects undermining and re-drawing them. Sports and media, therefore, interact dynamically as cultural and social agents, with the only current certainty being that, together and separately (the latter increasingly difficult to imagine), the media sports cultural complex shows not the slightest sign of ossification or retreat.

Notes

1 Two Australian Research Council-supported Discovery Grants helped provide the foundation for this chapter. The first, *Handling the "Battering Ram": Rupert Murdoch, News Corporation and the Global Contest for Dominance in Sports Television*, was concerned with the development of broadcast sports television across the world. The second, *Struggling for Possession: The Control and Use of Online Media Sport* (with Dr. Brett Hutchins, Monash University) is yet to be completed, but engages with analytical issues surrounding sports "after television." I would like to acknowledge the research assistance of Callum Gilmour, Janine Mikosza and Genna Burrows in this program of sports media research.

2 A trend discernible also with regard to the sales of many "hit" pop songs and cinema attendances for "big box office" movies.

3 In this regard, television shares a trend evident in the case of another "old" medium – the newspaper – which, according to the World Association of Newspapers (2008), is undergoing unprecedented expansion in the developing world while being pronounced moribund in the developed world.

4 Urry (2000, p. 6) notes, in particular, that the "relative autonomy of American society throughout the twentieth century" precipitated "a universalization of the American societal experience." While his specific disciplinary target is sociology, the self-declared "science of society," it is worth reflecting on the extent to which sports media scholarship has been dominated by the US. It is certainly the case that most academic work on media sports, ranging from economics, management, and marketing to psychology, politics and sociology, and incorporating "studies" domains such as media, communication, sports and leisure, has been produced in the U.S. context. The main reasons for this state of affairs are both the scale of the American higher education system and the size and influence of its sports media. However, substantial Anglophone work has been produced in the UK, Canada and Australasia, and in other countries and languages, but tends to suffer from Anglophone and/or Western hegemony in sports media studies. Although challenges to this intellectual formation are making only limited progress in the international research sphere, the significant growth of sports and its attendant media in regions such as the Asia-Pacific are demanding a greater focus on non-Western sports media contexts (Rowe & Gilmour, 2008).

5 The mobility here is intellectual as well as technological, the use of a fictional character as "evidence" indicating a move towards transdisciplinarity and the diversification of analytical approaches that has registered also in sports studies in, for example, the use of imaginative techniques to bring ethnographic life to sports-related issues and experiences (see, for example, Denison & Markula, 2003).

6 A further ironic twist lies in the aforementioned declaration by Andrews and Ritzer (2007, p. 149) that "the study of the globalization of sports requires that researchers and analysts look at all of the key elements, without *a priori* elevating the significance of one or more and denigrating the importance of others." Andrews's speculation on the motives and meanings of U.S. fan responses to EPL marketing is, perhaps, one such example of the practice that Andrews and Ritzer see as undesirable in the light of their approving citation of Grossberg's (1992) critique of "interpretive logics, and indeed frameworks, through which researchers' *a priori* assumptions are confirmed through their filtered engagement with the empirical."

References

Andrews, D.L. (2009). Of American slouch and English fervour. *FlowTV, 11*(3). Retrieved January 27, 2010, from http://flowtv.org/?p=4564

Andrews, D.L. & Giardina, M.L. (2008). Sport without guarantees: toward a cultural studies that matters. *Cultural Studies* ↔ *Critical Methodologies, 8*(4), 395–422. doi: 10.1177/1532708608321573.

Andrews, D.L. & Ritzer, G. (2007). The grobal in the sporting glocal. *Global Networks, 7*(2), 135–53.

Appadurai, A. (Ed.). (2001). *Globalization.* Durham, NC: Duke University Press.

Australian Government, Department of Broadband, Communications and the Digital Economy. (2009). *Sport on television: A review of the anti-siphoning scheme in the contemporary digital environment.* Retrieved February 28, 2010, from www.dbcde.gov.au/television/antisiphoning_and_antihoarding/sport_on_television-review_of_the_anti-siphoning_scheme_discussion_paper

Bairner, A. (2001). *Sport, nationalism, and globalization: European and North American perspectives.* Albany: State University of New York Press.

Bauman, Z. (2000). *Liquid modernity.* Cambridge: Polity.

Bauman, Z. (2002). *Society under siege.* Cambridge: Polity.

Bernstein, A. & Blain, N. (Eds.). (2003). *Sport, media, culture: Global and local dimensions.* London: Frank Cass.

Birrell, S. & McDonald, M.G. (Eds.). (2000). *Reading sport: Critical essays on power and representation.* Boston: Northeastern University Press.

Boyle, R. & Whannel, G. (Eds.). (2010). Sport in new media cultures special issue. *Convergence: The International Journal of Research into New Media Technologies, 16*(3).

Brookes, R. (2002). *Representing sport.* London: Arnold.

Brunt, S. (2010, February 24). On a rare night, Canada gathered to watch one game. *The Globe and Mail.* Retrieved February 27, 2010, from www.ctvolympics.ca/news-centre/columnists/bruntscorner/newsid=51571.html#a+country+united+watch+canada

Carrington, B. & McDonald, I. (Eds.). (2001). *"Race," sport and British society.* London and New York: Routledge.

Carrington, B. & McDonald, I. (Eds.). (2009). *Marxism, cultural studies and sport.* London and New York: Routledge.

Cashmore, E. (2002). *Beckham.* Cambridge: Polity.

Caudwell, J. (Ed.). (2006). *Sport, sexualities and queer theory.* London and New York: Routledge.

Chessell, J. (2010, February 13). Networks jostle as TV rights season kicks off. *The Australian Business.* Retrieved February 14, 2010, from www.theaustralian.com.au/business/networks-jostle-as-tv-rights-season-kicks-off/story-e6frg8zx-1225829862967

Coad, D. (2008). *The metrosexual: Gender, sexuality, and sport*. Albany: State University of New York Press.

Conn, D. (2010, February 23). Premier League clubs owe 56% of Europe's debt. *Guardian*. Retrieved February 27, 2010, from www.guardian.co.uk/football/2010/feb/23/premier-league-clubs-europe-debt

Denison, J. & Markula, P. (Eds.). (2003). *"Moving writing": Crafting movement in sport research*. New York: Peter Lang.

DePauw, K. & Gavron, S. (2005). *Disability sport* (2nd Ed.). Champaign, IL: Human Kinetics.

Ellis, J. (2002). *Seeing things: Television in the age of uncertainty*. London and New York: I.B. Taurus.

English, J. (2005). *The economy of prestige: Prizes, awards, and the circulation of cultural value*. Cambridge, MA: Harvard University Press.

Fixmer, A. & Pulley, B. (2010, February 8). Super Bowl is most watched U.S. show ever, CBS says. *Bloomberg.com*. Retrieved February 13, 2010 from www.bloomberg.com/apps/news?pid=newsarchive&sid=aShTcum5rYw

Grossberg, L. (1992). *We gotta get out of this place: Popular conservatism and postmodern culture*. London: Routledge.

Hall, S. (1986). The problem of ideology: Marxism without guarantees. *Journal of Communication Inquiry, 10*(2), 28–44.

Held, D. & McGrew, A. (Eds.). (2007). *Globalization theory: Approaches and controversies*. Cambridge: Polity.

Hoggart, R. (1957). *The uses of literacy: Aspects of working class life*. London: Chatto and Windus.

Hutchins, B. & Rowe, D. (2009a). "A battle between enraged bulls": The 2009 Australian senate inquiry into sports news and digital media. *Record of the Communications Policy & Research Forum 2009* (pp. 165–75). Sydney: Network Insight Institute. Retrieved from www.networkinsight.org/events/cprf09.html/group/6

Hutchins, B. & Rowe, D. (2009b). From broadcast rationing to digital plenitude: The changing dynamics of the media sport content economy. *Television & New Media, 10*(4), 354–70.

Hutchins, B., Rowe, D., & Ruddock, A. (2009). "It's fantasy football made real": Networked media sport, the internet, and the hybrid reality of MyFootballClub. *Sociology of Sport Journal, 26*(1), 89–106.

Katz, E. & Scannell, P. (Eds.). (2009). The end of television? Its impact on the world (so far). *The Annals of the American Academy of Political and Social Science Series, 625*(6). doi: 10.1177/0002716209337796.

Kenny, C. (2009, November/December). Revolution in a box. *Foreign Policy*. Retrieved February 13, 2010 from www.foreignpolicy.com/articles/2009/10/19/revolution_in_a_box?page=full

Krüger, A. (1989). The "sportification" of the world: Are there any differences left? (guest editorial). *International Journal of Comparative Physical Education and Sport, 11*(2), 4–5.

Lane, F.S. (2006). *The decency wars: The campaign to cleanse American culture*. Amherst, NY: Prometheus.

Leonard, D. (Ed.). (2009). New media and global sporting cultures special issue. *Sociology of Sport Journal, 26*(1).

Lotz, A.D. (2007). *The television will be revolutionized*. New York and London: New York University Press.

Luo, Q. & Richeri, G. (Eds.). (2009). *Encoding the Olympics: Comparative analysis on international reporting of Beijing 2008: A communication perspective*. Lausanne, Switzerland: International Olympic Committee. Retrieved March 28, 2010 from http://doc.rero.ch/record/12568?ln=en

Maguire, J. (1999). *Global sport: Identities, societies, civilizations*. Cambridge: Polity.

Maguire, J. (2005). *Power and global sport: Zones of prestige, emulation and resistance.* London: Routledge.

Mickle, T. & Ourand, J. (2010, January 18). NBC readjusts games sales goals. *Sports Business Journal.* Retrieved March 28, 2010 from www.sportsbusinessjournal.com/article/64590

Miller, T. (2006). *Cultural citizenship: Cosmopolitanism, consumerism, and television in a neoliberal age.* Philadelphia, PA: Temple University Press.

Miller, T., Lawrence, G., McKay, J., & Rowe, D. (2001). *Globalization and sport: Playing the world.* London: Sage.

Miller, T., Rowe, D., & Lawrence, G. (2010). The new international division of cultural labour and sport. In M. Falcous & J. Maguire (Eds.), *Routledge handbook of sport and migration* (forthcoming). London: Routledge.

MyFootballClub. (2010). Retrieved February 27, 2010 from www.myfootballclub.co.uk/

News Corporation. (2009). *NewsCorp annual report.* Retrieved February 14, 2010 from www.newscorp.com/AR2008Flash/NC08.html

Nielsen. (2008, September 5). Beijing Olympics draw largest ever global TV audience. Retrieved February 13, 2010 from http://blog.nielsen.com/nielsenwire/media_entertainment/beijing-olympics-draw-largest-ever-global-tv-audience/

Parliament of Australia, Senate Standing Committee. (2009, May). *The reporting of sports news and the emergence of digital media.* The Senate Standing Committee on Environment, Communications and the Arts, Commonwealth of Australia. Retrieved February 15, 2009, from www.aph.gov.au/senate/committee/eca_ctte/sports_news/report/index.htm

Pronger, B. (1998). Post-Sport: Transgressing boundaries in physical culture. In G. Rail (Ed.), *Sport and postmodern times* (pp. 277–98). New York: State University of New York Press.

Reuters. (2010, February 23). Watching the games? Switch on your cellphone. Retrieved February 28, 2010, from www.reuters.com/article/idUSTRE61M6PV20100223

Roche, M. (2000). *Mega-events and modernity: Olympics and expos in the growth of global culture.* London and New York: Routledge.

Romero, J.M. (2008, May 17). Sounders FC announce fan association. *The Seattle Times.* Retrieved March 28, 2010 from http://seattletimes.nwsource.com/html/sounders/2004420604_sounders17.html

Rose, A. & Friedman, J. (1997). Television sports as mas(s)culine cult of distraction. In A. Baker & T. Boyd (Eds.), *Out of Bounds* (pp. 1–15). Bloomington: Indiana University Press.

Rowe, D. (2003). Sport and the repudiation of the global. *International Review for the Sociology of Sport, 38*(3), 281–94.

Rowe, D. (2004). *Sport, culture and the media: The unruly trinity* (2nd Ed.). Maidenhead, UK: Open University Press.

Rowe, D. (2009). Media and sport: The cultural dynamics of global games. *Sociology Compass, 3/4,* 543–58. doi: 10.1111/j.1751–9020.2009.00225.

Rowe, D. & Gilmour, C. (2008). Contemporary media sport: De- or re-westernization? *International Journal of Sport Communication, 1*(2), 177–94.

Rowe, D. & Gilmour, C. (2009). Global sport: Where Wembley Way meets Bollywood Boulevard. In A. Moran & M. Keane (Eds.), *Cultural adaptation* (pp. 171–82). London: Routledge.

Rowe, D. & Stevenson, D. (2006). Sydney 2000: Sociality and spatiality in global media events. In A. Tomlinson & C. Young (Eds.), *National identity and global sports events: Culture, politics, and spectacle in the Olympics and the football world cup* (pp. 197–214). New York: State University of New York Press.

Roy, A. (1997). *The god of small things.* London: Flamingo.

Ruddock, A., Hutchins, B., & Rowe, D. (2010). Contradictions in media sport culture: "MyFootballClub" and the reinscription of football supporter traditions through online media. *European Journal of Cultural Studies, 13*(3), 323–39. (Forthcoming).

Schechner, S. & Ovide, S. (2010, February 7). Record draw for Super Bowl: An audience of 106.5 million bucks trend of declining viewership for networks. *The Wall Street Journal: Media and Marketing*. Retrieved February 13, 2010 from: http://online.wsj.com/article/SB10001424052748703615904575053300315837616.html

Scherer, J. & Whitson, D. (2009). Public broadcasting, sport, and cultural citizenship: The future of sport on the Canadian Broadcasting Corporation? *International Review for the Sociology of Sport, 44*(2–3), 213–29.

Stelter, B. (2010, February 23). Water-cooler effect: Internet can be TV's friend. *New York Times*. Retrieved February 27, 2010 from www.nytimes.com/2010/02/24/business/media/24cooler.html?hp

Street, J. (2005). Showbusiness of a serious kind: The cultural politics of the arts prize. *Media, Culture and Society, 27*(6), 819–40.

Tay, J. & Turner, G. (2010). Not the apocalypse: Television futures in the digital age. *International Journal of Digital Television, 1*(1), 31–50. doi: 10.1386/jdtv.1.1.31/1.

Thomas, L. (2010, February 25). BBC's news coverage of Tiger Woods' apology sparks "dumbing down" backlash. *Mail Online*. Retrieved March 28, 2010 from www.dailymail.co.uk/news/article-1253598/BBCs-news-coverage-Tiger-Woods-apology-sparks-dumbing-backlash.html#ixzz0jRxYpheR

Urry, J. (2000). *Sociology beyond societies: Mobilities for the twenty first century*. London and New York: Routledge.

Urry, J. (2003). *Global complexity*. Cambridge: Polity.

Urry, J. (2007). *Mobilities*. Oxford: Blackwell.

Wenner, L.A. (2004). Recovering (from) Janet Jackson's breast: Ethics and the nexus of media, sports, and management. *Journal of Sport Management, 18*, 315–34.

Wenner, L.A. (2008). Super-cooled sports dirt: Moral contagion and Super Bowl commercials in the shadows of Janet Jackson. *Television & New Media, 9*(2), 131–54.

Whannel, G. (2008). *Culture, politics and sport: Blowing the whistle, revisited*. London: Routledge.

World Association of Newspapers. (2008, June 2). World press trends: Newspapers are a growth business. Retrieved February 15, 2010 from www.wan-press.org/article17377.html

World News Australia. (2010, February 21). Free-to-air tax cut sharpens. Retrieved February 21, 2010 from www.sbs.com.au/news/article/1199286/Conroy-draws-Abbott-to-media-mogul-bout

7

TWEETS AND BLOGS

Transformative, adversarial, and integrative developments in sports media

Jimmy Sanderson

ARIZONA STATE UNIVERSITY

Jeffrey W. Kassing

ARIZONA STATE UNIVERSITY

Social media have increased the availability of sports information while simultaneously allowing athletes to become more active in producing news content. This capability enables athletes to conveniently bypass sports organizations and the mass media in breaking news to the public. In doing so, athletes become more accessible to fans in computer-mediated environments while actual social interaction opportunities between fans and athletes remain increasingly guarded. Social media encompass a multitude of formats, but in this essay we focus on two that are permeating the sports world – blogs and an extremely popular variant of blogs – Twitter. Whereas athletes use other social media outlets such as Facebook, message boards, or wikis, blogs and Twitter appear to be the predominant social media "of choice" for athletes – and therefore, are the focus of the current work.

While social media possess many fruitful directions for sports media and communication research, this essay centers on three ways in which blogs and Twitter significantly impact sports media: (a) transformative; (b) adversarial; and (c) integrative. We contend that blogs and Twitter afford athletes more control over the release of sports news while also increasing their self-presentation management. The ability to circumvent sports media and sports organizations in breaking news shifts sports media and consumption practices and directly connects fans and athletes with one another. However, while the capability to release information empowers athletes, it correspondingly creates conflict between athletes and sports reporters, as journalist see their sports media relevance shrink (Weintraub, 2007), and sports organizations lose their ability to tightly regulate the public release of information. Finally, social media invite participation from fans through both commentary on sports media stories and posting information about athletes' activities for public consumption, which allows both mass media entities and sports organizations to benefit from free labor.

Traditionally, athletes and fans have been comparatively non-influential in the production of sports media. They are actors in and consumers of the storyline, but uninvolved in how those stories get shaped and presented. That task has been reserved for sports information directors, publicists, agents, and sports reporters who shape and nurture sports news. But the forms of social media considered here have unhinged this traditional architecture, in unprecedented ways, shifting how sports stories unfold. We explore how this is occurring in this essay, but first we provide a brief overview of blogs and Twitter.

Blogs and Twitter

Blogs have been defined as "frequently modified web pages in which dated entries are listed in reverse chronological sequence" (Herring, Scheidt, Bonus, & Wright, 2004, p.1). Blogs have become extremely popular and according to Blogpulse.com, a site that tracks blogging trends, there are 126,861,574 blogs in existence, 42,234 blogs created every 24 hours, and 889,254 blogs posts occurring every hour ("Blogpulse Stats," 2010). Blogs popularity can be attributed to minimal entry barriers – creating a blog is inexpensive (in most cases free) – and blogs give individuals a communicative channel in which they can conveniently disseminate information to broad groups of people (Wei, 2009).

While traditional blogs certainly possess communicative advantages, there may be circumstances when people need to relay brief, concise messages, and for those who follow blogs, one must generally visit the blog to ascertain if new content has been posted. While these actions are not unreasonable, they have been mitigated by an emerging variant of blogging – Twitter. Messages sent by Twitter are limited in length and people can configure their Twitter accounts to be notified when a person has posted a message via this medium. Thus, Twitter offers people a platform in which they can conveniently post messages from their cellular phone or other portable technological device, and gives others the ability to be immediately notified when an update has been posted.

Twitter is clearly one of the most popular social media forums at the present time (Weingarten, 2008). Twitter allows individuals to create "microblogs" wherein they can construct and distribute communicative messages to others (Goodyear, 2009). One's Twitter account is linked to a username preceded by the @ symbol, and messages, termed "tweets," are limited to 140 characters per message. People become connected to others by choosing to "follow" another user, and thus, each "tweet" that person sends is transmitted to each of their "followers" who can respond by sending a "re-tweet." There has been an exponential increase in the number of celebrities, journalists and other media personnel "tweeting" to their fans across the globe. Perhaps no other group has more prominently adopted blogs and Twitter as communication tools than athletes, whose recurrent use of these social media sites appears to be redefining sports media practices.

Blogs and Twitter as transformative

One of the foremost ways that blogs and Twitter are transforming sports media is by allowing athletes to take an active role in content production, essentially providing them with the opportunity to "break" news, which is *subsequently* reported by the mass media. This shift in sports news reporting aligns with media scholars' (Kenix, 2009; Reese, 2009; Wall, 2005) contentions that the ability to produce news content via blogs is creating a "new genre of journalism" (Wall, 2005, p. 154). This emergent trend is characterized by people gaining a voice in online news stories through commentary. Such commentary enables them to contest mass media news reports and to invoke alternative explanations for events (Reese, 2009), while at the same time constructing and distributing meaningful and idealistic preferred self-images (Chonchuir & McCarthy, 2008). Athletes appear to be part of this trend too. Blogs and Twitter give them the capability to break their own news stories, and allow them to retain control over how these stories are initially transmitted to the public. This capability and increased control promote an alternative lens for public interpretation of the story. Several examples powerfully depict how these social media forums enable athletes to create their own "genre of journalism" (Wall, 2005, p. 154).

One of the hallmarks of traditional sports media architecture is the retirement-announcement press conference. Accordingly, at the twilight of a professional athlete's career the athlete's current team calls a press conference to showcase the retirement announcement. Historically, these events are predicated upon press members' availability; typically involve a question-and-answer session between the athlete and sports reporters, and finish with sports journalists reporting the retirement, speculating on the legacy the athlete will leave behind. However, on March 23, 2009, Boston Red Sox pitcher Curt Schilling posted an entry to his blog announcing his retirement from the game. There was no fanfare and no press conference. Schilling simply posted an entry to his blog entitled "Calling it quits." In blogging his retirement, Schilling provided fans with a public forum in which they could not only consume his message directly, but also contribute to "build" upon his legacy through comment participation (there were 1,261 messages posted to this blog entry). Fans, who would be absent from any press conference covering such an announcement, became instant and direct contributors to the social construction of Schilling's retirement.

Considering that Schilling is one of the most active electronic media users amongst athletes, and also has an adversarial relationship with sports reporters (Sanderson, 2008b), his decision to blog his retirement is not surprising. Nevertheless, Schilling's decision to announce his retirement online, retaining control over how this significant career-punctuating and potentially career-defining moment would be presented, demonstrates an important, direct, and deliberate circumvention of traditional sports media practices. It vividly depicts how athletes may begin taking more control in disseminating meaningful information for public consumption instead of relying on sports journalists or the sports organization to break and initially frame legacy-building moments. It will be interesting to see if Schilling's announcement serves as an anomaly or if it becomes the forerunner for a trend that transforms a ritualized event into a virtual communiqué that both sports reporters and fans learn about simultaneously.

Although blogging one's retirement could be viewed as an exception rather than a rule, athletes are nonetheless increasingly breaking news via blogs and Twitter. For instance, on September 9, 2009, National Basketball Association (NBA) superstar Allen Iverson, a free agent at the time, informed fans via his Twitter feed, that he would be signing a contract with the Memphis Grizzlies franchise (*Toronto Sun*, 2009). The mainstream media quickly picked up the story; however, Twitter enabled Iverson to "break" the story in a manner and at a time of his choosing. While the Grizzlies organization eventually reported Iverson's signing, those who followed him on Twitter gained access to this information directly from Iverson *before* it was distributed via more traditional media outlets.

While professional athletes regularly utilize social media to report about themselves, they at times employ these tools to make organizational information publically available. For example, on June 16, 2009, Kevin Love, an NBA player with the Minnesota Timberwolves franchise, sent a tweet that his head coach, Kevin McHale, had just been fired by the organization (Pucin, 2009). Surprisingly, this information had not yet been disclosed by the organization. When sports journalists learned of Love's tweet, they directed a barrage of questions at Timberwolves executives, placing the organization in an unanticipated reactive position (Associated Press, 2009a). In this particular situation, not only was the mass media circumvented, but the Timberwolves organization was caught off guard by how the story broke and needed to respond quicker than they presumably would have anticipated was necessary.

Thus, in utilizing these social media technologies, athletes gain more control over both *how* they are represented, as well as in deciding *what* information gets presented. It will be interesting to observe how this trend plays out in the future, and what outcomes result for current sports production and consumption processes. For instance, to what degree do fans turn to athletes' blogs, Twitter feeds, and other social media platforms instead of traditional media outlets to obtain news? While many sports reporters are now using social media to connect with fans and break news, it seems plausible that fans may prefer to go directly to "the source." Cycling fans, for example, learned of dangers in the course design at the 2009 edition of the Tour of Italy via tweets from a host of riders. The tweets transpired over several days, demonstrating increased disgust with the lack of concern for rider safety, and precipitated a full-blown rider protest during the middle of the race. The cycling media covered the rider protest, but fans following their favorite riders on Twitter learned of building rider discontent directly and days before the protest (Kassing & Sanderson, 2010).

In breaking news, athletes eschew typical sports media distribution processes and gain a sympathetic forum where they can offer an alternative voice to counteract media framing. Here too Twitter proved helpful to protesting cyclists. Several immediately posted apologetic justifications for the protest and their misgivings about detracting from the event's prestige. While it seems a stretch to predict the death of sports journalism, there is little question that athletes' social media use has prompted a shift in sports reporting as athletes now have forums available to directly communicate with fans, domains that fans overwhelmingly support with their participation.

While social media certainly empower athletes, they correspondingly exacerbate tensions for athletes in their relationships with both sports journalists and sports organizations. It is easy to understand why sports reporters would resent athletes taking a more active role in sports media production. Sports organizations, on the other hand, have to contend with athletes divulging information that the organization would prefer to remain "in house" (as with Kevin Love). One way sports organizations have addressed these concerns is by adopting social media policies that govern when athletes can use these tools. Yet these policies often prove too restrictive, as organizations regularly fine athletes for violating social media policies.

Blogs and Twitter as adversarial

Relational conflict between athletes and sports reporters and athletes and sports organizations is certainly not a new phenomenon. With social media, however, athletes can interject their own commentary about the disagreements they are having with these entities, directly soliciting and involving fans in the process. In the past athletes and sports journalists have traded barbs during press conferences and interviews. Now these disagreements surface via electronic channels, and the autonomy blog postings and tweets afford athletes enables them to be more assertive in rebutting perceived inaccuracies in sports reporting.

Consider the case of NFL wide receiver Chad Johnson, later to be known as Chad Ocho Cinco. Prior to the 2009 season, he used his Twitter account to spar with FoxSports.com journalist Mark Kriegel. Apparently, Johnson was upset over critical comments Kriegel made about him. Kriegel contended that Johnson was indicative of a culture of "chump ballplayers who think they're fabulous and interesting – who believe their personal minutiae has actual merit – despite never having won a thing ... " (*USA Today*, 2009). Johnson responded by tweeting, "Mark Kriegel you're an idiot, you want a Lil [sic] fame I'll help, because your story today sucked just like you did in school!!!" and "Mark Kriegel you can come work for me, you're wasting away as a writer for foxsports, from me and my followers you get a 'Child Please!!!'" (Kriegel, 2009). Johnson also has had similar encounters via Twitter with ProFootballTalk.com reporter Mike Florio and ESPN NFL analyst Mark Schlereth (*USA Today*, 2009).

Similarly, former Boston Red Sox pitcher Curt Schilling utilized his blog to respond to accusations by Baltimore Orioles play-by-play commentator Gary Thorne that Schilling faked an injury during the 2004 American League Championship Series (ALCS). During a Red Sox–Orioles broadcast on April 25, 2007,

Thorne alleged that Doug Mirabelli, Schilling's teammate, had told Thorne that Schilling faked an ankle injury that resulted in his sock bleeding while he was pitching in the 2004 ALCS, and that Schilling essentially devised the injury as a publicity stunt. On April 27, 2007, Schilling created an entry on his blog entitled "Ignorance has its privileges," a 1,549 word open letter to fans, in which he lambasted Thorne and directed criticism towards specific sports journalists and media coverage in general.

Schilling received considerable social support from fans commenting on this blog entry (Sanderson, 2010). His blog, in turn, served as a space where he could construct rebuttals that accurately reflected his perspectives free from filtering by the Red Sox organization and sports reporters. Additionally, by airing their grievances in this manner, Schilling and Johnson fostered opportunities for fans to become involved in their disagreements with sports reporters. Thus, by inviting audience members into the news story, they enabled fans to weigh in on their conflicts, which in Schilling's case, generated substantial support for his decision to assertively combat sports reporters (Sanderson, 2010).

Although Johnson and Kriegel's feud has simmered down, and Schilling has since retired, their arguments with the sports journalists serve as poignant exemplars that depict how conflict emerges as athletes employ blogs and Twitter to counteract information reported by sports journalists. While an athlete could criticize a sports journalist through traditional media outlets, such commentary can be filtered or framed in a way that does not accurately reflect their position, particularly if the athlete has a contentious relationship with sports reporters (as Johnson does and Schilling did). Additionally, considering that sports journalists tend to be critical in their assessment of athletes' behavior (Sanderson 2008b), social media provide athletes with a forum where they can respond to these critiques, provide alternative explanations, question the veracity of sports journalists' reporting, and generate support from the public.

Athletes' blogs and tweets also initiate conflict with sports organizations. This seems to stem from the organizations' inability to control information that is being released via these social media channels. For example, on September 28, 2009, Texas Tech University head football coach Mike Leach banned players from using Twitter or Facebook (Associated Press, 2009b). Leach's decision seemed to result from players posting critical messages about Leach via Twitter that made national sports headlines. Specifically, linebacker Marlon Williams posted a tweet asking why he was wasting his time sitting in a meeting room, waiting for the head coach, who was unable to be on time, while offensive lineman Brandon Carter tweeted after a loss to the University of Houston, that the team's current performance had not matched pre-season expectations. In explaining his decision, Leach referred to social media as "stupid distractions" (Associated Press, 2009b). And yet, now that Leach has been fired for alleged misconduct towards a Texas Tech player, perhaps those tweets were harbingers of a larger issue, problems that Leach conveniently suppressed through his social media policy.

Moving forward, it will be interesting to observe how relational conflict between athletes with both sports reporters and sports organizations plays out via social media, and how audience participation contributes to or nullifies these disagreements. For instance, do fans tend to support athletes' decisions to contest media reports? Or do fans tend to side with journalists? It also seems plausible that these arguments may drive traffic to mass media websites as well as to athletes' blogs or Twitter feeds. It would be worthwhile to consider what types of conflict increase audience participation and the extent to which the agendas built by both athletes and journalists resonate with, and are confirmed or contested by audience members.

Given that social media can serve as a site of conflict, it is not surprising that athletes use these media to build support among fans against a common enemy (Kassing & Sanderson, in press). Discredited American cyclist Floyd Landis, who was stripped of his Tour de France title after a positive doping test for testosterone, used his blog to repeatedly attack the U.S. Anti-Doping Agency (USADA), the World Anti-Doping Agency (WADA), and the French lab that conducted the tests for what he deemed to be flawed testing policies and procedures. He campaigned via his blog for transparency in the process and garnered considerable support from fans in doing so. Fans' ability to offer commentary confirming or contesting athletes' accounts, then, provides a unique opportunity for public contributions to the framing of sports stories. Additionally, social media enable fans to become content creators. Technology has made it easier for fans to capture athletes' off-field activities, which they can then broadcast for public consumption without the athletes' knowledge.

Blogs and Twitter as integrative

As athletes' and sports reporters' accounts compete in social media forums, fans benefit by receiving sports information from multiple sources. Additionally, through audience participation and commentary, social media integrates the perspectives of athletes, sports journalists, and fans into sports media stories. While the integration of audience members into the sports media process provides content for mass media organizations, it also benefits sports organizations. Mass media outlets have capitalized on the blogging phenomenon by opening access for fans to comment on sports stories. This invitation is not altruistic, as participation and commentary on these stories enable mass media organizations to benefit from free labor performed by audience members who drive the story, converse about the story's salience, and contribute to the dissemination of the story. Mass media organizations have long relied on audience labor to strengthen media consumption processes (Cohen, 2008; Yahr, 2007); however, the invitation extended to individuals to share and comment on these stories via social media, allows mass media entities to obtain content evaluation and distribution services that are enacted under the guise of participation.

Although mass media outlets have traditionally informed sports organizations of player misconduct, fans now have the capacity to do this as well. For instance,

Sanderson (2009) examined how audience labor performed online alerted sports organizations to the conduct of three professional athletes (NBA players Josh Howard and Greg Oden, and NFL player Matt Leinart). Interestingly, all three incidents took place on the athletes' personal time, one of which occurred at the athlete's private residence (Leinart). Yet the ability for people to access these athletes and report their activity (in some cases with video and photographic evidence) not only facilitated the organizations' censuring of these athletes, but also enhanced the organizations' ability to monitor their private lives.

Fans' willingness to engage in these practices is likely grounded in identity. Sport is strongly linked to one's social identity (Boyle & Magnusson, 2007; Hirt, Zilmann, Erickson, & Kennedy, 1992; Zagacki & Grano, 2005), and some fans become so identified with a sports team that they base their social belonging and self-esteem on the sports team's success (Smith & Stewart, 2007). Thus, when athletes engage in behavior that fans perceive to threaten the team's ability to be successful, fans may feel obligated to publicly report this information, as these actions affect the fans' identification with the team (Fink, Parker, Brett, & Higgins, 2009). In other words, when a team's success and a fan's self-worth become so intermeshed it may seem appropriate and even prudent for a die-hard fan to police and monitor athletes' behavior to ensure that both the team's and the fan's identity will not be compromised.

As social media integrate fans into the sports media world, several important implications arise from this merger. First, while there is vast participation from audience members on mass media websites, there also have been a number of independent sites developed by fans (e.g., Profootballtalk.com), which mass media organizations now draw from in reporting stories. It would be worthwhile to explore how extensively mass media organizations (e.g. ESPN) utilize these sources in their reporting, as well as to determine where fans perceive independent sites to reside in the information source hierarchy. In other words, do fans consider the information reported on independent sites to be more accurate or unbiased than information reported on established mass media sites? Or do they believe these sources are secondary to established media outlets? And perhaps even more compelling, which sites do fans first turn to when seeking sports information?

Second, it would be important to investigate how fan "reporting" contributes to sports organizations' monitoring of athletes' private lives, and what ramifications this holds for athletes' personal decisions. Clearly athletes cannot be expected to hide away from public view (though most do maintain very private lives), yet athletes must be aware of the implications that social media hold for them. Two recent examples in the NBA vividly highlight this issue. On January 27, 2010, Portland Trailblazers player Greg Oden issued a public apology after nude pictures of Oden appeared on the Internet (Associated Press, 2010a). Oden acknowledged that he had taken the pictures of himself on his cellphone and sent them to an ex-girlfriend in 2008. A little over a week later, on February 9, 2010, San Antonio Spurs player George Hill issued a public apology for nude pictures he had taken of himself that ended up online (Associated Press, 2010b).

Athletes cannot prevent fans from photographing and videotaping them while in public places. But clearly they need to be conscientious about the possibility that messages, particularly those of a private and suggestive manner, sent via social media may surface elsewhere and at some time in the future. These situations raise key questions regarding organizational control, censorship, and freedom of expression, all of which arise from the integration of athletes and fans into sports media processes.

Conclusion

The capabilities that social media offer to athletes in producing their own content and retaining control over self-presentation, coupled with fans' ability to directly access athletes via these sites, offer unique interaction opportunities that have heretofore been unavailable when consuming sports media. We conclude this essay by discussing one important implication arising from athletes' social media use and the larger ramifications this phenomenon holds for sports media in general. Again, while there are many implications stemming from athletes' social media use, we contend that one compelling outcome is that blogs and Twitter serve as new mechanisms for evolving parasocial interaction (PSI) within virtual sports communities.

PSI refers to media users interacting with media personae in ways that resemble actual social interaction (Horton & Wohl, 1956). While much PSI research has examined relationships between audience members and media figures occurring via traditional media (Palmgreen, Wenner, & Rayburn, 1980; Rubin & McHugh, 1987; Rubin, Haridakis, & Eyal, 2003), the Internet and its computer-mediated communication (CMC) forums are gaining ground as prominent sites for PSI (Bae & Lee, 2004; Goldberg & Allen, 2008; Konijn, Utz, Tanis, & Barnes, 2008). Moreover, recent research has started to examine how PSI manifests between fans and athletes, particularly via social media (Kassing & Sanderson, 2009, 2010; Sanderson, 2008a).

Recent scholarship provides several explanations that illuminate why social media possess valuable utility for fans to display PSI with athletes. For instance, research indicates that audience members become so absorbed in media programming that they mentally transport themselves into media narratives (Dal Cin, Zanna, & Fong, 2004; Green & Brock, 2000). Building on this construct, scholars have posited that PSI and transporting oneself into media narratives are conceptually related (Green, Brock, & Kaufman, 2004; Greenwood, 2008). Others have argued that the need to belong and strong attachments with media figures predict PSI (Cohen, 2004; Cole & Leets, 1999; Greenwood & Long, 2009).

Given these findings there are several plausible explanations for why social media have become prominent sites for PSI between fans and athletes. First, fans develop strong identification towards athletes and these attachments may fuel a desire to become involved in the athlete's media narrative (blog/tweet). And social media enable fans to *physically* intervene in these narratives by providing commentary, guidance, advice, and praise to athletes. For instance, Kassing and Sanderson (2009) examined fan postings to American cyclist Floyd Landis' blog during his comeback bid to win the 2006 Tour de France. They found that fan postings displayed traditional PSI dimensions such as inspiration and affection, relationally appropriate behaviors which included sympathy, encouragement, praise, apology, and congratulations, and active social interaction behaviors such as giving advice, expressing gratitude, and displaying playfulness. In other work, Sanderson (2008c) investigated PSI occurring on Dallas Mavericks owner Mark Cuban's blog while he participated on the popular American Broadcasting Corporation (ABC) reality show *Dancing with the Stars*. In this case, fans' PSI reflected a significant emotional investment in Cuban's performance, which included mentally agonizing during his performances, procrastinating over work and family responsibilities to ensure they watched Cuban perform, and initiating persuasion campaigns to increase his vote count so he would remain on the show.

Second, social media provide a platform by which users can engage and interact with the objects of PSI. Such social engagement in turn fosters PSI as fans feel "closer" to and involved with athletes. For example, Kassing and Sanderson (2010) found that cyclists in the Tour of Italy interacted directly with fans via Twitter by requesting their suggestions for warm-up music and by inviting them to participate in merchandise giveaways. They also shared what it was like to ride through treacherous conditions and at excessive speeds, giving fans an insider perspective unavailable through other media outlets. Fostering interactivity and cultivating insider perspectives were key elements of how PSI manifested between cyclists and their respective fans. Closeness and involvement characterize PSI and seem to be enhanced by the immediacy, both temporal and psychological, afforded by these media.

PSI occurring between fans and athletes via social media likely contributes to how dominant athletes' social media presence becomes, and could shape how intertwined social and sports media become. For instance, Whannel (1999) observed that sports organizations seek to regulate players' lifestyles to exert maximum production from athletes, which ultimately benefits the organization's financial viability. However, if athletes turn to social media to disclose such constraints, support could be generated amongst fans to publicly call such practices into question. It is equally possible however, that athletes' disclosures will be met with criticism from their fan base. Fans may contest and debate athletes' grievances. Sanderson (2008a) found this to be the case with Curt Schilling when fans criticized his political pontifications and his excessive religious commentary. In such cases, social media provide a battleground of sorts, a place where both positive and negative facets of PSI will emerge and compete. Additionally, some scholars have observed that sports journalism is trending towards celebrity journalism (Rowe, 2007; Whannel, 2001) and social media may amplify this view as fans capture and broadcast intimate aspects of athletes' private lives.

Moreover, as the bonds grow between athletes and fans via social media, athletes' social media use may receive more acceptance as a legitimate sports media source. As more athletes promote themselves and their perspectives via social media, sports media will need to turn to these outlets as legitimate sources for sporting news. Miller (2009) coined the term "Media 3.0" (p. 6) to characterize media studies that are shaped by collective identity and group experiences of social spaces. Athletes' social media sites provide a unique space where collective identity is expressed and where fans and athletes cooperatively make sense of sports media stories. Thus, sports media expands into a host of spheres, a format which Hutchins and Rowe (2009) refer to as a "digital plentitude" (p. 354). They add that the broadcasting capability offered by the Internet "demands adjustment and reorganization in both media and sports industries" (p. 355) and that the Internet extinguishes the notion that there is a scarcity of sports distribution channels. Thus, athletes' increasing adoption of social media populates what was once a restricted and tightly controlled sports media sphere with innumerable new sources of content; thereby limiting the monopolizing forces of traditional sports media.

The shifting of power in sports reporting is not limited merely to content and access, however. It may also hold serious financial implications. If fans increasingly turn to athletes' social media broadcasts, athletes potentially could market their social media sites to advertisers (some already have) and draw sponsors away from sports organizations and mass media outlets. This emerging sports media environment is likely to prove chaotic (Rowe, 2004) and it will be worthwhile to see how each of these entities responds to this sports media reconfiguration. Some sports organizations have already adopted social media use policies. How diligently these policies are enforced and which sports organizations follow the NFL and NBA's lead will be interesting. The practices that emerge from social media's intrusion into sports media will likely influence societal perceptions and regulation of athletes' social media use (Hutchins & Rowe, 2009). Communication and sports media scholars will see many opportunities to observe how the reshaping of sports media economy plays out (Hutchins & Rowe, 2009; Hutchins, Rowe, & Ruddock, 2009).

Final thoughts

The social media discussed in this essay have clearly reshaped our conceptions of sports media and fans' consumption of them. Whether athletes use them to "set the record straight" or fans participate by vilifying or exonerating athletes, it is clear that social media have proven influential. They are transformative and adversarial, while also being integrative and community-building. How social media continue to shape and reconfigure sports media, sports journalism, and sports reporting will be questions to consider for some time. We look forward to seeing where these current social media, and those yet to surface, will take us.

References

Associated Press. (2009a, June 17). Love: McHale won't return. Retrieved on September 22, 2009, from http://sports.espn.go.com/nba/news/story?id=4265512

Associated Press. (2009b, September 28). No twitter use for Tech players. Retrieved from http://sports.espn.go.com/ncf/news/story?id=4511880

Associated Press (2010a, January 27). Oden sorry photos have surfaced. Retrieved on February 17, 2010, from http://sports.espn.go.com/nba/news/story?id=4861469

Associated Press (2010b, February 9). Hill apologizes for nude photos. Retrieved on February 17, 2010, from http://sports.espn.go.com/nba/news/story?id=4900803

Bae, H.S. & Lee, B. (2004). Audience involvement and its antecedents: An analysis of the electronic bulletin board messages about an entertainment-education drama on divorce in Korea. *Asian Journal of Communication, 14*(1), 6–21.

Blogpulse Stats. (2010, updated daily). Retrieved on January 28, 2010, from www.blogpulse.com

Boyle, B.A. & Magnusson, P. (2007). Social identity and brand equality formation: A comparative study of collegiate sports fans. *Journal of Sport Management, 21*(4), 497–520.

Chonchuir, M.N. & McCarthy, J. (2008). The enchanting potential of technology: A dialogical case study of enchantment and the internet. *Personal & Ubiquitous Computing, 12*(5), 401–9.

Cohen, J. (2004). Parasocial break-up from favorite television characters: The role of attachment styles and relationship intensity. *Journal of Social and Personal Relationships, 21,* 187–202.

Cohen, N.S. (2008). The valorization of surveillance: Towards a political economy of Facebook. *Democratic Communique, 22*(1), 5–22.

Cole, T. & Leets, L. (1999). Attachment styles and intimate television viewing: Insecurely forming relationships in a parasocial way. *Journal of Social and Personal Relationships, 16,* 495–511.

Dal Cin, S., Zanna, M.P., & Fong, G.T. (2004). Narrative persuasion and overcoming resistance. In E.S. Knowles & J.A. Linn (Eds.), *Resistance and persuasion* (pp. 175–91). Mahwah, NJ: Erlbaum.

Fink, J.S., Parker, H.M., Brett, M., & Higgins, J. (2009). Off-field behavior of athletes and team identification: Using social identity theory and balance theory to explain fan reactions. *Journal of Sport Management, 23*(2), 142–55.

Goldberg, C.B. & Allen, D.G. (2008). Black and white and read all over: Race differences in reactions to recruitment websites. *Human Resource Management, 47*(2), 217–36.

Goodyear, S. (2009, March 21). Just one word: Fake and that's a good thing. *Toronto Star.* Retrieved on September 1, 2009, from the Lexis-Nexis academic database.

Green, M.C. & Brock, T.C. (2000). The role of transportation in the persuasiveness of public narratives. *Journal of Personality and Social Psychology, 79,* 701–21.

Green, M.C., Brock, T.C., & Kaufman, G.F. (2004). Understanding media enjoyment: The role of transportation into narrative worlds. *Communication Theory, 14,* 311–27.

Greenwood, D.N. (2008). Television as escape from self: Psychological predictors of media involvement. *Personality and Individual Differences, 44*(2), 414–24.

Greenwood, D.N. & Long, C.R. (2009). Psychological predictors of media involvement: Solitude experiences and the need to belong. *Communication Research, 36*(5), 637–54.

Herring, S.C., Scheidt, L.A., Bonus, S., & Wright, E. (2004). Bridging the gap: A genre analysis of weblogs. *Proceedings of the 37th Hawai'i International Conference on System Sciences (HICSS-37).* Los Alamitos, CA: IEEE Computer Society Press.

Hirt, E.R., Zilmann, D., Erickson, G.A., & Kennedy, C. (1992). Costs and benefits of allegiance: Changes in fans' self-ascribed competencies after team victory versus defeat. *Journal of Personality and Social Psychology, 63*(5), 724–38.

Horton, D. & Wohl, R.R. (1956). Mass communication and para-social interaction. *Psychiatry, 19,* 215–29.

Hutchins, B. & Rowe, D. (2009). From broadcast scarcity to digital plentitude: The changing dynamics of the media sport content economy. *Television & New Media, 10*(4), 354–70.

Hutchins, B., Rowe, D., & Ruddock, A. (2009). "It's fantasy football made real": Networked media sport, the internet, and the hybrid reality of MyFootballClub. *Sociology of Sport Journal, 26*(1), 89–106.

Kassing, J.W. & Sanderson, J. (2009). "You're the kind of guy that we all want for a drinking buddy": Expressions of parasocial interaction on floydlandis.com. *Western Journal of Communication, 73*, 182–203.

Kassing, J.W. & Sanderson, J. (2010). Tweeting through the Giro: A case study of fanathlete interaction on Twitter. *International Journal of Sport Communication, 3*(1), 113–28.

Kassing, J.W. & Sanderson, J. (in press). "Is this a church? Such a big bunch of believers around here!": Fan expressions of social support on Floydlandis.com. *Journal of Communication Studies.*

Kenix, L.J. (2009). Blogs as alternative. *Journal of Computer-Mediated Communication, 14*(4), 790–822.

Konijn, E.A., Utz, S., Tanis, M., & Barnes, S.B. (Eds.). (2008). *Mediated interpersonal communication.* New York: Routledge.

Kriegel, M. (2009, August 4). On the Mark: Please, not more ocho. *Foxsports.com.* Retrieved on September 30, 2009, from http://msn.foxsports.com/nfl/story/9888346/On-the-Mark:-Please,-not-more-Ocho

Miller, T. (2009). Media studies 3.0. *Television & New Media, 10*(1), 5–6.

Palmgreen, P., Wenner, L.A., & Rayburn II, J.D. (1980). Relations between gratifications sought and obtained: A study of television news. *Communication Research, 7*(2), 161–92.

Pucin, D. (2009, June 18). Athletes turn to Twitter to get message out: Whether it's breaking news by Kevin Love or an update from Shaq, the sports world has never been the same. *Los Angeles Times.* Retrieved on September 22, 2009, from the Lexis-Nexis academic database.

Reese, S.D. (2009). The future of journalism in emerging deliberative space. *Journalism, 10* (3), 362–64.

Rowe, D. (2004). *Sport, culture and the media: The unruly trinity* (2nd Ed.). Maidenhead, UK: Open University Press.

Rowe, D. (2007). Sports journalism: Still the "toy department" of the news media? *Journalism, 8*(4), 385–405.

Rubin, A.M., Haridakis, P.M., & Eyal, K. (2003). Viewer aggression and attraction to television talk shows. *Media Psychology, 5*(4), 331–62.

Rubin, R.B. & McHugh, M. (1987). Development of parasocial interaction relationships. *Journal of Broadcasting and Electronic Media, 31*(3), 279–92.

Sanderson, J. (2008a). "You are the type of person that children should look up to as a hero": Parasocial interaction on 38pitches.com. *International Journal of Sport Communication, 1*(3), 337–60.

Sanderson, J. (2008b). The blog is serving its purpose: Self-presentation strategies on 38pitches.com. *Journal of Computer-Mediated Communication, 13*(4), 912–36.

Sanderson, J. (2008c). Spreading the word: Emphatic interaction displays on BlogMaverick. com. *Journal of Media Psychology: Theories, Methods, and Applications, 20*(4), 157–68.

Sanderson, J. (2009). Professional athletes' shrinking privacy boundaries: Fans, ICTs, and athlete monitoring. *International Journal of Sport Communication, 2*(2), 240–56.

Sanderson, J. (2010). "The Nation stands behind you": Mobilizing social support on 38pitches.com. *Communication Quarterly, 58*, 188–206.

Smith, A.C.T. & Stewart, B. (2007). The travelling fan: Understanding the mechanisms of sport fan consumption in a sport tourism setting. *Journal of Sport Tourism, 12*(3/4), 155–81.

Toronto Sun. (2009, September 8). A.I. inks deal with Memphis. Retrieved on September 15, 2009, from the Lexis-Nexis academic database.

USA Today. (2009, August 4). Chad Ochocinco in battle with media on twitter, calls writer "idiot." Retrieved on September 30, 2009, from http://content.usatoday.com/communities/thehuddle/post/2009/08/68496123/1

Wall, M. (2005). "Blogs of war": Weblogs as news. *Journalism, 6*(2), 153–72.

Wei, L. (2009). Filter blogs vs. personal journals: Understanding the knowledge production gap on the internet. *Journal of Computer-Mediated Communication, 14*(3), 532–58.

Weingarten, G. (2008, September 7). Brevity ... is the soul of a twit. *Washington Post.* Retrieved on August 22, 2009, from the Lexis-Nexis academic database.

Weintraub, R. (2007). Play (hard) ball!: Why the sports beat must evolve. *Columbia Journalism Review, 46*(3), 14–16.

Whannel, G. (1999). Sports stars, narrativization and masculinities. *Leisure Studies, 18*(3), 249–65.

Whannel, G. (2001). *Media sports stars: Masculinities and moralities.* London: Routledge.

Yahr, E. (2007). Crowded house. *American Journalism Review, 29*(5), 8–9.

Zagacki, K.S. & Grano, D. (2005). Radio sports talk and the fantasies of sport. *Critical Studies in Media Communication, 22*(1), 45–63.

8

FROM ANALYSIS TO AGGRESSION

The nature of fan emotion, cognition and behavior in Internet sports communities

Lance V. Porter

LOUISIANA STATE UNIVERSITY

Chris Wood

JWA PUBLIC COMMUNICATIONS

Vincent L. Benigni

COLLEGE OF CHARLESTON

At the intersection of passionate college football fans and their use of the World Wide Web as an ultimate means of free speech and expression is a phenomenon transforming media and sport seamlessly within our society. What began organically as yet another application of this new technology by a select few has morphed into an economic and cultural development – part revelation and part revolution – utilized by the masses. Fueling this "expression express" is the insatiable appetite for information and need for identity among those that have galvanized their collective affinity for their favorite teams into Fan-Based Internet Sports Communities (FBISCs) (Benigni, Porter, & Wood, 2009). In addition to multi-million dollar budgets and state-of-the-art facilities, now we can add "football forums" to the list of attributes of today's big-time football factories as well. The World Wide Web has unarguably empowered fans as a noisy Greek chorus in the weekly drama that is college football. And that chorus can be deafening when college football fans make their way online to seek information or give an opinion. This study will examine these communities and the fans that populate them through a season-long content analysis and an online fan survey.

Literature review

Motives for fans forming Internet sports communities

Sports fans are notably different media consumers than their contemporaries who favor other types of programming and entertainment. As Gantz, Wang, Bryant, and

Potter (2006) note, when compared to TV viewers of other programming types, sports fans are more likely to prepare for the viewing experience beforehand, analyze the experience afterward, and remain highly focused on the action on the screen during the games, as emotionally engaged and active viewers like no others.

What are the motives driving the sports fan to these prevalent FBISC sites? Raney (2006) notes that consumers tend to report three broad categorizations for sports media consumption – emotional, cognitive, and behavioral/social. Web site traffic and related data, as well as message board threads, certainly provide evidence that fan enjoyment and entertainment are inherent in the formation and growth of FBISCs. In addition, the need for fans to obtain the latest information and to expand knowledge about beloved teams, players, and coaches fulfills Raney's notion that cognitive motives add to our understanding of the utilitarian function of these sites. Finally, behavioral motives are apparent because FBISCs provide an accessible platform for fans to celebrate and commiserate with those who hold similar allegiances, especially following sports contests.

As Raney (2006) explains, enjoyment of viewership, or in the case of this study the continual consumption of online media content, "is a function of the outcome of the game in relation to the strength and valence of the dispositions held toward the competitors" (p. 316). The disposition theory of sports spectatorship (Zillmann, Bryant, & Sapolsky, 1989; Bryant & Raney, 2000) is critical, then, to understanding the motives for fans consuming and posting content on FBISC sites. This theory focuses on the accumulation of expectations, as well as resulting victories and losses, of favorite teams over time. It may be argued, theoretically, that disposition could have predicted the conception of the fan sites themselves.

In addition, sports fandom, at least, has been shown as a means for escape or release from over-stimulation or under-stimulation (stress or boredom) in one's everyday life (Wann, Allen, & Rochelle, 2004). Suspense is another contributor to the enjoyment of sports media, whether via commentary that reflects the building suspense of games (Bryant, Rockwell, & Owens, 1994), or the notion that men and women enjoy the closest, most suspenseful games to different degrees (Su-lin Gan et al., 1997). Furthermore, consumers enjoy suspenseful sports contests even more so than suspenseful fictional drama, because of the unpredictable nature and unforeseen outcome of a highly competitive game as it unfolds (Peterson & Raney, 2008).

Finally, exciting and entertaining sports contests are often aggressive and violent in nature, one of the common assumptions regarding the popularity of college football. Raney and Kinnally (2009) found that rivalry games were perceived to be more violent and impacted enjoyment of games won versus games lost. Some fans feel strong connections with their favorite team(s) beyond disposition, even to the extent that team success or failure may influence a fan's self-esteem, or at least self-identity. Cialdini et al. (1976) first introduced the notion of fans "basking in reflected glory" (BIRG). BIRGing, however, is most likely confined to sports and not as readily evident in other settings, such as post-victory celebrations of winning candidates for public office (Sigelman, 1986).

Conversely, fans also have shown a tendency to distance themselves from teams viewed as losers through a concept labeled as cutting off reflected failure or CORFing (Wann & Branscombe, 1990; Wann et al., 1995). A motivation behind CORFing is, again, to maintain the self-esteem and self-identity of the fans of sports teams, with the difference being under circumstances when their favorite team loses. Wann and Branscombe (1990) label BIRGing and CORFing tendencies as means for fans to demonstrate strategic self-presentation. Furthermore, Wann et al. (1995) identify a third type of self-identity and preservation strategy for fans that they classify as cutting off future failure (COFF) where fans of successful teams temper their celebrations to preserve their ego in the future, should their teams experience failure in future games.

The notion of fans BIRGing, CORFing, or COFFing can be documented through the monitoring of traffic and analysis of content on FBISCs, especially blogs, posts, or other types of messages displayed by identifiable fans for public consumption. One study used registered traffic from Web sites of respective soccer teams following championship game outcomes to measure tendencies for BIRGing and CORFing (Boen, Vanbeselaere, & Feys, 2002). As expected, this study found that team Web sites had significantly more visitors after that team had won than after the team had lost. Another indication of fans being more prone to BIRGing on FBISCs was found in a study of highly identified soccer fans who also failed to engage in "blasting" or overly criticizing other teams or fans (Bernache-Assollant, Lacassagne, & Braddock, 2007).

In addition to emotional motives for fans forming and enjoying these sites, there are cognitive and behavioral motives as well. Madrigal (1995) noted that there are three cognitive antecedents – expectancy disconfirmation, team identification, and quality of opponent – that are related to two affective states – enjoyment and basking in reflected glory. Most relevant to this discussion is the finding that team identification had the dominant influence on affect, while enjoyment had the dominant influence on fan satisfaction.

Another cognitive motive for fan consumption of FBISC content is the opportunity to obtain information, garner additional knowledge, or perhaps even participate in analysis and discussions with fellow fans. Madrigal and Chen (2008) note that fans seek causal attributions for a game outcome; that is, they seek reasons for why things turned out the way they did. This perspective reinforces the idea that FBISCs provide fans with a forum for sports commentary and analysis. As Madrigal and Chen note: "Given its centrality to human nature, it is therefore not surprising that fans put so much effort into identifying the reasons behind a preferred team's victory or defeat. One need only (to) listen to sports talk radio or read a sports blog on the day after an important game to appreciate the prevalence of such behavior among fans" (p. 717).

Any study of FBISC content, especially message board threads, should consider the tone of the message and temperament of the messenger, especially examining the person's aggressive nature. While the notion of a catharsis effect of media on the consumer has been repeatedly refuted, some have seen limited effects under specific conditions, such as a highly identified fan's belief that watching aggressive sports, such as football, could lead to a reduction in aggressive behavior (Wann et al., 1999). In the context of this study on FBISCs, the interest is in how team identity might influence verbal aggression – say among participants in online chats or forums. Online aggression may prove more prevalent among fans because of the protection that personal anonymity provides. One study found evidence that highly identified fans – those with strong affiliations with specific teams – were not necessarily more aggressive in general; however, these fans did show more intense signs of aggression toward players or coaches of rival teams (Wann, Peterson, Cothran, & Dykes, 1999). A significant finding in this study is of particular interest to those examining online aggression among fans of particular teams. Wann, Peterson, Cothran, and Dykes (1999) identified fandom of individual teams as the most prominent indicator of violence: "With respect to sport fan aggression ... the key individual difference variable is the fan's level of identification with the team" (p. 598).

For the sake of measuring online aggression by fans of respective FBISCs, this study will utilize scales with internal consistency for measuring verbal aggression, as devised by Buss and Perry (1992), since verbal aggression is so closely associated with written correspondence of message board posts that is aggressive in nature.

Internet sports communities from the fan's perspective

Wann and Pierce (2005) provided further evidence of Wann's Team Identification– Social Psychological Health Model when they found that social well-being was more strongly related to one's identification with a local sports team – professing to be a fan of a team – rather than identification with a distant team or as a fan (of sports) in general. In addition, some researchers have proposed that being a sports fan contributes to popularity, at least among males (End, Kretschmar, & Dietz-Uhler, 2004).

As might be expected, there is evidence to support the role of gender orientation (masculinity significantly more so than femininity) as a predictor, and even to a greater degree than anatomical sex, of sport fandom (Wann, Waddill, & Dunham, 2004). For some time, it has been assumed that men and women prefer different sporting fare, with evidence that men enjoy the more physical, competitive sport of football, for example, to a much greater degree than do women (Sargent, Zillmann, & Weaver, 1998). This study of the demographic and psychographic nature of the college football fan within the defined parameters of FBISCs should, on this evidence, confirm that this audience of sports fans, independent of team affiliation, is predominantly male. Interestingly, in a study examining a potential connection between dysfunctional fans and their dislike for rivals (Smith & Wann, 2006), those considered dysfunctional – with a propensity for confrontations that would be assumed to be aggressive – were more likely to be identified as fans of a favorite team, though surprisingly, not likely to express dislike for their rivals to any significant degree ... a representation of "fanatics" for, rather than against, specific teams, perhaps.

Wann (1995) noted that eight factors are believed to contribute to sport fandom – eustress, self-esteem, escape, entertainment, economic, aesthetic, group affiliation, and family needs. In developing an empirical test to develop a measure of sport fandom, Wann (1995) found validity for the construction of a Sport Fan Motivation Scale, which we are using in this current study. To better measure a fan's psychological commitment to a particular team, Kwon and Trail (2003) suggested improvements to the Psychological Commitment to Team (PCT) scale devised by Mahony, Madrigal, and Howard (2000). Kwon and Trail (2003) also note that the Team Identification Index and the Psychological Commitment to Team Scale may use single-item measures under certain circumstances.

Research questions

General

Because this study is the first of its nature to examine fan-based Internet sports communities, we will examine the actual content on both the front pages and the message boards of these sites. In answering these questions, we will provide a systematic overview of the types of content frequently encountered over the course of a select football season.

RQ1:   What type of content is featured on FBISC front pages?
RQ2:   What type of content is featured on the message boards of FBISCs?

Cognitive

To go beyond just examining the content of these sites and to provide further analysis of the impact of FBISCs, this study asks fans about how they think these sites are influencing the most important stakeholders in college sports.

RQ3:   What do fans think about the influence of FBISCs on fellow fan bases, administrations, student-athletes, and media who are cognizant of the content of these respective sites?

Emotive

In an attempt to study more than fan assumptions of the influence of these sites, this study investigates emotional content from a few angles. We will first ask fans their motives for visiting these sites. Then we will examine closely the content fans and publishers post on the pages of the sites. Lastly, we will look at how the use of FBISCs affects their attitudes towards both their teams and the sport of college football.

RQ4: Why do fans visit FBISCs?

RQ5: How do people express themselves on the message boards of these sites?

RQ6: How does the use of FBISCs affect fans' psychological commitment to or disposition toward their teams?

RQ7: How does the use of FBISCs affect sport fandom?

Behavioral

Finally, this study attempts to advance the review of demographic and psychographic profiles of those who come to these sites while examining their subsequent behaviors while they are online. We will examine further the ultimate implications of this site behavior toward others on the site.

RQ8: What level of involvement do fans have on their respective team websites?

RQ9: What kind of bridging behavior on other team sites or bonding behavior with fellow fans on favorite team sites takes place to create a sense of community among fans?

RQ10: To what extent does the use of FBISCs by fans with different levels of involvement facilitate online aggression?

Methods

To explore the research questions, we conducted both a season-long content analysis of 35 FBISCs dedicated to teams in the Southeastern Conference (SEC) and an online fan survey of these same sites. The SEC's popularity in college football is unmatched in terms of attendance and television ratings, with the conference recently signing the richest television deal in the history of college sports at $3 billion (Wolverton, Lopez-Rivera, & Killough, 2009). The content analysis covered both the front pages of these FBISCs and the most popular message boards on each site.

Sample

To find the best representation of FBISCs in the 12-team SEC, we identified the two most highly trafficked online networks of Web sites dedicated to college sports – Yahoo!-owned Rivals.com and Fox Sports' Scout.com (Recruiting Websites Booming, 2007). In addition, we identified through Google rankings and observation of site activity, the most-trafficked independent and free FBISCs dedicated to each team in the conference. Therefore, we analyzed three sites for each of the 12 teams in the SEC – the Rivals, Scout, and independent sites (Vanderbilt had no independent site).

Code sheet development

On both the front pages and the message board threads, coders determined whether the page contained criticism, praise or neutral analysis of (a) coaching decisions,

(b) player performance, (c) officiating, (d) media content, and (e) fan behavior. In addition, the coders noted content such as (f) rumors, (g) recruiting, (h) gambling, (i) injuries, (j) predictions, and (k) politics. They also examined the sites for the presence of (l) original or linked video, (m) photos, and (n) audio. Finally, the coders classified (o) emotions on the message board threads according to a code sheet developed by Macias and Lewis (2003) in their examination of health-related message boards. These emotions such as happiness, fear, and disgust were supplemented with additional emotions identified by the researchers that were common to FBISC message boards such as joking/humor and boredom.

Procedure

Coders met with the research team during non-conference play – the conference preseason and early regular season in August and September – to observe behavior on these sites and alter the code sheet accordingly. The coders examined both the sites' front pages as well as randomly selected threads from the most popular message board. The coders accessed the sites and coded both the front pages and three threads from each message board at least five days per week.

Reliability

Two of the trained coders independently coded a hard copy of the front pages and message boards from a randomly selected sample of the sites. Reliability scores averaged .83 for front-page analysis and .95 for message board analysis under the Holsti (1969) method indicating intercoder reliability. All disagreements were resolved between coders prior to actual coding during the conference season/duration of the study.

Survey

During the last month of the football season, we asked the publishers of each of the teams' Rivals, Scout, and independent sites to "pushpin" a link to an online survey in their most trafficked message board for 30 days. Most publishers provided an endorsement of our survey by posting an introductory and explanatory message themselves, which encouraged site visitors to participate (see Table 8.1). See the Appendix to this chapter for a full description of the survey instrument.

TABLE 8.1 Sites examined

	Content analysis	Fan survey
Rivals	12	12
Scout	12	11
Free independent	11	9

Results

We collected 3,816 survey responses from 32 different sites. For the content analysis, we analyzed 1,579 message board threads and 1,318 front pages on 35 different sites over the entire regular season. In terms of survey respondents, 97% of the respondents indicated they were Caucasian, and 95% were male. Approximately 9% of respondents were 18–24 years of age, 26% age 25–34, 24% age 35–44 and 41% age 45 and over. In terms of education, 84% indicated they held at least a bachelor's degree, while only 10% earned less than $50,000 a year, and 55% earned more than $100,000 a year.

Tests of research questions

RQ1:   What type of content is featured on FBISC front pages?

In terms of coaching, 42.4% of front pages featured some sort of original analysis of coaching decisions of the home team, but only 7.7% of pages featured original analysis of opposing teams. While only 2.7% of front pages attacked home team coaches, even less, at 1.3%, attacked opposing coaches. However, 7.4% praised the home team coaches and less than 1% praised opposing coaches.

As for players, 84.1% of of front pages included recruiting information. In addition, 55.4% of front pages featured original analysis of home team player performance, but only 9.5% analyzed opposing player performance. However, 26.5% of front pages contained some sort of original analysis of opposing teams. Approximately 2.7% of front pages featured original criticism of the performance of their own team's players, while less than 1% criticized the play of opposing players. Approximately 16.3% of front pages praised the home team's players, but only 1% praised the opposing team's players. Approximately 9.8% of front pages provided content related to player injuries on their team. Rivalries also figured prominently, with 14.3% of front pages including information about their main rivals. Finally, 37.3% of front pages included content related to former players of the team.

In terms of media content, 22.3% of front pages featured some sort of original analysis of mainstream media coverage. Furthermore, 32.3% of front pages included some sort of link to or summary of mainstream media stories about the team, while only 3% of front pages included some sort of link to a rumor or unsubstantiated story. Only 1.7% contained original "breaking news" stories. For original content, 30.7% included original photography, and 27.3% included original video, while only 4.9% included photos or links to mainstream media photos and 25.9% included video or links to video from mainstream media. A total of 86.7% of front pages linked directly to content featured on their message boards, and only 2% of front pages provided information related to gambling (point spread, etc.). RQ1 is answered as most front pages of these sites contain mostly content about the home team, dominated by recruiting information. Original content mostly concerns recruiting as well.

RQ2:   What type of content is featured on the message boards of FBISCs?

In terms of coaching, 28.2% of threads featured some sort of original analysis of coaching decisions of the home team, and 10.6% of threads featured original analysis of opposing teams. In contrast to the front pages, 15.3% of threads analyzed attacked home team coaches, and 4.9% attacked opposing coaches. Furthermore, 10.3% of threads praised the home team coaches and less than 3.7% praised opposing coaches.

As for players, 8.7% of threads included recruiting information. In addition, 37.7% of threads featured original analysis of home team player performance, and 12.9% analyzed opposing player performance. However, 21.4% of threads contained some sort of criticism of opposing teams. Approximately 11.4% of threads featured attacks on players on the home team, and only 3.4% criticized the play of opposing players. Approximately 17% of threads praised the home team's players, but only 3.6% praised the opposing team's players. Approximately 5% of threads provided content related to player injuries on their team. Rivalries figured even more prominently on message boards with 19.8% of threads including information about their main rivals. Finally, 3% of threads included content related to former players of the team.

For media content, 13.6% of fans posting on threads included some original analysis of mainstream media coverage. In addition, 14% of threads included some sort of link to, or summary of, mainstream media news stories. Only 5.7% included a link to a rumor or unsubstantiated story, and less than 1% posted "breaking news." In terms of original content, less than 1% included links to original photos, photos taken by mainstream media or original video, while 1.1% linked to video produced by mainstream media.

In terms of predictions, 29.5% of threads included some sort of prediction about the outcome of the game, and like the front pages, only 2% of threads provided any information related to gambling. RQ2 is answered as most FBISC message boards seem to provide more of a balanced amount of information about opposing teams, less information than the front pages about recruiting, and more critical information in general.

RQ3:   What do fans think about the influence of FBISCs on fellow fan bases, administrations, student-athletes, and media who are cognizant of the content of these respective sites?

Approximately 81.7% "agree" or "strongly agree" that Internet communities strengthen fan bases of college teams. In addition, 4% "strongly agree," 38.9% "agree," 18.9% are "undecided," 31.9% "disagree," and 6.2% "strongly disagree" that Internet communities influence university athletic department decisions. However, 66.9% "strongly agree" or "agree" that Internet communities influence student-athletes. Finally, 80.8% "agree" or "strongly agree" that Internet communities influence reporters. Therefore, RQ3 is answered as fans feel that FBISCs strongly influence fans, student-athletes and reporters, but not athletic department decisions.

RQ4:   Why do fans visit FBISCs?

In answer to the open-ended question "Why did you visit this site today?", fans responded with "information" about coaches, players and recruiting in large numbers. BIRGing and CORFing seems the norm on these sites with approximately 72.4% of fans surveyed say that they are more likely to post on a sports message board after a win, while only 37.6% post after a loss. Furthermore, 85% of fans said they were more likely to visit after a win, while only 15% said they were more likely to visit after a loss. We must note, however, that numerous fans indicated in the open-ended portion of these questions that they were displeased with the forced-choice nature, often stating they wished we had provided them with the opportunity to say "neither" or "equally after a win or loss." Finally, approximately 75% of fans said they visit "several times a day" during the season as opposed to only 33% visiting "several times a day" during the off-season. In addition, 66% of fans said they visit "several times a day" during recruiting season. The open-ended question "What do you like best about this site?" yielded an overwhelming response of "good information." Therefore, RQ4 is answered as most fans visit these sites largely for informational purposes.

RQ5:   How do people express themselves on the message boards of these sites?

On the message boards, 29% posted positive emotions in their threads, while 31% posted negative emotions, and 40% posted neutral emotions. (See Figure 8.1 for full range of emotions.)

Furthermore, "Analytical" postings outpaced all other types of postings (19%) on FBISCs, with similar "Interest/Curious" posts ranking second (13%). In terms of negative emotions, while "Frustration" (7%) and "Anger" (6%) topped the list, "Joking/Humor" (6%) and "Pride," (5%) "Happy/Joy" (5%) and "Camaradarie" (5%) were at similar, though slightly lower, levels. Fans also overwhelmingly responded to the open-ended question "What do you like least about this site?" with the answer "negative posters." Therefore, RQ5 findings show that the emotions expressed on message boards are fairly balanced between positive, negative and neutral.

RQ6:   How does the use of FBISCs affect fans' psychological commitment to or disposition toward the team?

Fans who use FBISCs at levels higher than average exhibit a significantly higher psychological commitment to the team ($M = .103$) than fans that use FBISCs at lower than average levels ($M = -.164$, $F(1, 3815) = 66.278$, $p < .01$).

RQ7:   How does the use of FBISCs affect sport fandom?

Fans who use FBISCs at higher-than-average levels exhibit significantly higher levels of sport fandom ($M = .164$) than fans that use FBISCs at lower-than-average levels ($M = -.260$, $F(1, 3815) = 170.215$, $p < .01$).

RQ8: What level of involvement do fans have on their respective team websites?

In terms of time spent on FBISCs "yesterday," 6.5% of fans report that they spent more than three hours, 36.2% spent one to three hours, 37.8% spent a half hour to one hour, and 19.6% spent less than a half hour. In terms of how often fans post on these sites overall, during off-season, 33.3% of fans post several times a day, 28.6% post about once a day, 14.6% post three to five days a week, 14.7% post one to two times a week, 5.3% post every few weeks, and 3.5% post less often. During recruiting season (spring), 63.2% post several times a day, 20.2% post about once a day, 8.1% post three to five days a week, 5.9% post one to two times a week, 1.8% post every few weeks, and .9% post less often. However, during football season, 75.3% post several times a day, 18.9% post about once a day, 4.3%

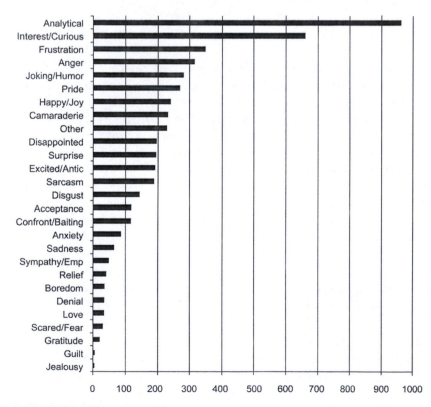

FIGURE 8.1 Emotions expressed

post three to five days per week, 1% post one to two times a week, 0.4% post every few weeks, and 0.1% post less often.

Fans varied in their response to how often and where (on what sites) they post, with 14.8% "lurking" or never posting, 38.1% posting only on one fan-based site, 22.8% posting on two sites, and 13.8% posting on three sites. However, they varied even more with regard to the number of sites from which they obtain information, with only 10.6% getting information from one site; 15.9% get information from two sites, 22.4% get information from three sites, 14.9% get information from four sites, and 16.2% get information from five sites. Regarding paying for subscriptions, 52% of respondents subscribe to one site, 29.7% do not subscribe to any sites, 15.3% subscribe to two sites, and 2.4% subscribe to three sites. Thus, results of RQ8 reveal that fans are heavily involved in their sites, especially during football and recruiting seasons.

RQ9:   What kind of "bridging" behavior on other team sites or bonding behavior with fellow fans on favorite team sites takes place to create a sense of community among fans?

In terms of how often fans bond by posting on their own sites, blogs or forums, 9.9% always post on their own team's blog, 17.7% very often post, 35.9% sometimes post, 25% rarely post, and 11.4% never post. As for bridging to other teams' sites, blogs or forums, 56.5% never post on another team's blogs, 30% rarely post, while 10.9% sometimes post, 2% very often post, and 0.7% always post. Therefore, in answering RQ9, more bonding takes place on these sites than bridging.

RQ10: To what extent does the use of FBISCs by fans with different levels of involvement facilitate online aggression?

To investigate the relationship between FBISC use, team record and online aggression, we subjected *online aggression* index scores to a two-way ANOVA, having two levels of FBISC use (high, low) and team record (winning, losing). The analysis yielded a main effect for FBISC use, $F (1, 3,815) = 8.4$, $p < .01$, indicating that online aggression was significantly higher for subjects using FBISCs at higher levels than for subjects using FBISCs at lower levels. The main effect for team record was not significant $F (1, 3,815) = .55$, $p > .05$. In addition, there was no interaction between the two factors. The means and standard deviations for the four groups are displayed in Table 8.2. Therefore, the results of RQ10 reveal that fans using FBISCs at high levels tend to exhibit higher levels of online aggression.

Discussion

Fan-based online communities are largely anonymous, mostly homogeneous, and often filled with animus. We see an interesting dichotomy in that more fans visit and post messages after a victory than in defeat, yet overall feelings of frustration and

TABLE 8.2 Means and standard deviations of differences in online aggression between groups

	Mean	SD
Low FBISC use/losing record (n = 330)	–.07	.95
Low FBISC use/winning record (n = 1,145)	–.10	.96
High FBISC use/losing record (n = 448)	–.01	.97
High FBISC use/winning record (n = 1,893)	–.07	1.0

anger outweigh emotions of pride and joy. Does that suggest that fans are hard to please, even in victory?

In any case, the new community craves more analysis – pre- and post-event – than traditional media have proffered in the non-immediate past. FBISCs satiate college football fans' never-ending hunger for information. If referencing the three categories of media consumption identified by Raney (2006) as emotional, cognitive, and behavioral, cognitions appear to trump emotions and aggressive actions in this case.

Specifically, FBISCs want more information about their own players and coaches than traditional media are able to provide. The publishers of these sites have responded by focusing a substantial amount of their content on players, coaches, and even former players. However, a great deal of the content is lifted from traditional media sources. Analytically, we care more about our team than the opponent, and on their home pages, FBISCs unapologetically tilt coverage to fulfill our needs. Interestingly, message board venom regarding opponents stems more from team or school hatred, and less from hostility toward individual coaches or players. Even so, fans spend more time on these sites attacking opposing teams' coaches and players than those on their own teams. The skew toward partisan content certainly fits fans' motivations for visiting these sites.

While it is obvious that the function of message boards is social and therefore behavioral, we thought the finding that most posts were "analytical" and regarding "interest/curious" in nature was surprising. Madrigal and Chen (2008) have noted that fans seek causal attributions for the outcomes of games – an observation supported by the FBISC front page and message board traffic this study also revealed.

FBISCs often have the reputation among sports administrations, coaches and the mainstream media as being volatile and emotional environments. Our findings refute this belief somewhat in that a large part of the content on these sites was neutral or information-seeking. However, we must point out that the leading emotional categories were "frustration" and "anger." Even so, the cognitive motive for visiting these sites seems to outweigh the emotional. Most fans seem to hunger more for information than for interaction, which may explain the low numbers of visitors who actually take the time to post on the message boards.

In-season, more sites serve as a repository to house existing coverage (by other media) than in breaking stories, with the majority of new material coming in the form of game analysis. However, the sites' founding core competence, recruiting coverage, remains a loyal mainstay for readers. Message board posters are nearly twice as likely to regularly contribute during recruiting season, and more original site content comes during this time than any other. These findings make sense in that the mainstream media do not have the resources to devote to covering recruiting, which these fans obviously value. In line with the research questions regarding information subsidy (RQs 1 and 2) and involvement (RQ7), the sites' recruiting coverage is a major precursor to online fan behaviors. Because recruiting is especially followed during the off-season, this presupposes a BIRGing component (RQ4) where satisfied or even previously CORFing fans can bond (RQ9) and brag about incoming (yet unproven) players.

Armed with this thirst for more information than the traditional media provide, these fan communities are powerful agents, according to their members. Student-athletes and reporters are perceived to be highly influenced by site content. This finding runs counter to a study done by Benigni, Porter, and Wood (2009) of sports journalists, who perceive fan sites as much less impactful on those two groups. Fans' perception of lurking by athletes and reporters is significant in a variety of ways, ranging from institutional control and site policing (now currently done by many top-level athletic programs), to ethical principles ranging from self-determination to categorical imperative that are challenged by fluid reporting norms caused by new technology and societal shifts.

Finally, FBISCs influence fan behavior, thus indicating a possible cultivation effect. Despite their regular expressions of analytical content and thirst for new information, regular users are more likely to show online aggression, regardless of team record. Further evidence obtained in this study supports what Wann, Peterson, Cothran, and Dykes (1999) have noted: that individual team fandom is the most prominent indicator of sports fan aggression.

In addition, heavier users show a more intense spirit of fandom and a deeper psychological commitment to their team. While it's obvious that more intense fans would gravitate toward FBISCs, the online aggression part of the equation is a bit unclear. Perhaps the anonymous nature of FBISCs allows fans the freedom to wear their emotions on their sleeve. Despite the trend toward BIRGing and CORFing, the prevalance of "homer" content, and the lack of bridging going on here, fans seem more than willing to verbally attack fans of their own team. Is aggression simply the nature of these communities, or is it a result of something else? Future research should delve more deeply into online aggression and its effects.

Conclusion

This study of fans in the nation's most publicized college football conference provides more than just emotional context. While the research is limited in that it covers just one region of the country in one sport, it offers a baseline glimpse into issues of information subsidy, media and reader displacement, and race and class issues (the majority of FBISC members are white and well educated, mirroring the sample of the 2009 Benigni et al. study of reporters). These sites provide an important source of information for avid college football fans. Fans who visit these sites perceive the sites as highly influential. Few people post and provide content, but most visitors are looking for information not available through regular channels. Despite the lack of visitors from outside of the fan base of their favorite team, visiting these sites is related in some way to online verbal aggression. However, this sort of behavior seems to be the thing that most fans say they like least about these sites. Implications for site operators would mean taking steps to curb this type of behavior and asking their visitors to remain civil toward each other.

Future research could account for other issues outside of fandom, ranging from workplace productivity (it's naïve to assume that subscribers solely access sites from home), to credibility and journalistic integrity of FBISC content, as well as privacy of sports figures and site users. The 2010 NFL draft could be a notable case study in that character issues were paramount in player evaluation and selection. Perceived high-character quarterbacks with significant questions about durability (overall top draft pick Sam Bradford) and technique (first-round pick Tim Tebow) were highly coveted by certain teams. Conversely, some NFL-readier players with perceived character flaws were passed over by skeptical general managers. Future research should note whether teams at the next level utilize FBISCs to track player issues (in college or high school), and if today's e-reporters and site contributors/posters provide acute (albeit often unvetted and anonymous) information subsidies to team administrators about players' or even coaches' off-field behaviors.

For anyone seeking a platform that offers empowerment, but not at the expense of enjoyment, FBISCs provide just that. More specifically, for the managers and owners of these sites, FBISCs attract target audiences apparently more concentrated and highly engaged in sport than fans of any other media or entertainment fare – a retailer's gold mine, perhaps? For those coaches, players, and administrators of the sport, FBISCs reinforce the watchdog function of the media as the fourth estate. For sports fans, FBISCs provide a means for furthering their journey of self-preservation and self-identity. Finally, for fans of sports teams, especially those of college football's Southeastern Conference, these sites provide insights and information bringing them closer to understanding the nature and performances of their beloved teams. SEC fans, at least, have shown that the FBISC serves as a contemporary, mediated locale similar to golf's "19th hole" – a clubhouse, of sorts, conducive for rumination, celebration, and keeping score. And just as those birdies and great golf shots provide one with memorable stories and incentives to play on, so too do FBISCs keep the active, vociferous sports fan coming back for more.

References

Benigni, V.L., Porter, L.V., & Wood, J.C. (2009). Handoff: A multi-method examination of the move from print to new media of college sports reporters and fans. Presented at the International Communication Association Conference, Chicago.

Bernache-Assollant, I., Lacassagne, M.F., & Braddock, J.H. (2007). Basking in reflected glory and blasting differences in identity-management strategies between two groups of highly identified soccer fans. *Journal of Language & Social Psychology, 26*(4), 381–88.

Boen, F., Vanbeselaere, N., & Feys, J. (2002). Behavioral consequences of fluctuating group success: An Internet study of soccer-team fans. *The Journal of Social Psychology, 42* (6), 769–81.

Bryant, J. & Raney, A.A. (2000). Sports on the screen. In D. Zillmann & P. Vorderer (Eds.), *Media entertainment: The psychology of its appeal* (pp. 153–74). Mahwah, NJ: Erlbaum.

Bryant, J., Rockwell, S., & Owens, J. (1994). "Buzzer beaters" and "barn burners": The effects of enjoyment of watching the game go down to the wire. *Journal of Sport & Social Issues, 18*(4), 326–39.

Buss, A. & Perry, M. (1992). The aggression questionnaire. *Journal of Personality and Social Psychology, 63*(3), 452–59.

Cialdini, R.B., Borden, R.J., Thorne, A., Walker, M.R., Freeman, S., & Sloan, L.R. (1976). Basking in reflected glory: Three (football) field studies. *Journal of Personality and Social Psychology, 34*, 366–75.

End, C.M., Kretschmar, J.M., & Dietz-Uhler, B. (2004). College students' perceptions of sports fandom as a social status determinant. *International Sports Journal, 8*(1), 114–23.

Forrest, S., Eatough, V., & Shevlin, M. (2005). Measuring adult indirect aggression: The development and psychometric assessment of the indirect aggression scales. *Aggressive Behavior, 31*(1), 84–97.

Gantz, W., Wang, Z., Bryant, P., & Potter, R.F. (2006). Sports versus all comers: Comparing TV sports fans with fans of other programming genres. *Journal of Broadcasting & Electronic Media, 50*(1), 95–118.

Holsti, O. (1969). *Content analysis for the social sciences and humanities*, Reading, MA: Addison-Wesley.

Kiousis, S. (2001). Public trust or mistrust? Perceptions of media credibility in the information age. *Mass Communication and Society, 4*(4), 381–403.

Kwon, H.H. & Trail, G.T. (2003). A reexamination of the construct and concurrent validity of the Psychological Commitment to Team Scale. *Sport Marketing Quarterly, 12*, 88–93.

Kwon, H.H. & Trail, G.T. (2005). The feasibility of single-item measures in sport loyalty research. *Sport Management Review, 8*, 69–89.

Macias, W. & Lewis, L.S. (2003). A content analysis of direct-to-consumer (DTC) prescription drug Web sites. *Journal of Advertising, 32*(4), 43–56.

Madrigal, R. (1995). Cognitive and affective determinants of fan satisfaction with sporting event attendance. *Journal of Leisure Research, 27*(3), 205–27.

Madrigal, R. & Chen, J. (2008). Moderating and mediating effects of team identification in regard to causal attributions and summary judgments following a game outcome. *Journal of Sport Management, 22*(6), 717–33.

Mahony, D.F., Madrigal, R., & Howard, D. (2000). Using the Psychological Commitment to Team (PCT) Scale to segment sport consumers based on loyalty. *Sport Marketing Quarterly, 9*, 15–25.

Peterson, E.M. & Raney, A.A. (2008). Reconceptualizing and reexamining suspense as a predictor of mediated sports enjoyment. *Journal of Broadcasting & Electronic Media, 52*(4), 544–62.

Porter, L.V. & Sallot, L. (2003). The Internet and public relations: Investigating practitioners' roles and World Wide Web use. *Journalism & Mass Communication Quarterly, 80*(3), 603–22.

Raney, A.A. (2006). Why we watch and enjoy. In A.A. Raney & J. Bryant (Eds.), *Handbook of sports and media* (pp. 319–29). Mahwah, NJ: Erlbaum.

Raney, A.A. & Kinnally, W. (2009). Examining perceived violence in and enjoyment of televised rivalry sports contests. *Mass Communication & Society, 12*(3), 311–31.

Recruiting websites booming, also under fire (2007, April 7). Retrieved April 28, 2010, from the NBC Sports Site: http://nbcsports.msnbc.com/id/17973156/

Sargent, S.L., Zillmann, D., & Weaver III, J.B. (1998). The gender gap in the enjoyment of televised sports. *Journal of Sport & Social Issues, 22*(1), 46–64.

Sigelman, L. (1986). Basking in reflected glory revisited: An attempt at replication. *Social Psychology Quarterly, 49*(1), 90–92.

Smith, J. & Wann, D.L. (2006). Relationship of dysfunctional sport fandom with dislike for rivals in a sample of college students. *Perceptual & Motor Skills, 102*(3), 719–20.

Sweetser, K.D., Porter, L.V., Chung, D., & Kim, E. (2008). Credibility and the uses of blogs among professionals in the information industry. *Journalism & Mass Communication Quarterly, 85*(1), 169–85.

Su-lin, G., Tuggle, C.A., Mitrook, M.A., Coussement, S.H., & Zillmann, D. (1997). The thrill of a close game: Who enjoys it and who doesn't? *Journal of Sport & Social Issues, 21* (1), 53–64.

Wann, D.L. (1995). Preliminary validation of the Sport Fan Motivation Scale. *Journal of Sport & Social Issues, 19*, 377–96.

Wann, D.L., Allen, B., & Rochelle, A.R. (2004). Using sport fandom as an escape: Searching for relief from under-stimulation and over-stimulation. *International Sports Journal, 8*(1), 104–13.

Wann, D.L. & Branscombe, N.R. (1990). Die-hard and fair-weather fans: Effects of identification on BIRGing and CORFing tendencies. *Journal of Sport & Social Issues, 14* (2), 103–17.

Wann, D.L., Carlson, J.D., Holland, L.C., Jacob, B.E., Owens, D.A., & Wells, D.D. (1999). Beliefs in symbolic catharsis: The importance of involvement with aggressive sports. *Social Behavior and Personality, 27*(2), 155–64.

Wann, D.L., Hamlet, M.A., Wilson, T.M., & Hodges, J.A. (1995). Basking in reflected glory, cutting off reflected failure, and cutting off future failure: The importance of group identification. *Social Behavior & Personality: An International Journal, 23*(4), 377–89.

Wann, D.L., Peterson, R.R., Cothran, C., & Dykes, M. (1999). Sport fan aggression and anonymity: The importance of team identification. *Social Behavior and Personality, 27*(6), 597–602.

Wann, D.L. & Pierce, S. (2005). The relationship between sport team identification and social well-being: Additional evidence supporting the Team Identification–Social Psychological Health Model. *North American Journal of Psychology, 7*(1), 117–24.

Wann, D.L., Waddill, P., & Dunham, M. (2004). Using sex and gender role orientation to predict level of sport fandom. *Journal of Sport Behavior, 27*(4), 367–77.

Wolverton, B., Lopez-Rivera, M., & Killough, A. (2009). A powerful league piles up its advantages. *Chronicle of Higher Education, 56*(2), A1–A28.

Zillmann, D., Bryant, J., & Sapolsky, B. (1989). Enjoyment from sports spectatorship. In J.H. Goldstein (Ed.), *Sports, games, and play: Social and psychological viewpoints* (2nd Ed., pp. 241–78). Hillsdale, NJ: Erlbaum.

Appendix: survey instrument

First, we asked fans about the influence of FBISCs. Measuring items on a five-point Likert type scale, ranging from "Strongly Agree" to "Strongly Disagree," we asked respondents whether FBISCs "strengthen fan bases of college teams," and whether they "influence university athletic department decisions," "student-athletes," and "reporters." In addition, we asked whether these sites "make fans more informed about sports," and whether they "contribute to fan enjoyment of sports." To measure media credibility, we adapted two items from Kiousis (2001) and added one item regarding whether fans preferred "objective and unbiased information rather than fan or 'homer' information."

Using questions adapted from Porter and Sallot (2003) and Sweetser, Porter, Chung, and Kim (2008), the self-reported use questions asked how often respondents used sports Web sites devoted to the "team(s) I cover," what types of sites the respondent read and how often access occurred during the "average workday," "during the season," "during the recruiting season," and "during the off-season." We measured these items on a five-point Likert scale with semantic differentials ranging from "Always" to "Never." We adapted Web use questions asked by Porter and Sallot (2003), adding items regarding how often they used a range of sports sites from ESPN.com to FBISCs during the "off-season," "recruiting season," and "football season." These items were measured on a 5-point Likert scale from "Strongly Disagree" to "Strongly Agree." We also asked a series of questions relating to how often fans posted on their favorite teams' sites as well as opposing teams' sites.

We used Wann's (1995) sport fan motivation scale (SFMS) to measure general sports fandom (alpha = .77) and Kwon and Trail's (2003; 2005) adaptation of Mahony, Madrigal, and Howard's (2000) Psychological Commitment to Team (PCT) scale to measure specific team fandom (alpha = .79). To measure online aggression, we constructed a scale (alpha = .75) combining and adapting items relating to verbal aggression from Buss and Perry's (1992) aggression scale and the indirect aggression scale from Forrest, Eatough, and Shevlin (2005).

9

THE LESS YOU SAY

An initial study of gender coverage in sports on Twitter

Lauren Reichart Smith

AUBURN UNIVERSITY

> It is our desire to promote, encourage and support female ski racers, but to this end the ladies must work with us and help themselves. … Lady skiers must learn to promote themselves, make themselves available for happy, uncritical and positive TV interviews. They must show themselves – helmet and goggles off in the finish area – play on their youth and pretty faces. Everyone loves a winner – and a glamorous winner is a big bonus.
>
> (Federation Internationale de Ski, 2005, p. 1).

The above quote, from the Federation Internationale de Ski (International Ski Federation), is a telling example of how attitudes toward female athletes still remain centered around one theme: looks. For many years, girls were generally not encouraged to participate in sports, because sports were deemed to be masculine. Femininity was not a trait associated with any aspect of sport or athleticism. Clasen (2001) argued that, since sports are a typically masculine social environment, women end up having to showcase their feminine qualities rather than their athletic ability. Even after the success of female athletes in the 1996 Summer Olympic Games (in which the U.S. women won more medals than the U.S. men), their presence in American sports media continued to be underrepresented and they were shown in stereotypical and traditional ways, focusing on their femininity rather than their athletic ability.

The mass media can have significant impacts on the thoughts and ideas of individuals. Kane (1988) stated, "The mass media have become one of the most powerful institutional forces for shaping values and attitudes in modern culture" (pp. 88–89). This idea was reinforced again with the argument that media are a driving force in the determination of what is right and important within society (Greenburg & Hier, 2001; Kane, Traub, & Hayes, 2000). The theory of hegemonic masculinity

(Duncan & Brummett, 1993) explains how males are framed as the dominant group in athletics through various displays including air time, story count, and photographic images (Hardin, Chance, Dodd, & Hardin, 2002; Messner, 1988). This framing may result in a belief that women are not as important in the area of sports because of their lesser exposure in the media.

Real (2006) stated the World Wide Web has become an ideal medium for sports fans because of its accessibility, interactivity, speed, and multimedia content. Social networking and social media are changing the way individuals receive information; in fact, Twitter, the microblogging social networking tool, was said to lead the pack in breaking news (O'Conner, 2009).

The purpose of this study is an initial examination of the social media platform Twitter, to determine if gender coverage of women changes to a level more equivalent to their male counterparts. Traditional media platforms are limited by constraints of space, time and money; the only restriction within Twitter is a limit on how long each individual tweet should be (140 characters). The question arises as to whether or not traditional media biases, with respect to gender, will continue to exist on a new media platform not limited by the same constraints.

Theoretical basis

Past sports research has used framing (Fortunato, 2001; Goffman, 1974; Parker & Fink, 2008) and agenda-setting (Falkheim, 2008; McCombs & Shaw, 1972; Seltzer & Mitrook, 2009) to analyze broadcasts of sporting events. Previous scholarship has also used Foucault's (1971) discourse theory, which holds that statements define who and what male and female athletes are (MacKay & Dallaire, 2009; Pirinen, 1997; Wright & Clarke, 1999). However, in the comparison of genders in sports context, hegemonic theory (Gramsci, 1971; Sage, 1998) and more specifically hegemonic masculinity (Duncan & Brummett, 1993) are widely used theories. Gramsci's (1971) notion of hegemony centers around ideas of winning, power, and domination of a ruling class portrayed through the media and accepted as normal and natural. These ideas become societal norms; in the case of masculinity, norms stress values such as courage, toughness in mind and body, mastery, skill, adventure, and aggression in certain forms (Carrigan, Connell, & Lee, 1985).

Hegemonic masculinity explains how males are guaranteed the dominant position in society over women based on cultural norms (Connell, 2005). Scholarship concludes hegemonic masculinity is a specific strategy that is constructed through economics, culture, and dependence on social arrangements for the subordination of women (see Carrigan et al., 1985; Connell, 2005; Messner, 1988). Connell (2005) goes on to further claim hegemonic masculinity may be the most socially endorsed form of male expression through the applauding of characteristics such as aggressiveness, drive, ambition, self-reliance, and strength in males, but discouraging those same characteristics in females.

In the world of sports, male and female athletes are perceived and covered in drastically different ways. Sports have traditionally been associated with males and deemed to be masculine endeavors (Kane, 2007). Despite an increasing number of women participating in sports throughout the world, sport remains a male dominated field in terms of everything from access to media exposure (Schell & Rodriguez, 2000). Hegemonic masculinity may be one explanation for the different media portrayals. Messner (1988) notes, "There is a continuing marginalization, or downright ignoring, of women's sports by media" (p. 1). Under-representation and marginalization of female athletes in the media serve to create an illusion that females are nonexistent in the sporting world, which ultimately supports the notions of hegemonic masculinity (Kane & Greendorfer, 1994).

The mass media play a strong role in the maintenance of sport as a masculine hegemonic domain (Duncan & Messner, 1998; Harris & Clayton, 2002; Pirinen, 1997). The historical under-representation and marginalization of female athletes in traditional mass media could potentially negatively influence how society views women and women's sport. Hegemonic masculinity could be used to account for diminished word counts in stories about female athletes (Kane & Lenskyj, 1998), fewer pictures of female athletes ("Newspaper sports staff continue to slight women," 1991, p. 3), and pictures that frame female athletes in a passive role (Hardin, Chance, Dodd, & Hardin, 2002). The following section outlines different scholarship that supports this notion of hegemonic masculinity.

Hegemonic masculinity in the mass media

Female athletes in the media have been shown to consistently take a "runner up" status. Media researchers have criticized media coverage of sports with regard to gender and the dominance of males on the sports pages (Hardin, Chance, Dodd, & Hardin, 2002). Researchers have demonstrated women's athleticism is primarily based within cultural values of femininity and sexuality (see Hargreaves, 1994; Kane & Greendorfer, 1994; Lenskyj, 1986, 1992, 1994). Sports media have helped define male athletes as strong, courageous, and competent, while the female athlete has been defined through the creation of a picture of sexual appeal, femininity, and not as physically capable (Kane, 1996; Willis, 1982). Mass media play an important role in the world of sports because the majority of spectators watch the event via mass media (Koivula, 1999).

Research produces the same conclusions with regard to the differences in media coverage; women's teams typically receive less coverage than men's teams, and the coverage women receive is marginal (see Coakley, 1998; Fink & Kensicki, 2002; Kane & Parks, 1992; Tuggle, 1997). Coverage of women and women's teams is increased when the sport is considered traditionally feminine or "socially acceptable," like figure skating or gymnastics (Bissell & Duke, 2007). Women who participate in sports deemed to be more masculine, like soccer and rugby, receive less coverage (Cramer, 1994; Fink & Kensicki, 2002).

Though older research (Lumpkin & Williams, 1991; Sabo & Jansen, 1992) found that women were underrepresented, the following studies show some promising differences. Kinnick's (1998) examination of five major U.S. newspapers found some evidence for gender bias; however, females generally received equal story amounts, photo amounts, and story prominence. Vincent, Imwold, Masemann, and Johnson (2002) found females and males in British newspapers received relatively equal amounts of coverage, and comparable coverage in the descriptive language used within the articles, suggesting major international events boost coverage of women's sports. Yu (2009) examined news coverage of Asian female Olympic athletes and found Asian females were more likely to be covered in individual sports – like diving and the marathon events – while successes in other sports were ignored. A longitudinal examination of British national newspaper coverage of male and female track and field athletes found females remained underrepresented until 2004, and equality in coverage has only occurred from that point to the present (King, 2007). In an analysis of daily newspapers, Hardin, Chance, Dodd, and Hardin (2002) found that photos of male and female athletes were almost equal in number and, though female athletes were more often shown in passive roles, they were framed in a more neutral manner than in a sexualized manner.

Just as women's sports participation has increased since the passage of Title IX in 1972, the number of media channels distributing sports information has also increased. In the past, traditional media (television, newspapers, radio, magazines, etc.) primarily reported on sporting events. Since the Internet became publicly available in the mid-1990s and technology has become more advanced and mobile (wireless Internet, smart phones, etc.), not only can sports news be viewed electronically through online content, but also consumers can participate in certain sporting events and create their own sports media.

Online sports content

Social media and social networking are changing the face of sports consumption, though not without controversy and conflict between traditional media outlets and new media opportunities. With respect to the World Wide Web becoming a new delivery mechanism for sport, Real (2006) noted "Like an unanticipated child, the newest member of the sports media family has disrupted everything" (p. 171). Leonard (2009) cites several conflicts involving traditional media outlets and bloggers (Abbott, 2008; Jaschik, 2007), and later stated "those spaces and mediums that encompass new media technologies operate as contested spaces, where meaning, narrative, and representation are increasingly challenged by and from the spectrum of constituencies that form the sports media complex" (p. 2). What is clear is that this medium of delivery is still in its infancy, different tools of delivery come in and out of popularity in the blink of an eye, and the eventual outcomes and effects are still unknown.

Scholars have begun to consider the new sports media world as a community-based world, made possible by new media platforms. Wikipedia has been theorized to allow for increased communication for sports fans as well as supplement existing mainstream media storylines (Dart, 2009). Delivery of sports media has expanded beyond one channel (or medium) at a time; instead, new media platforms allow for networked media that enable supporters to build their own communities around a team or player (Hutchins, Rowe, & Ruddock, 2009).

In the limited scholarship available that examines whether traditional media gender biases extend to the Internet, the conclusions remain a mixed bag of findings. Kian, Mondello, and Vincent (2009) found that language on two popular websites during March Madness did not include gender specific descriptors that uphold hegemonic masculinity. However, other scholars have found that discrepancies in coverage and language continue to exist (Jones, 2004; Kian, Mondello, & Vincent, 2009; Sagas et al., 2000). Oates (2009) also hints at notions of hegemonic masculinity being upheld through corporate branding across multiple platforms of delivery, stating the "ability to signify and legitimatize gender hierarchy's remains potent" (p. 34).

Social media platforms

To date, hundreds of social networking sites are in existence. The most popular and familiar names include Facebook, MySpace, and YouTube, each boasting over 40 million users (Alexa.com, 2009). The Pew Internet and American Life Project (Pew, 2009) reported 35% of all adults and 65% of all teens/young adults use social networking sites. Boyd and Ellison (2007) defined social networking sites (SNS) as

> web-based services that allow individuals to (1) construct a public or semi-public profile within a bounded system, (2) articulate a list of other users with whom they share a connection, and (3) view and traverse their list of connections and those made by others within the system.
>
> *(p. 1)*

Twitter is one such social media platform that is heralded for information delivery. In an April, 2010 conference, Chirp (the Twitter developer conference) stated there were over 105 million registered users, with 300,000 new users signing up per day. Evan Williams, co-founder and CEO, stated "We think of Twitter as it's not a social network, but it's an information network. It tells people what they care about as it is happening in the world" (Williams, 2009). O'Conner (2009) noted, "In short order, and in a world where legacy media is downsizing and shutting bureaus worldwide, Twitter has become a go-to source of news you can use when and where you want and need it – often when and where the legacy media cannot yet or no longer supplies it" (p. 3). Initial studies have focused on the social and information functions of Twitter, such as Sanderson and Kassing's offering in Chapter 7 of this volume.

As previously outlined, research findings consistently reach the same conclusions with respect to coverage differences between genders. Realizing newspapers, magazines, and television are bound by the constraints of time and space, and are driven more by profit than a sense of fair and equal coverage, the question arises as to whether or not coverage will change when moved to a medium in which similar restrictions fail to exist, such as the Internet. Looking specifically at Twitter, the only restriction set forth is the 140-character limit of posts. As noted, there is no limit as to how many times a day a user may post updates, and there are certainly no restrictions on what type of content can be posted. The explosive growth of Twitter users shows that Twitter is becoming a prominent social networking tool, and the number of users continues to grow. Twitter will not be the next medium where sports information is presented; the coverage of sports is already happening on Twitter, making it necessary to study that presentation of information. When looking at how sport information is presented, Twitter seems to be a fairly equal playing field with respect to gender. It is in the context of the above ideas that the following research questions are advanced:

RQ1: How does the overall number of tweets differ by gender?
RQ1a: How do links to articles differ by gender?
RQ1b: How do links to videos differ by gender?
RQ1c: How do links to pictures differ by gender?
RQ2a: How does the overall number of tweets differ by sport?
RQ2b: How does the overall number of tweets by sport differ across gender?
RQ3: What are the differences in gender in number of retweets, both overall and by conference?

Method

Procedure

Content analysis was used to analyze coverage of gender across the Twitter feeds of four major United States sports conferences comprised of Division 1A universities. The conferences were the Southeastern Conference ("SEC"), the Pacific 10 ("Pac-10"), the Big Ten, and the Big 12. Originally, the Big East and Atlantic Coast Conferences were to be included as well, but were discarded because of insufficient information available within the Twitter feeds. These six conferences were selected because of the extreme media prominence that teams within these particular conferences receive. Though teams from other conferences receive media coverage, it is often the exception and not the norm, and usually only occurs when something unusual happens, such as the upsetting of a major football team in a game. The purpose of this project was to analyze differences in coverage by gender through the number of tweets and number of links to articles, videos and photographs. In analyzing the tweets from each conference, a census sample was obtained. The researcher decided to use a census, as all four conferences began their Twitter feeds in the year 2009, and it was not believed that a random sample would accurately portray what was posted.

The unit of analysis was the tweet, meaning each post was considered an individual tweet and was coded on one line. Two coders trained on an individual school's sport Twitter feed. Overall intercoder reliability was .92, with all intercoder reliability being calculated using Cohen's *kappa* (Cohen, 1960). The census was coded by one coder, with the total sample being 6,149. A second coder coded approximately 20% (1,231 tweets) of the census. The 20% was comprised of a random sample of tweets from each of the four conferences – approximately 20% of all tweets from each conference were coded; breakdown was 75 tweets for the Pac-10, 215 tweets for the Big 10, 433 tweets for the SEC, and 508 tweets for the Big 12. Overall intercoder reliability was .95 using Cohen's *kappa*.

Coding categories

Tweets were analyzed by employing several criteria: overall number of tweets (determined by looking at the total number of tweets listed in the conference's main profile), sport (what sport the tweet was about), gender (male, female, both, or no gender listed), if there was a link to an article, a link to a video, or a link to a picture (yes or no), what the action of the picture was (game active – the subject in play; game passive – the subject during a game, but on the sidelines or watching; passive – a posed media photo; headshot – a shot which might be used for a player profile; coach – if the photo showed the coach of the team in any capacity; and other – any subject other than a player or coach), the race of the subject in the picture/video, which was coded based on perceived skin pigmentation (Caucasian, African American, Asian, Hispanic, Other, Can't be determined), and if the tweet was a "retweet" (yes or no). A retweet is defined as content which is written by a third party, and copied by another user (in this case, the athletic conference) and shared. A retweet is designated by the letters "RT," followed by the "@username" symbol, finalized by the different user's original content.[1] One important point to note is if the tweet had a link to an article, but the article included a picture or video, then the tweet was said to link to both an article and a photo/video. This is a distinction from tweets coded as linking to video, such as to a clip on YouTube, with no accompanying article. Chi-square analysis and frequency distributions were used to analyze all data.

Results

Descriptives

The Twitter feeds of four major United States sports conferences comprised of Division 1A universities were analyzed in this study. In total, 6,159 total tweets

TABLE 9.1 Total number of tweets and links to articles/videos/photos

	Male (%)	Female (%)	Both (%)	No gender (%)	Total (%)
Links to articles	1,537 (62%)	719 (29%)	89 (4%)	124 (5%)	2,468 (40%)
Links to videos	255 (66%)	45 (12%)	1 (<1%)	81 (21%)	386 (5.9%)
Links to photos	762 (70%)	261 (24%)	25 (2%)	34 (3%)	1,085 (17.6%)
Total tweets	4,333 (70%)	1,313 (21%)	169 (3%)	353 (6%)	6,159 (n/a)

Note: n = 6,159

were coded and analyzed (n = 6,159). The Pac-10 had the fewest number of tweets with 382. The Big Ten had 1,077 tweets, the SEC had 2,163 tweets and the Big 12 had 2,537.

RQ1 asked how the overall number of tweets differed by gender, and RQ1a–c asked how overall links to articles, videos and pictures differed by gender. Table 9.1 provides complete frequency distributions for the previous questions. Notably, the gender split between males and females was large, with males receiving 70% of the total tweets across all four conferences, and females receiving only 21%. For article links, males received 62% of the links, and females 29%. Males accounted for 66% of the links to videos, and females accounted for only 12%; videos not featuring a specific gender, such as promotional conference videos, accounted for 21% of those links. Finally, with respect to photographs, males accounted for 70% of the links to photos, and females accounted for 24%. Chi-square analysis revealed significant *Phi* (1.50) and Cramer's *V* (.87) values the previous four items analyzed. Consequently, this set of RQs was confirmed as having significant differences in tweets, articles, videos and photos by gender.

RQ2a asked how total tweet number differed by sport. The sports of football and basketball received the greatest number of tweets. Football garnered 36% of the total tweets in the sample, while basketball received approximately 30% of all tweets. All other sports received less than 5% of all tweets. RQ2b examined how tweet number by sport differed across gender. Though direct comparison of male and female sports were limited to soccer, swimming and diving, track and field, basketball, gymnastics, golf, tennis, and cross country, in all of these sports males received a greater number of tweets. Chi-square analysis revealed significant *Phi* (1.33) and Cramer's *V* (.77) values for each of the previously listed eight sports. Therefore, this set of RQ's confirms significant differences in number of tweets by sport and sport by gender.

RQ3 analyzed one unique element within Twitter, the retweet. Table 9.2 provides complete frequency distributions of the total number of retweets, and the number of retweets by conference. Though the overall percentage of retweets is small (15%), the differences in gender, both overall and in each conference, is quite large. Overall, males account for 77% of all retweets, while females only account for 17%. The smallest ratio within the conferences comes from the Big Ten, with 64% of the retweets going to the males, and 24% going to the females. The largest split is

TABLE 9.2 Retweet breakdown

	Male (%)	Female (%)	Both (%)	No Gender (%)	Total (%)
Pac-10	7 (88%)	1 (13%)	0	0	8 (2 %)
Big Ten	122 (64%)	47 (24%)	16 (8%)	7 (4%)	192 (18%)
SEC	572 (76%)	109 (15%)	8 (1%)	22 (3%)	712 (33%)
Big 12	24 (75%)	1 (3%)	0	7 (22%)	32 (1%)
Total retweets	725 (77%)	158 (17%)	24 (3%)	36 (4%)	944 (15%)

Note: n = 944

found in the Pac-10, with males receiving 88% of the retweets, and females receiving 13% of the retweets. The most interesting finding comes from the Big 12, in which non-gender specific retweets outnumber the retweets about females. Consequently, RQ3 confirms significant differences in the numbers of retweets by gender.

Discussion

The purpose of this initial study was to determine how gender was being covered on a recent social networking tool. Based on the results, it can be concluded that coverage between genders is not anywhere approaching equal. From overall tweet, article, video, picture, and retweets, to conference-specific breakdowns, coverage of men's athletics outperforms coverage of women's athletics. What is shown here by the various breakdowns is this medium and method of reporting sports information may actually be a step backward with respect to the equality of gender coverage in sports media. This suggests that despite the difference in format and lack of restrictions within Twitter, the producers of the content are perhaps simply repeating what traditional media have done, and are not using the tool to level the playing field with respect to gender coverage.

The set of RQ1s was an attempt to determine gender coverage across all of the conferences. With an approximate 70/20 split for total tweets, as well as links to articles, videos, and photos made about men versus women (with the remaining 10% being given to either coverage of both sexes or non-gender specific coverage), the numbers fall more in line with the majority of past research, and less in line with recent scholarship which has pointed to more equal coverage. An interesting finding within this data set is in the comparison of links to videos; men dominate, garnering 66% of all links to videos. However, non-gender specific videos claimed 21% of those links, leaving females in third place with only 12%. These non-gender specific videos tended to be conference promotional videos, videos featuring mascots, or crowd/spectator videos. What needs to be considered is the significance of coverage devoted to revenue-generating sports, namely football and basketball. Overall, and within each conference, football and basketball consistently receives somewhere between 30–40% of all tweets. Obviously there is no direct gender comparison possible with football, and when football tweets account for approximately one-third of the entire tweet stream, it becomes very difficult for women's sports to close the gap. In further examining the breakdown of gender within basketball, it was found the men's team also received the lion's share of the coverage, with approximately 60% of all basketball-related tweets. Combining those numbers with football means the two male sports are essentially making up over 50% of the tweets over the four conferences' Twitter feeds. Again, this is a substantial gap for women to overcome. In using the theory of hegemonic masculinity, the overall coverage numbers of the Twitter feeds would support the theory's conclusions and underlying notions. By the sizable gap in coverage, these Twitter feeds may be doing nothing more than simply reinforcing the dominant position of males over females in the sports arena. Women, in the four aspects analyzed, receive less than one-quarter of the coverage in all four conferences' feeds. Messner's (1988) statement that women are marginalized and even ignored seems to be supported in all four elements analyzed of the Twitter feeds. Observationally, the majority of tweets were nothing more than an update of some sort (e.g. a score in a game, a reference to the latest poll within a sport, a quote from a coach, or even an update as to what former players from the conference are doing in respective professional leagues). Football received the most tweets across the board, largely because of the game score updates, quotes from Media Days, and updates from the 2009 NFL draft. Basketball accounted for the second highest number of tweets, with the majority of their coverage coming from March Madness and the Media Days events. These tweets were nothing more than what one would see on a Facebook status update, and essentially help position each of the conferences to fall under the category of a "Broadcaster" user in the Twitter world.

The set of RQ2s was an attempt to determine gender coverage differences by sport. Perhaps the most eye-catching difference is in the direct comparison of men's and women's basketball. Tweets about men's basketball significantly outnumber tweets about women's basketball, with an approximate 75/25 split within each conference. Though the SEC, the Pac-10, and the Big Ten all covered "Basketball Media Days" for the men for their respective conferences, the Big 10 was the only conference to cover the Media Day event for the women. Additionally, it is of interest to note that within the SEC, six teams from the conference were selected for the NCAA women's basketball tournament in 2009. Half as many teams from the conference made the NCAA men's basketball tournament, yet the men received approximately 78% of the overall basketball coverage. This finding falls directly in line with previous research conclusions that women's sports, and successes, tend to be downplayed within the media.

Basketball is a high visibility sport and one of the only listed sports where each conference offers the opportunity for both men and women to play. An important point to note is that these numbers can be skewed by the fact that not all of the conferences offer equal sporting opportunities for men and women. For example, gymnastics in the SEC is limited to women, whereas the Big Ten, Big-12, and Pac-10 offer the sport to men and women. However, even with that discrepancy, the male gymnasts received more tweets than the female gymnasts. Of the eight mentioned sports, soccer was the only one in which women received more tweets than men. As with other sports, soccer does not typically offer equal opportunities for men and women to play across all conferences.

RQ3 was an attempt to analyze one of the unique elements of Twitter – the retweet, or the conference's copying of another user's content, and posting it to their own feed. The retweet has significance to this study; this is one characteristic that separates this type of information source from traditional media. In traditional media forms, the message is broadcast by the media outlet. With the retweet, the person responsible for maintaining the conference's Twitter feed is actively reading other users' Twitter feeds, and pulling those posts they find interesting or pertinent to use for their own purposes. It is unheard of for a television news anchor to take a phone call mid-broadcast, then repeat to the viewing audience what the person on the phone said. However, this practice is fully accepted within the Twitter community.

What was being retweeted was not specific to any one user. Major media outlets, such as ESPN, CBS and ABC were retweeted within the conference's Twitter feeds. Specific conference sport feeds, such as the University of Michigan's women's volleyball Twitter feed, were retweeted. Individuals connected to the sport, school or conference (i.e., the coaches, players, or school officials) received retweets. Media outlets such as Rivals.com were retweeted. Finally, the conference also retweeted fans and followers of the Twitter feed. This suggests the individuals responsible for the Twitter feed are not limiting themselves to one specific type of content to re-broadcast.

In the examination of the retweets, a major discrepancy between genders was found. Overall, male sports received 77% of the retweets, and women's sports received only 17%. The conferences all individually featured very high discrepancies, with the biggest being found in the Pac-10; here men's sports received 88% of the retweets, and women's sports received 13%. This suggests, despite the ability to select from a variety of content and a variety of sources, the Twitter feeds of the conferences are conforming to the traditional biases found with respect to gender and mass media. This is interesting in that it is widely recognized that traditional media produces for profit; if there is no profit, the coverage disappears. A Twitter feed is not a media source concerned with profit; instead a Twitter feed should, by the social network aspect, be more concerned with conversation, interaction, and openness. The question then shifts to whether Twitter feeds are accurately providing what their audience wants.

As an exploration, this study is not without limitations. This was a comparison of just gender and coverage amount. Factors such as the quality of the posts, the action being portrayed in the photographs, and race were not analyzed. When there was a link, what was linked to was not specifically analyzed. Further, the ideas of profitability and brand viability, which could have an influence on the type of content posted, were not considered. A final limitation to consider is that, within the Twitter feeds themselves, there is an issue with man/womanpower running the feed. The job of running a Twitter feed is not a typical 40-hour per week job. If it were, the feeds might look a lot different. Instead, there may be a limitation on who is available at what time to produce tweets, which may impact how many tweets are being published to the individual feeds.

Conclusions

Previous research on gender has focused on traditional media outlets: newspaper, magazines, and television. Research with respect to sports online is in its early infancy, and has many diverse areas to study. Research on social networking has been emerging over the past few years, and research on Twitter is very limited. Twitter is a relatively new entry into the social media world, and though it serves as the "buzz" of the moment, its future remains uncertain. However, Twitter is an example of a social media platform, and the basic components that comprise Twitter will serve as a precedent for future social media platforms and new social media tools.

Operating under the assumption that Twitter offers the opportunity for more expressive coverage than traditional media, albeit with the 140-character per post limit, the gender inequity can be viewed as troubling. Coverage of men's athletics outpaces women's sports from the standpoint of overall tweet count, secondary materials such as articles, videos, and pictures, and in retweets.

By any measure of the breakdowns discussed there seems to be a move toward further gender disparity rather than equity in terms of coverage. This is especially troubling in that it leaves a suggestion that, even at the conference level, there exists a persistent degree of hegemonic masculinity. One might think that, of any interested parties, the conferences would certainly want to highlight their wide variety of sports for both genders for both awareness and athletic and fan recruitment. This shortcoming, if it persists, cannot be blamed solely upon a media set upon its own agenda, audience demand or the power of the dollar. The gender bias belongs to those at the conference level whose goal, as the Big Ten says, is to "emphasize the values of integrity, fairness and competitiveness in all aspects of its student-athletes' lives."

This study was one attempt to consider gender coverage within a new media environment, specifically in the form of a social networking site. Interestingly, it seems the conferences are using this tool more as an update mechanism, and fall into the category of broadcasters, while perhaps lacking the intention of the "social" part of the social network. However, considering the only limitation is the character length of each tweet, the conference feeds show a major discrepancy in the cover-age of males and females. The avenues for future research, not just on Twitter, but social media in general, are numerous. Future research could examine the quality of coverage received by males and females, as well as how males and females are por-trayed within this type of media. Additionally, the idea of profitability needs to be examined, and the question of why a non-profit media source would be following the same model as media sources concerned with profit.

With no reason to not provide a more equitable coverage, perhaps the discrepancy is best summed up by the following tweet from the Big Ten Twitter feed: "Sounds like an exciting game, but if we tweeted every game in every sport in the conference it would be a pretty dull feed." It cannot be determined, from this quote, what game was being talked about, but it seems to be an interesting self-admission that there is not only a bias, but knowledge of a bias.

Note

1 The explanation of the retweet was current at the writing of the paper. Since then, Twitter has changed the retweet format. By using the new retweet feature the conference can add a third party's content, link and avatar into the collection of Twitter feeds you follow or "Twitter stream."

References

Abbott, H. (2008, March 11). The Mavericks vs. the bloggers. Retrieved February 13, 2010 from http://myespn.go.com/blogs/truehoop/0-31-29/The-Mavericks-vs-the-Bloggers.html

Alexa.com (2009a). *Facebook.com* (Electronic Version). Retrieved December 3, 2009 from www.alexa.com/siteinfo/facebook.com

Alexa.com (2009b). *MySpace.com* (Electronic Version). Retrieved December 3, 2009 from www.alexa.com/siteinfo/myspace.com

Alexa.com (2009c). *YouTube.com* (Electronic Version). Retrieved December 3, 2009 from www.alexa.com/siteinfo/youtube.com

Bissell, K.L. & Duke, A.M. (2007). Bump, set, spike: An analysis of commentary and camera angles of women's beach volleyball during the 2004 summer Olympics. *Journal of Promotion Management, 13*(1/2), 35–53.

Boyd, D. & Ellison, N.B. (2007). Social network sites: Definition, history and scholarship. *Journal of Computer Mediated Communication, 1*, 210–30.

Carrigan, T., Connell, B., & Lee, J. (1985). Toward a new sociology of masculinity. *Theory & Society, 14*(5), 551–604.

Clasen, P.R.W. (2001). The female athlete: Dualisms and paradox in practice. *Women and Language, 24*(2), 7–13.

Coakley, J.J. (1998). *Sport in society: Issues and controversies*. New York: Irwin/McGraw-Hill.

Cohen, Jacob (1960). A coefficient of agreement for nominal scales. *Educational and Psychological Measurement, 20*, 37–46.

Connell, R.W. (2005). *Masculinities* (2nd Ed.). Berkeley and Los Angeles: University of California Press.

Cramer, J.A. (1994). Conversations with women journalists. In P.J. Creedon (Ed.), *Women, media, and sport: Challenging gender values* (pp. 159–80). Thousand Oaks, CA: Sage.

Dart, J.J. (2009). Blogging the 2006 FIFA World Cup finals. *Sociology of Sport Journal, 1*(29), 107–26.

Duncan, M.C. & Brummett, B. (1993). Liberal and radical sources of female empowerment in sport media. *Sociology of Sport Journal, 10*(1), 57–72.

Duncan, M.C. & Messner, M.A. (1998). The media image of sport and gender. In L.A. Wenner (Ed.), *MediaSport: Cultural sensibilities and sport in the media age* (pp. 170–85). London: Routledge.

Falkheim, J. (2008). Events framed by the mass media; Media coverage and effects of America's Cup preregatta in Sweden. *Event Management, 11*(1–2), 81–88.

Federation Internationale de Ski. (2005). *Promotion of female competitors.* Letter sent to all national ski associations from the Ladies' Alpine Sub-Committee, FIS. Oberhofen, Switzerland: Ladies' Alpine Sub-Committee, FIS.

Fink, J.S. & Kensicki, L.J. (2002). An imperceptible difference: Visual and textual constructions of femininity in *Sports Illustrated* and *Sports Illustrated for Women. Mass Communication and Society, 5,* 317–39.

Fortunato, J.A. (2001). The television framing methods of the national basketball association: An agenda-setting application. *Atlantic Journal of Communication, 9*(2), 166–81.

Foucault, M. (1971). Orders of discourse. *Social Science Information, 10*(2), 7–30.

Goffman, E. (1974). *Frame analysis: An essay on the organization of experience.* New York: Harper & Row.

Gramsci, A. (1971). *Selections from the prison notebooks.* New York: International Publishers.

Greenburg, J. & Hier, S. (2001). Crisis, mobilization, and collective problems: "Illegal" Chinese migrants and the Canadian news media. *Mediaweek,* 20–22.

Hardin, M., Chance, J., Dodd, J.E., & Hardin, B. (2002). Olympic photo coverage fair to female athletes. *Newspaper Research Journal, 23*(2/3), 64–79.

Hargreaves, J. (1994). *Sporting females: Critical issues in the history and sociology of women's sports.* London: Routledge.

Harris, J. & Clayton, B. (2002). Femininity, masculinity, physicality and the English tabloid press: The case of Anna Kournikova. *International Review for the Sociology of Sport, 37*(3–4), 397–413.

Hutchins, B., Rowe, D., & Ruddock, A. (2009). "It's fantasy football made real": Networked media sport, the Internet, and the hybrid reality of MyFootballClub. *Sociology of Sport Journal, 1*(26), 89–106.

Jaschik, S. (2007, June 12). NCAA vs. bloggers. Retrieved February 13, 2010 from www.insidehighered.com/news/2007/06/12/blogger

Jones, D. (2004). Half the story? Olympic women on ABC news online. *Media International Australia, 110,* 132–46.

Kane, H.D., Traub, G.E., & Hayes, B.G. (2000). Interactive media and its contribution to the constructive and destruction of values and character. *Journal of Humanistic Counseling, Education, and Development, 2,* 87–99.

Kane, M.J. (1988). Media coverage of the female athlete before, during, and after Title IX: *Sports Illustrated* revisited. *Journal of Sport Management, 2,* 58–65.

Kane, M.J. (1996). Media coverage of the post Title IX female athlete. *Duke Journal of Gender Law and Policy, 3,* 95–127.

Kane, M.J. (2007). Sociological aspects of sport. In J. Parks, J. Quarterman, & L. Thibault (Eds.), *Contemporary sport management* (3rd Ed.) (pp. 389–413). Champaign, IL: Human Kinetics.

Kane, M.J. & Greendorfer, S.L. (1994). The media's role in accommodating and resisting stereotyped images of women in sport. In P.J. Creedon (Ed.), *Women, media, and sport* (pp. 3–27). Thousand Oaks, CA: Sage.

Kane, M.J. & Lenskyj, H.J. (1998). Media treatment of female athletes: Issues in gender and sexualities. In L.A. Wenner (Ed.), *MediaSport* (pp. 186–201). New York: Routledge.

Kane, M.J. & Parks, J.B. (1992). The social construction of gender difference and hierarchy in sport journalism: Few new twists on very old themes. *Women in Sport and Physical Activity Journal, 1,* 49–83.

Kian, E.M., Mondello, M., & Vincent, J. (2009). ESPN – the women's sports network? A content analysis of Internet coverage of March Madness. *Journal of Broadcasting & Electronic Media, 53*(3), 477–95.

King, C. (2007). Media portrayals of male and female athletes: A text and picture analysis of British national newspaper coverage of the Olympic Games since 1948. *International Review for the Sociology of Sport, 42*(2), 187–99.

Kinnick, K.N. (1998). Gender bias in newspaper profiles of 1996 Olympic athletes: A content analysis of five major dailies. *Women's Studies in Communication, 21*(2), 212–37.

Koivula, N. (1999). Gender stereotyping in televised media sport coverage. *Sex Roles,* October, 589–610.

Lenskyj, H.J. (1986). *Out of bounds: Women, sport and sexuality.* Toronto: The Women's Press.

Lenskyj, H.J. (1992). Unsafe at home base: Women's experiences of sexual harassment in university sport and physical education. *Women in Sport and Physical Activity Journal, 1,* 19–33.

Lenskyj, H.J. (1994). Sexuality and femininity in sport contexts: Issues and alternatives. *Journal of Sport & Social Issues, 18*(4), 356–76.

Leonard, D.J. (2009). New media and global sporting cultures: Moving beyond the clichés and binaries. *Sociology of Sport Journal, 26,* 1–16.

Lumpkin, A. & Williams, L. (1991). Mass media influence on female high school athletes' identification with professional athletes. *International Journal of Sport Psychology, 18,* 231–36.

MacKay, S. & Dallaire, C. (2009). Campus newspaper coverage of varsity sports: Getting closer to equitable and sports-related representations of female athletes? *International Review for the Sociology of Sport, 44*(1), 25–40.

McCombs, M.E. & Shaw, D.L. (1972). The agenda-setting function of mass media. *Public Opinion Quarterly, 36,* 176–87.

McCombs, M.E. & Shaw, D.L. (1993). The evolution of agenda-setting research: Twenty-five years in the marketplace of ideas. *Journal of Communication, 43*(2), 58–67.

Messner, M.A. (1988). Sports and male domination: The female athletes as contested ideological terrain. *Sociology of Sport Journal, 5*(1), 197–211.

Newspaper sports staff continue to slight women in their coverage (1991, March/April). *Media Report to Women* (no byline), p. 3.

Oates, T.P. (2009). New media and the repackaging of NFL fandom. *Sociology of Sport Journal, 26*(1), 31–49.

O'Conner, R. (2009). Facebook and Twitter are reshaping journalism as we know it (Electronic Version). Retrieved November 25, 2009 from www.alternet.org/mediaculture/121211/facebook_and_twitter_are_reshaping_journalism_as_we_know_it/

Parker, H.M. & Fink, J.S. (2008). The effect of sport commentator framing on viewer attitudes. *Sex Roles, 58*(1–2), 116–26.

Pew (2009). Adults and social network websites (Electronic Version). Retrieved November 18, 2009 from www.pewinternet.org/Reports/2009/Adults-and-Social-Network-Websites. aspx?r=1

Pirinen, R.M. (1997). The construction of women's positions in sport: A textual analysis of articles on female athletes in Finnish women's magazines. *Sociology of Sport Journal, 14*(3), 290–301.

Real, M. (2006). Sports online: The newest player in mediasport. In A. Raney & J. Bryant (Eds.), *Handbook of sports and media* (pp. 171–84). Mahwah, NJ: Lawrence Erlbaum Associates.

Sabo, D. & Jansen, S.C. (1992). Images of men in sport media. In S. Craig (Ed.), *Men, masculinity and the media* (pp. 169–84). Thousand Oaks, CA: Sage.

Sagas, M., Cunningham, G.B., Wigely, B.J., & Ashley, F.B. (2000). Internet coverage of university softball and baseball websites: The inequity continues. *Sociology of Sport Journal, 17,* 198–205.

Sage, G.H. (1998). *Power and ideology in American sport: A critical perspective* (2nd Ed.). Champaign, IL: Human Kinetics.

Schell, L.S. & Rodriguez, S. (2000). Our sporting sisters: How male hegemony stratifies women in sport. *Women in Sport & Physical Activity Journal, 9*(1), 15–35.

Seltzer, T. & Mitrook, M. (2009). The role of expert opinion in framing media coverage of the Heisman Trophy race. *Journal of Sports Media, 4*(2), 1–29.

Tuggle, C.A. (1997). Differences in television sports reporting of men's and women's athletics: ESPN *SportsCenter* and CNN *Sports Tonight. Journal of Broadcasting & Electronic Media, 41*(1), 14–24.

Vincent, J., Imwold, C., Masemann, V., & Johnson, J.T. (2002). A comparison of selected "serious" and "popular" British, Canadian, and United States newspaper coverage of female and male athletes competing in the Centennial Olympic Games. *International Review for the Sociology of Sport, 37*(3–4), 319–35.

Williams, E. (2009). A conversation with Evan Williams. Retrieved March 1, 2010 from www.youtube.com/watch?v=p5jXcgZnEa0& fmt=18

Willis, P. (1982). Women in sport and ideology. In J. Hargreaves (Ed.), *Sport, culture, and ideology* (pp. 117–35). London: Routledge & Kegan Paul.

Wright, J. & Clarke, G. (1999). Sport, the media and the construction of compulsory heterosexuality: A case study of women's rugby union. *International Review for the Sociology of Sport, 34*(3), 227–43.

Yu, C.C. (2009). A content analysis of news coverage of Asian female Olympic athletes. *International Review for the Sociology of Sport, 44*(2–3), 283–305.

10

SPORT, IDENTITIES, AND CONSUMPTION

The construction of sport at ESPN.com

Lindsey J. Meân

ARIZONA STATE UNIVERSITY

As witnessed in previous chapters of this book, sport is a key site for the re/production of culture and associated ideological forms and practices, notably as a major site for identities and as a demarcating force for gender and sexuality (Duncan & Messner, 1998; Vertinsky, 2006). However, sport has also become a prominent component of the media, another highly influential cultural form. Indeed, sport in the media has experienced enormous growth over the last two decades, rendering the cultural impact of these combined forces highly significant. As such, the unprecedented socio-cultural influence of the relationship between sport, culture, and media has been widely acknowledged and referred to as "the unruly trinity" by Rowe (2004).

Nonetheless, a consequence of this relationship has been that sport has also become mediatized, meaning it has effectively become part of media culture (Hutchins, Rowe, & Ruddock, 2009). Indeed, the intersection of sport and media has become so blurred that we should now conceptualize "sport as media" (Hutchins et al., 2009, p. 89) or *MediaSport* (Wenner, 1998). Consequently, media-sport itself has become a site of ideological significance as a powerful re/producer[1] of cultural meanings and forms and entrenched as a valued intertextual referent within what Wernick (1991) describes as promotional culture (Meân, Kassing, & Sanderson, 2010).

Consumption of mediasport is highly relevant for the performance of identities (Horne, 2006) – a reflection of sports prominence as a site for male identity construction (Messner, 1988). The shared distinctiveness provided by mediasport consumption and its practices, knowledge, understandings, etc. (Mehus, 2005) is therefore linked to *habitus* (Bourdieu, 1978), *imagined communities* (Anderson, 1991), and *interpretive communities* (Lindlof, 1988). Yet, potentially different impacts and influences are likely given differences across how mediasport forms are consumed (Mehus, 2005); although the increasing move towards integrated marketing means that the same self-referential narrative (Jansson, 2002) will be consumed across related mediasport.

Digital mediasport

The substantive growth of new media and the proliferation of sport in digital spaces have added a level of complexity to the discussion of mediasport. Questioning the distinction between old and new media forms, Leonard (2009) notes new media are not disruptive or contesting of contemporary sport, and that the established mediasport have "interfaced" with new media (p. 4). Consequently, the traditional, dominant sport narratives of white, male, heterosexual supremacy have continued to be re/produced in mainstream new digital mediasport (Dart, 2009; Meân, 2010; Oates, 2009).

The dominance of the traditional mediasport institutions (e.g., ESPN) in the new media landscape is evident in their large audience numbers compared to alternate forms (Dart, 2009). This potentially arises from their position as sites of authority and familiarity, but it is also significant *because* of this authority over sport as a category. ESPN.com is the foremost new mediasport site, consistently noted to reach the largest audiences (ESPN Fact Sheet, 2010), including the typically elusive 18–34-year-old men (Lowry, 2005). At a broader level, ESPN is lauded as the most successful sports enterprise in the world (Pérez-Peña, 2007), although its dominance in other countries remains speculative. Nonetheless, ESPN.com and its affiliates (e.g., ESPN television channels, *ESPN The Magazine*) consistently have the biggest audience of any U.S. mediasport site, where its main focus continues to be American sports for American audiences – a powerful, authoritative position given that identities are prominently linked to sport and the consumption of mediasport.

Categories and identities

The significance of sporting identities (Messner, 1988) and their emotional connection to sporting discourses (Meân, 2001, 2010; Oates, 2009) has been observed to render sports audiences especially vulnerable to the meanings in mediasport (Scherer, 2007; Wenner, 1991, 1993). This arises because the consumption of sport, mediasport, and related merchandising and activities *is* part of identity performance (Rowe, 2004; Walsh & Giulianotti, 2001). Thus, vulnerability manifests as being highly subject to the influence and collaborative co-construction of shared meanings and understandings (with mediasport as well as other significant category members). Consequently, the dominant constructions, narratives, and shared understandings (i.e., discourses) re/produced within the persuasive context of new mediasport become of particular concern given the vulnerable interpretive communities of sport (Meân, 2010; Scherer, 2007; Wenner, 1991, 1993).

Digital mediasport provide a site through which new or re-invented imagined or interpretive communities can arise that reflect lifestyles and interests (Crawford,

2004), but communities and identities can also remain embedded within traditional forms and "expert" texts. This renders the intersection of sporting identities, mediasport consumption, and the discursive meanings of old media in new digital forms highly relevant for continued and consistent scrutiny. Accordingly, this chapter will provide an analysis of the discourses re/produced within the re/presentational content and practices at ESPN.com, focusing on the ways in which these serve to construct sport and sports fandom (consumers) for a vulnerable interpretive community. However, to frame this analysis better, the key concepts and processes outlined above are first considered in more detail.

Mediasport, identities and consumption

The power of mediasport arises, in part, from the manner in which it is consumed by audiences as a function of identities (Scherer, 2007; Walsh & Giulianotti, 2001; Wenner, 1991) within a cyclical process that links emotions, identities, discourses, and ideologies (Meân, 2001, 2009, 2010; Meân & Kassing, 2008; Oates, 2009). However, while this re/produces particular definitions and understandings (hence power relations) these are not fixed but actively constructed to maintain the status quo and resist change (Foucault, 1972). Identities therefore render individuals motivated to re/produce the shared definitions and categories of the discourses from which their identities arise (Meân, 2001, 2003; Meân & Kassing, 2008); an impetus that manifests as collaboration or resistance to authoritative or powerful discourses and definitions re/produced within authoritative texts, sites, etc. Consequently, the narrowing of sporting discourses available in digital space means the re/presentation of fewer and less varied definitions and identities (Dart, 2009) with the integration of old and new mediasport into increasingly cross-referenced and self-referential integrated media narratives (Jansson, 2002).

Digital mediasport and interpretive communities

Mediasport in digital space is prolific, making it a significant site for sport consumption as identity while its accessibility and availability (at least to consumers with constant high-speed internet access) also renders it ideal for both casual and serious sports consumers (Real, 2006). But the persuasive elements of digital media make it a site of critical concern. Digital media provide many of the persuasive characteristics of television, providing access to video as "live" coverage or news that has been edited into spectacular visuals and compelling narratives (Sullivan, 2006). Yet, in contrast to television, it enables a detailed, complex narrative more typical of print media. Content is also apparently consumed self-selectively and not subject to scheduling, enacting a problematic illusion of active participation and democracy since digital sites are actually packaged and designed to guide consumption (Graham & Hearn, 2001). As a result the influence of moderators and journalistic content remains obscured (Dart, 2009).

Combined, these features render digital sites highly persuasive, especially for sports audiences – or interpretive communities – given their potential vulnerability and susceptibility to the meaning-making and persuasive content of such sites (Scherer, 2007; Wenner, 1991, 1993). Interpretive communities are audiences sharing an identity constructed through the consumption of particular texts, which renders them also motivated to *read* (e.g., understand and make meanings) in ways that collaborate with the discourses and discursive practices re/produced despite the availability of multiple readings.

New mediasport encompasses a variety of media sites characterized as (pre-dominantly) digitized and interactionally dynamic, such as internet sites for sports news (e.g., ESPN.com, sportsbusinessdaily.com) and sport organizations (e.g., NFL.com), games (e.g., Madden NFL) and fantasy leagues. However, new mediasport also comprise prime sites for *enhanced* shared narratives, meanings, branding and platform-jumping (Oates, 2009) as consumers are cross-referred to multiple sites to consume related texts and meanings (Jansson, 2002). This is especially relevant assuming sport audiences are highly likely to collaborate with these narratives and meaning-making – especially of authoritative mediasport texts – since misinterpretation or failure to collaborate risks exclusion from the category (Meân, 2001; Potter, 1996). Further, mediasport features powerful aids to assist and guide shared under-standings and meaning-making (Wenner, 1991, 1993), effectively disciplining or gatekeeping the category (Foucault, 1977; Gumperz, 1982). These concerns become increasingly relevant with moves towards greater integration of promotional content, notably advertising, into the main narratives of digital mediasport; a practice that led ESPN.com's recent redesign to enable more "special" advertisement integration (Klaassen, 2009).

Constructing sport at ESPN.com

The *meanings* of sport have wide social and cultural significance, and the prevalence of new mediasport as a key site for the re/production of these meanings warrants a continued focus on the discursive and rhetorical content of authoritative or dominant digital sites (Leonard, 2009). Thus ESPN.com's content and practices are of interest as an established, wider integrated mediasport narrative that con-sistently draws the largest audiences of U.S. digital mediasport (ESPN Fact Sheet, 2010; Lowry, 2005), rendering it an authoritative, gatekeeping mediasport text. Equally, its dominant audience of younger males (median age 31.8, McDavid, 2008) and growing audiences (ESPN Fact Sheet, 2010), alongside the characteristics that render digital media highly persuasive, make the continued scrutiny of ESPN's sporting definitions and practices particularly relevant. But ESPN is also an authoritative sport text that is familiar to non-sporting communities, hence it is also likely to be used by casual visitors, alongside sports fans and *fanatics* (Real, 2006), rendering its re/presentational practices persuasive to a wide range of interpretive communities.

Since re/presentational practices serve to re/produce discourses in invisibly persuasive ways, the analysis reported focused on the definitions and sport category membership (notably authority and expertise) enacted at ESPN.com. A significant part of the discursive construction of meaning involves who and what is normatively framed as *the category* within routine and everyday re/presentational practices. Thus, who and what comprised sport, and how it was constructed as a site for consumption, were important aspects for analyzing the re/production of sport as a category at ESPN.com. Central membership (as opposed to peripheral members or excluded groups) is significant for understanding how category definitions, meanings, and memberships are enacted, and even deployed as a right (given dominant discourses, such as sport as male category, Meân, 2001). Consequently, while central members still have to work to maintain their position, they also have greater power to define, given their category entitlements such as knowledge, expertise, etc.

Since sport is consistently re/produced as a predominantly white male heterosexual category, gendered constructions were a specific focus of the analysis. But analysis also focused on the wider construction of sport as a category, of ESPN as a category member, and on the discursive construction of audience as members, participants and guided consumers, given that sport audiences are likely to be highly subject to the meanings and the disciplinary actions of identity performance and category membership constructed at ESPN.com.

This analysis of ESPN.com occurred during football season. In America, football is viewed as having a unique prominence in the U.S. mediasport marketplace (Oates, 2009), as opposed to the predominance of soccer elsewhere in the world. Thus "American" football (as it is widely known outside the U.S.) is a premium and defining sport within the U.S., constructing it as a central member and organizing force within American sport and wider U.S. culture – making its re/presentation highly relevant for study. However, football is also noted to re/produce traditional power relations, meaning the selection of football season may seem to load the dice in favor of findings that will find the predominance of an uncontested form of white hyper/masculinity.

But, the *big four* sports within the US are all noted to re/produce these traditional forms. And selecting a period that focused on a more gender balanced sport event like the Winter Olympics (Billings, 2008) would be to select for an exceptional, intermittent mega-mediasport event. As such, rather than exceptionality, ESPN. com during football season could be viewed as a routine and ordinary mediasport text alongside which all other sports and athletes are routinely positioned, making it relevant for the study of everyday constructions (Potter, 1996). Equally, as a dominant category, it seems relevant to study how and if football is constructed as lifestyle for consumption as identity. Yet, it should be noted that football as *the* sport is not *natural*, but a cultural definition and category that has to be continually re/produced to maintain its status and category membership. As such, a lack of change (like shift in meanings and practices) is actively achieved, part of a cyclical process since category definitions have to be re/produced to stay the same.

Method

Critical discourse analysis (CDA) with an emphasis on discursive and rhetorical analysis (Potter, 1996) was used to explore category construction and re/presentational practices at ESPN.com. The analytical process followed ESPN.com from an audience-position, giving attention to the re/presentational features and practices that guided consumption and signified main content (such as premium positioning, size, hyperlinks, and other production techniques on the homepage) alongside primacy in terms of Western reading patterns. While this privileged the analysis of articles and texts symbolically prioritized by ESPN.com, this was appropriate since ESPN.com enacted them as key category interests which, in turn, framed their content as significant for consumption (hence identity performance) and meaning-making.

Text sampling: visiting ESPN.com

ESPN.com was selected for analysis given its centrality and familiarity as a dominant U.S. mediasport site. The analysis period was November 23 to December 2, 2009, providing a limited but relevant sample. ESPN.com was visited and content recorded at random times that reflected researcher availability to visit the site over the course of the 10 days, potentially matching wider audience strategies of convenience sampling.

Analysis and discussion

Since category construction is a process that is continual and recurrent, elements of this arise throughout the analysis. Thus, the initial analysis and discussion focuses on the construction of ESPN.com and the category of sport, followed by more detailed analysis of the discursive practices that construct and manage expertise, consumption, and membership (of ESPN.com and the sport category). The final section then addresses the construction of sport as lifestyle at ESPN.com.

Re/producing ESPN and sport as a category

News and main features

The banner statement "ESPN: the worldwide leader in sports" at the top of the homepage positioned ESPN as a global mediasport power, hence a central authority for sport, framing ESPN as possessing a global audience. However, ESPN.com predominantly re/presented U.S.-oriented or -focused sports. The homepage main stories and dominant visual images that occupied the prime position: (American) football, men's basketball, and NASCAR (seasonality is addressed shortly below). Golf was featured inconsistently, although its inclusion concerned Tiger Woods and his domestic life, suggesting this was more about celebrity than golf and for the general reader rather than golf fans per se. Over the time sampled, ESPN.com constructed the main sport news and current events within a narrow range of uniquely U.S. sports or domestically focused events, re/producing sport as American (despite its global claims). Equally, ESPN's self-framing as the "world leader" intertextually positioned U.S. sport as worldwide and leading the sports world, mobilizing discourses of American exceptionalism and global significance. Together, this re/produced ESPN as the dominant (global) mediasport authority and American sport as *the* central category member.

While men's football and basketball were re/produced as the dominant sports, receiving much more substantive main page coverage than all the other sports, the images of football dominated physically and numerically – positioning football as the dominant, central sport and thus as *the* American sport. This effectively rendered other sports as peripheral category members, while simultaneously re/producing (these) U.S. sports as central category members. Of course, this emphasis may be considered merely seasonal – an argument potentially supported by the absence of the key American sport of baseball (MLB) – and as reflective of sport audience interests. In fact, the major U.S. team sports are now considered effectively 12-month media events, since out-of-season action has become an increasingly significant part of promotional circuits and fan consumption. This can be seen in the 62% increase in NFL draft viewing between 2002 and 2008 (Gorman, 2009), with an audience of over 5 million for ESPN's 2009 draft coverage (Friedman, 2009) and live streaming of the draft at NFL.com. As such, the MLB was represented as off-season gossip (see below), a commonly acknowledged strategy in mediasport to maintain interest and consumer participation out of season. But more relevant to this issue was the consistent absence of other seasonal sports, including women's basketball (WNBA) and soccer (MLS), a notable absence in the months building up to FIFA's 2010 World Cup tournament.[2] Thus, to account for this dominance as seasonal vagaries is to discount the in-season sports rendered invisible by these practices. Equally, to suggest that it merely reflected audience interests and demand ignores sport audience building and maintenance strategies (Duncan & Messner, 1998) and agenda setting capabilities (Billings, 2008).

The exclusivity of men's and male sex-typed sports as main news and the absence of women's versions (e.g. WNBA) re/produced men and men's sport as central members of the category. In fact, the predominant exclusion of women athletes on the homepage, and the absence of hyperlinks for and to women's sports, further re/produced sport as a male category, effectively rendering women invisible and excluded from the category. These exclusions re/produced wider, dominant mediasport representational practices that consistently exclude or peripheralize women (Hardin, 2005; Kane & Lenskyj, 1998; Meân, 2010). For example, on one day the *last* amongst ten "HEADLINES" (stories/links provided without photographs) comprised one of the few main articles concerning women's sport, listed below with the other "headlines" (spelling as in original, camera symbol indicated link to accompanying video):

- Irish QB Clausen punched by irate fan
- Bills reach out to Cowher, who declines
- 49ers drop tampering charges vs. Jets
- Mauer almost unanimous choice as AL MVP
- Purdue edges Tennessee for Paradise Jam title
- Gators' Meyer says Notre Dame not in plans
- Chargers' Cromartie under police investigation
- UNC falls to No. 12 in men's hoops poll
- Rodriguez's job at Michigan likely safe for now
- LPGA's Ochoa top player for fourth straight year.

Of course, it is easy to speculate on the positioning of such an achievement if she was the top PGA player for the fourth year. However, it is the possessive linguistic framing across the ten headlines that is worthy of attention. Ochoa is one of three athletes positioned as a possessive (Gators' Meyer and Chargers' Cromartie are the others). But while it is a discursively normative or familiar practice to position athletes as team members (as for Meyer and Cromartie), this practice does not extend to positioning *athletes* as belonging to regulating institutions. Positioning Ochoa as belonging to the LPGA arguably frames her as an object; the forefronting of LPGA could also be seen as a strategy to manage a lack of (consumer) familiarity with women golf players, arguably a consequence of lack of regular media coverage. Regardless, it is hard to conceive of any top male golf player being headlined as, for example, PGA's Tiger Woods.

The comparative absence of women also contrasted with the meaning-making discursive action of the visual images (photographs or videos) accompanying the main news: men's football and basketball. These images typically comprised athletes in aggressive, combative, and athletic action (rarely just standing). For example, the hard-hitting, "bodies as weapons" framing of mens' sports (Jansen & Sabo, 1994) was evident in a number of football images produced on one day: (a) a close-up of four NFL players in a head-on collision emphasized aggressive physical action; (b) three football players in the air to catch a ball emphasized competitive action, the low camera position enacted their athleticism (to jump so high) and framed their superiority (Goffman, 1976); (c) one player (with the ball) heading straight towards the camera closely pursued by two players emphasized the aggressive, competitive pursuit. Similarly, broadly two forms of action shot dominated the images of men's basketball: one athlete out-jumping other athletes while in the action of scoring; one or more athletes on the floor after being subject to physically aggressive action.

As a whole, the images of aggressive physical action served to re/produce men's basketball and football as sports of consistent and continued spectacular and competitive action, positioning the male athletes within traditional and hypermasculine sporting discourses by intertextually mobilizing discourses of war, weapons, and sanctioned competitive aggression. Of course, once again the argument that fans want to see such action is valid. However, the consistent framing of male sport in these active and spectacular ways contrasts with the re/presentation of women's sports. If it was merely about deploying the usual, spectacular sporting re/presentational practices, we would expect no differences between gendered forms (i.e., women's sports would also be "packaged" as action). As such, ESPN.com re/produced wider gendered practices of mediasport production that serve to re/produce sports as hypermasculine. Given the links between sport discourses, identities and ideologies (Meân, 2001, 2003, 2010) this can be seen as part of the self-referential and self-confirming re/production of identities by the (predominantly) male producers of mediasport (Hardin, 2005).

Other images accompanying the main stories on this day showed a male coach (talking), a male NASCAR driver (in uniform but not in action), a close-up head-shot of Tiger Woods (male), and an image that was a composition of an Iverson headshot (male) and a 76ers symbol. The Woods and Iverson stories were not concerned with actual games or events (i.e., not recap stories), but were commentary and analysis stories concerning Tiger Woods' personal life and whether Iverson could help his team ("Can A.I. help 76ers? Our experts debate"). Addressing Iverson as "A.I." suggested consumers knew to whom/what A.I. referred; an assumption, in the invitational form of a question, that served to discursively work up the *shared* category membership of ESPN.com (as authorial voice) and the consumer, while simultaneously positioning ESPN.com as having the "experts" to answer the question; i.e., to inform the already knowledgeable consumer.

Menus and peripheral articles

Menus serve a significant meaning-making and guidance function, strategically demarcating the significant forms of interests and knowledge (i.e., sub-categories, topics, etc.) and providing the navigational links for consumers to enact this entitlement. At ESPN.com's homepage, the main menu (across the top) and the "Scoreboard" menu (above the main menu but in smaller format denoting lesser significance) further framed the category's central sports and organizations. The "Full scoreboard" selection of "NFL," "NBA," "NHL," "NASCAR," and "All scores" worked (in conjunction with the central membership re/presented in the main stories) to further re/produce American sport and fan interests as football, basketball, hockey, and NASCAR. This positioned these as *the* content for audience consumption – disciplining sports identities and audience interests. Given the season, baseball was missing, but the MLB was evident in the off-season gossip (see below), and the mainstreaming success of NASCAR (and the shift to a "Big 5"[3]) was apparent in its routine inclusion as a central category member. Thus, the "Full scoreboard" continued to construct central membership as a narrow range of (male) American sports using language that framed the category as complete ("full").

In contrast, the main menu items were not linked to specific sports, instead re/producing traditional referents and newer lifestyle elements: "ALL SPORTS,"

"COMMENTARY," "PAGE 2," "FANTASY," "VIDEO," "SPORTSNATION," "CITIES," "THE LIFE." The mediatization and integrated nature of mediasport were embedded in these options, such as intertextual connections to traditional mediasport formats (e.g. Page 2) and newer forms of sports consumption, such as "Fantasy" sports leagues, as nation (imagined community of Sportsnation), and as lifestyle (e.g. sport as travel in The Life). The direct link to "Video" provided the spectacular and edited narratives of televisual action (without being subject to schedules). These rendered ESPN.com as a site at which a range of central features could be consumed as identity, whilst simultaneously constructing these activities as appropriate consumption for category membership. The construction and maintenance of the central narratives of category membership and identity performance re/produced at ESPN.com is significant, given the vulnerability of audiences to these definitions. Therefore, of particular interest in this menu were items that comprised the more recent manifestations of identities and fandom as imagined communities, consumption, and lifestyle – elements discussed in more detail later.

Experts, insiders, and guiding consumption

An integrated, interlinked self-referential narrative across ESPN as a wider text was explicitly part of the action at ESPN.com. Many articles were from or cross-referenced other ESPN sites (i.e., platform-jumping), and contributing journalists were often noted as staff at other ESPN sites (such as *ESPN The Magazine*, ESPN TrueHoops; see "Expert roundtable" below). This platform-jumping and explicit referencing of other established mediasport alongside a repeated self-referential narrative of sporting *expertise*, such as consistently referring to its staff as "experts" rather than journalists, reporters or writers, re/produced ESPN as *the* sporting authority. The explicit acknowledgement of content from other ESPN sources framed ESPN.com as offering more than merely a website, and as part of a larger team or franchise; mobilizing corporate discourses that appear widely accepted and routine in America as offering (benevolent) stability, authority, and power rather than problematic uniformity and self-referentiality. Indeed ESPN's strategy is to develop integrated marketing (evident in dedicated employee positions) and representation as a "truly multimedia package" (Binder, VP of Ad Sales at *ESPN the Magazine* quoted in McDavid, 2008).

Thus, appropriately, a menu provided explicit links to other ESPN products: "TV," "RADIO," "MAGAZINE," "INSIDER," "SHOP," "ESPN360," "SC" (SportsCenter). These links were repeated as small feeder articles (e.g., small image and tag line links) lower on the homepage. This effectively guided audience consumption via repetition, providing multiple opportunities or points at which to consume the same features, yet providing the illusion of choice and variety. Positioned as part of the main menu, the "Insider" was also linked through a small, detailed article. The term "Insider" mobilized desirable discourses of inner circle or in-group membership with entitlement to privileged information and status, enacted further by the subscription required to be an "insider." This was symbolically emphasized through visually contrasting "in" as white lettering with "sider" as grey, both on an orange background. Insider status was further enacted by language and topic choices that *worked up* the entitlement via detailed, informal, and trivializing style and content. Together these intertextually referenced gossip (as a genre increasingly familiar in mediasport), which traditionally comes from somebody placed centrally inside the category with key knowledge entitlement. Given ESPN's focus on cross-promotion, it is also worth noting that the "Insider" subscription includes a free *ESPN The Magazine* subscription.

The "Insider" feeder article referenced three stories: "Puck prospectus" (adding "Sid the Kid actually *hurts* the Penguins" [emphasis in original]); "MLB rumors"; and "Football outsiders." The language choices inferred facts ("actually") while using a nickname ("Sid the Kid") enacted familiarity with the category (insider status) and the consumer (shared knowledge and participation). Italicization emphasized and mimicked actual talk and tabloid genre, while also emphasizing the action (*"hurts"*). Similarly, the language choice "Rumors" suggested insider status and ironically worked up the *facticity* of the rumors without claim to facts, framing the information as (generally) reliable. "Football outsiders" explicitly contrasted with "insider" mobilizing discourses of exclusion and lower status to make insider status more desirable. Notably deployed in relation to football (during season), this becomes a provocative enticement to consumers, given the centrality of football and the significance of information or knowledge for sport identities.

"Insider" gossip further framed ESPN.com as having insider, and hence core, membership of the category, further working up its significance as a site of authority. Continual effort to re/produce as central and insider status is important, because power, status and definitions need to be maintained and disciplined (Foucault, 1972, 1977) and because it confers the entitlement to unquestioned, reliable knowledge (Potter, 1996); in real terms this links to the effective maintenance of market share and audience loyalty as *the* authoritative text. Thus ESPN.com can be seen to work up central category membership by explicitly demonstrated insider knowledge, while having insider knowledge simultaneously worked up its central membership. This was complemented by its other authoritative voices and explicitly acclaimed "experts" personified as ESPN's individualized journalists and commentators. Typically identified as "our experts," the deployment of "our" served to link them and their expertise to ESPN while also personalizing it. "Our experts debate" alongside the invitation to contribute suggested active participation and on-going debate, discursively positioning ESPN in a collaborative interaction with the consumer. However, these were not "live" debates but expert views on which consumers could comment. As such they enacted illusory, not actual, participation (Dart, 2009; Graham & Hearn, 2001).

The "experts" were typically linked to a specific ESPN product (or platform) and occasionally represented by a photograph, which revealed these experts to be (white) men. The re/production of expertise and knowledge as predominantly male and achievable solely through ESPN was also evident in the "Expert roundtable"

(December 2nd), which comprised: Henry Abbott, ESPN TrueHoop; J.A. Adande, ESPN.com; Chris Broussard, *ESPN The Magazine*; John Hollinger, ESPN.com; Chris Sheridan, ESPN.com; Marc Stein, ESPN.com. This rendered invisible the need for alternative narratives and positions on sport from outside ESPN, sustaining its framing of itself as the expert through a self-referential narrative that promoted ESPN as an integrated, authoritative text. The cross-referentiality also enabled the deployment of an apparent specialism by the inclusion of an expert from ESPN TrueHoops, a further enactment of expertise and provision for the *true* fan of basketball. Overall, the selection of the panel re/produced ESPN, sporting expertise and central category membership as male.

However, consumers were explicitly invited to participate by adding their own (electronic) comments, despite the lack of on-going interactivity. This served to enact consumers as part of the debate, framing them as expert and central to the category, while also enabling consumers to perform their expertise and membership as part of the expert panel. This illusion of participatory democracy was further mobilized through the common deployment of the legendary and heroic intertextual reference of the (Arthurian) roundtable as a site of integrity and equality, where no-one sits at the head. The forefronting of the experts' version on which the consumer could comment sat in contrast to this rhetorical claim. Nonetheless, the invitation to participate and the discursive appearance of interest and value in sharing the consumer's knowledge allowed consumers to explicitly perform their identity and entitlement to knowledge. Such participatory enactments discursively framed the consumer as a valued expert contributor. While this was achieved collaboratively, the collaboration was in one direction since consumers have to collaborate with ESPN.com (and any inappropriate posting can be removed). This makes the actual collaborative *production* of sports knowledge illusionary and ESPN.com's re/production as the authority effectively unchallengeable.

Beyond the homepage, the dominance of white, male expertise and commentary was apparent; effectively ESPN.com re/produced masculinity as central in the sport category, and central to ESPN.com. This is significant given ESPN.com's consistent self-referential narrative of its central membership and authority as an expert site and its vulnerable audience, notably of young males. Of course, there may have been female "experts" or journalists contributing to ESPN.com, but they were not explicitly re/presented. Since the white male dominance of sport production and journalism has been noted as problematic and the industry charged with increasing diversity (Hardin, 2005) the absence and apparent exclusion of women as experts or athletes remains problematic. Indeed, the uncritical re/presentational deployment of male dominance is indicative of a continued comfort with this perceived privilege and a failure to actively re/present alternative versions.

Lifestyle and rituals

As noted earlier, menus provide significant demarcations and guidance, and the main menu at ESPN.com framed a number of options as central to the category that reflected an integration of newer lifestyle with traditional sport rituals and practices. The deployment of imagined communities as nation through ESPN's "SportSNation" framed consumers as part of a large shared community. This also mobilized multiple familiar discourses deploying category knowledge (entitlements) and intertextual links to powerful fan communities denoted as *nation* (e.g. RedSox Nation) and the American nation. As such, this symbolized category membership characterized by the core values and practices of sports fandom in America.

While this simultaneously re/produced the U.S. (and U.S. sports) as *the* sporting nation and as ESPN.com (thus its consumers), it also constructed consumers as an interpretive community served by or functioning through ESPN's SportSNation (and "Insider"); i.e., re/produced shared values and interests fulfillable at ESPN. com, since they were discursively constructed by ESPN.com. Consistent invitations to join and make ESPN specific to you (MyESPN; MyNews, etc.) promoted the desirability of participation, enabling personalization that furthers the illusion of unique, personal consumption and participation; framing it as appropriate for identity performance and building a relationship with, and as part of, ESPN. (Indeed, increased personalization is an explicit marketing strategy for ESPN.com; ESPN Fact Sheet, 2010).

Similarly, "THE LIFE" intertextually mobilized a plethora of discourses, values and practices into action, immediately referencing idiomatic and iconic cultural references that suggest *the life* to be desirable. As such, "this sporting life" or "living the life" (of Riley, a true path or calling, the high life, etc.) mobilized a number of powerful discourses and values familiar in sport such as: dedication, fulfillment, happiness, luck, and/or religious faith (Butterworth, 2008; Meân & Kassing, 2008). In fact, Steven Binder, *ESPN The Magazine* Ad Sales VP, attributed its success in part to the equivalence of sport to religion for fans (McDavid, 2008). Thus, in the context ESPN's life is enacted as *the life*, making it achievable through consumption of/at ESPN.com. And, given the propensity of sport's consumers to collaborate with the meanings re/produced in (authoritative) sports texts, it could be assumed that this form would be seen as a desirous and positive life.

Through consistent links and central positioning, "FANTASY" framed participation in fantasy sports leagues as central to identity performance; arguably reflecting the popularity of these forms of consumption and ESPN's product involvement. The central positioning of "Fantasy" is also interesting given Oates' (2009) recent observation of ESPN's fantasy spaces as providing opportunities for platform-jumping, normalizing of corporate discourses, and gaining increased loyalty from fans. Equally, the centrality of "SHOP" as an explicit consumption activity linked to sport fandom is redolent of the newer lifestyle forms of commodification and identity performance. Such forms increasingly position sport as subject to inter-textual marketing strategies as fans become increasingly commodified and self-commodify as sites of/for consumption (Scherer, 2007; Walsh & Giulianotti, 2001). Indeed, a homepage feeder article entitled "Action sports" was accompanied by an image of men's fashion attire, not sports clothing, alongside the text "With so many action-sports brands stepping up, Black Friday may actually be appealing." This suggested shopping as appealing for men if connected to sport (even tenuously), framing sports fans as consumers of any and all sports related objects, effectively re/ producing an integrated identity narrative of sports fans that moves beyond team shirts and into a wider lifestyle of sport-related consumption.

The mobilization of stereotypically gendered shopping discourses by the connection of men's clothing to claims of shopping as unappealing unless sport-related in turn re/produced traditional gendered sport discourses by framing ESPN.com's and (hence) sports consumers as male. This further compounded the lack of women athletes and experts at ESPN.com. Equally, the additional female presence observed at ESPN.com conformed to traditionally commodified gendered framings. This was evident in a homepage feeder article for the "ESPN North Shore survival guide." The phrase "survival guide" intertextually referenced various genres and discourses linked to leisure, vacations, and extreme life or lifestyle events. The feeder included two images which, taking a left-to-right Western reading position, comprised: (a) a white woman lying on the beach in a bikini, wearing a baseball hat and earphones; (b) a surfer on large wave (too small to ascertain gender).

Consequently, while the consumer could interpret the woman as a surfer, she was not in *uniform* for competitive action. While it is possible that the woman was also shown in the action of surfing (small image), the first, predominant image was of her in a bikini and positioned for consumption as a sexual object and iconic (beach) lifestyle referent. Equally, the passivity of the primary image, alongside the anonymity of the second, provided no substantive basis for any connection between her and the surfer. As the only female image on the homepage at that time, ESPN.com can be seen as deploying the familiar discursive re/presentational practices (as passive and out of uniform) that frame women primarily for sexual, rather than athletic, consumption (Berger, 1972). Of course, being in uniform and in the semblance of an action-pose does not guarantee a lack of sexualization and, hence, trivialization.[4]

Further exploration of the linked "Survival guide" webpage (initially an attempt to establish the surfer's identity) revealed minimal written content and central visual images. The visuals comprised (clockwise from top left reflecting Western reading pattern): (a) a white male surfer on large wave; (b) national flags and a billboard with the Reef[5] logo; (c) two white guys (young and "surfer-ish") in a kitchen with coffee/tea mugs; (d) a surfer (gender unclear) on large wave. The linguistic choices ("survival guide") and visual images (kitchen scene, logos) constructed a narrative that framed surfing and surf consumption as lifestyle, rather than as a competitive athletic event. Integrating explicit corporate consumption through the inclusion of the Reef logo, arguably enacted as the world's brand via the multinational flags. The inclusion of the two white men (the experts perhaps) further framed it as white, male activity commodified for consumption by ESPN.com. The survival guide motif also functioned to construct ESPN.com as the expert (having the experts) on surf as a sport and a lifestyle, to guide the newer and older ESPN.com interpretive communities for surfing.

Other homepage links also connected to articles that framed sport fandom as *lifestyle* and, as a significant aspect of this, *rituals*. On December 3, "Building perfection rituals" linked to the ESPN.com travel index page (sports.espn-go.com/travel/index). This section effectively functioned to promote sport as the focus for travel and leisure, further enacting sport as lifestyle and explicitly promoting ritual as ideal or perfect fandom. Thus the increasingly familiar interlinking of sport and religion (Butterworth, 2008) was apparent at ESPN.com's travel and lifestyle pages. Consistent references to pilgrimages ("Rocky Top pilgrimage"), rituals ("Building perfection," "Best rituals," "Top traditions"), rivalry ("Rivalry week," "Revel in rivalry") effectively framed stadia as positive ("best," "top") sites for pilgrimage, hence as sites of epic glory, power and near-religious significance. The deployment of rituals and perfection framed the ritualistic and ritual-laden entitlements of sport as sacred and admirable, intertextually mobilizing familiar religious discourses, working up and normalizing the centrality of and loyalty to sport as a core way of life.

This pastiche of sports fandom also took other aspects of traditional sport performance reframing and integrating with the newer forms, such as travel and cultural tourism. Thus, tailgating was re/packaged together with visiting stadiums and interesting cities ("CITIES") where sports consumers should see the "sights" (e.g., cheerleaders, stadium) and participate in other cultural activities. This was evident in "Taste of town" by the "Food Guy" which was accompanied by images of Todd Blackledge in a local restaurant, describing him as "more than a college football analyst." This expanded the *expert* category at ESPN.com beyond sport to a wider definition of sporting lifestyle. Similarly, the "Road Warrior" and "Art of the pregame party" deployed familiar intertextual cultural references (to the hypermasculine character from the *Mad Max* films and the famous *Art of War*) and sporting discourses (of war, warriors, etc.) that effectively re/produced traveling to sport events and tailgating as hypermasculine sport lifestyle choices.

"Building perfection" linked to a series of sights and experiences framed as ideal cultural sporting achievements dominated by a large photograph of the University of Southern California Song Girls (band in background) captioned "The USC Song Girls give Trojans games one of college football's most indelible sights." Similarly, other smaller images included: Dallas Cowboys cheerleaders (in front of their stadium – the actual topic); a male fan barbecuing accompanied by a passively standing female fan. Together, these framed a narrative of desirable American sporting sights that the sport tourist or pilgrim should aspire to experience. However, these also framed women as part of the sights (commodified as objects alongside stadia), trivializing them as peripheral, sexualized, supportive objects for explicit consumption by men within the larger text of sport as lifestyle. Nonetheless, all these activities (travel, stadia, sights, etc.) were predominantly, if not exclusively, focused on football. This served to establish the quintessential American game as the central category member, as *the* sport worthy of such cultural attention.

Overall, the re-invention of sporting traditions and rituals and their framing within a narrative of cultural tourism functioned to shift the definition of such sport consumption as ESPN.com reconstructed activities often viewed as fanatical into a sophisticated fandom. That is, ESPN.com framed core fandom of (literally and digitally) following a team or sport as travel, lifestyle, and culture rather than as obsessive fanaticism. In turn, this normalized the consistent and continued consumption of sport, and all its activities, at ESPN. As such, ESPN.com constructed sport as a way of life, and itself as the source, guide, and path through which to consume the life.

Conclusion

During the short period of research, ESPN.com predominantly re/produced sport and its category membership as a narrow range of men's U.S. sports, positioning other sports, nations, and women as peripheral or excluded from the category. In working to position itself as the expert and authoritative text, ESPN consistently re/presented itself as a wider media site through an integrated self-referential narrative (Jansson, 2002) and cross-promotional platform-jumping (Oates, 2009). Using familiar discursive and re/presentational mediasport practices, ESPN.com worked up its position of knowledge (power) while it simultaneously positioned itself as collaborating with consumers/fans (solidarity) by enacting the illusion of participation (Dart, 2009; Graham & Hearn, 2001).

Many of the forms provided for consumption, including consistent invitations to participate in and personalize ESPN.com, served to render the consumer an active participant in their own consumption. Indeed, the collaborative discursive action of ESPN.com (such as invitations to comment alongside the experts, fantasy sports, shopping, travel, etc.) framed this expected consumption as identity performance. This in turn worked it up as a desirable part of the integrated narrative of sport identity performance and, therefore, as a valued part of the sporting action at ESPN.com; despite it being an illusionary collaboration. This invited inclusion also served to construct the consumer as a knowledgeable participant, while actually consistently positioning ESPN as the authoritative voice for the consumer.

Equally, ESPN.com was observed to represent sport as lifestyle and sacred rituals, framing itself as the guide for this consumption; albeit consumption constructed from a white, male perspective. In achieving this action, ESPN.com was observed to effectively deploy familiar narratives that re/produced sport within the narrow traditional discourses of sport and its rituals, while appearing to construct fandom along a newer narrative that integrated these into a wider, lifestyle definition of sport fandom. Thus, ESPN.com guided its interpretive communities to share in reformulated understandings of traditional sport practices (pilgrimages and rituals, such as tailgating) integrated and interfaced with newer definitions of sport as travel and cultural consumption (restaurants, cities). This effectively re/produced a sport identity that appeared less "fanatical" by enabling sport practices and rituals to become more integrated into other identity narratives.

However, the re/presentational practices at ESPN.com re/produced the newer lifestyle definitions of sport by using and re-inventing traditional and familiar gendered discourses, demonstrating little content or innovation to challenge these established forms and narratives (Dart, 2009; Leonard, 2009) or create different imagined communities for sport (Crawford, 2004). In fact, ESPN.com constructed the re-imagined interpretive community for sport as cultural tourism as white, male football fans. The exclusion of women as athletes, experts, and as the constructed consumer within the lifestyle and news content at ESPN.com was systemic and, hence, problematic. Thus, while new media have been argued to offer dynamic sites for the manifestation of the new imagined communities of sport, the lack of effort to include and re/present diversity at ESPN.com, and the re-invention of traditional practices as new yet traditionally gendered forms, suggested little substantive change in the dominant definitions and practices re/produced at this site.

Notes

1 The cycle of production and reproduction is referred to as re/production. Similarly, the constructed nature of presentation and representation is embedded in the usage of re/presentation.
2 FIFA's World Cup, a men's soccer (aka football) tournament, is arguably the biggest international sporting tournament. Held every four years, the June 2010 tournament is a key mediasport topic and promoted over an extended period outside the US (Meân, 2010).
3 The popularity, audience figures and media coverage of NASCAR has grown immensely in recent years, disrupting the dominance of the traditional "big 4" of U.S. sport (football, baseball, basketball, and hockey) and re/producing NASCAR as one of the big American sports.
4 The uniform itself, small as in beach volleyball or skin tight as in downhill skiing, combined with camera angles and other aspects, like head position and eye contact, all function together to primarily frame the athlete as presented for sexual or athletic consumption. The recent controversy over Lindsey Vonn's *Sports Illustrated* cover demonstrated this issue. In uniform and action skiing position, but not actually in action, Vonn had her face turned to the camera, eyes engaging the viewer, and was not wearing the proper face and headgear. This image suggests that problematic gendered representational practices may be shifting to more complex, subtle forms.
5 Reef is a trademarked brand of surf products and associated lifestyle leisure and fashion clothing and accessories.

References

Anderson, B. (1991). *Imagined communities* (2nd Ed.). London & New York: Verso.
Berger, J. (1972). *Ways of seeing*. New York: Penguin Books.
Billings, A.C. (2008). *Olympic media: Inside the biggest show on television*. London: Routledge.
Bourdieu, P. (1978). Sport and social class. *Social Science Information, 17*(6), 819–40.
Butterworth, M. (2008). Fox Sports, Super Bowl XLII, and the affirmation of American civil religion. *Journal of Sport & Social Issues, 32*, 318–23.
Crawford, G. (2004). *Consuming sport: Fans, sports and culture*. London: Routledge.
Dart, J.J. (2009). Blogging the 2006 FIFA World Cup finals. *Sociology of Sport Journal, 26*, 106–26.

Duncan, M.C. & Messner, M.A. (1998). The media image of sport and gender. In L.A. Wenner (Ed.), *MediaSport* (pp. 170–85). New York: Routledge.

ESPN Fact Sheet (January 10, 2010). *ESPN MediaZone*. (Retrieved from http://espnmediazone3.com/wpmu/).

Foucault, M. (1972). *The archaeology of knowledge*. London: Tavistock.

Foucault, M. (1977). *Discipline and punish: The birth of the prison*. London: Penguin.

Friedman, W. (2009). NFL draft is ratings boom for ESPN. *Media Daily News* (April 27). http://mediapost.com/publications/index.cfm?fa=Articles.showArticle&art_aid=104824. Retrieved May 22, 2010.

Goffman, E. (1976). *Gender advertisements*. Cambridge, MA: Harvard University Press.

Gorman, B. (2009). NFL draft viewership up 62% over 6 years. *Tvbythenumbers.com* (April 24). http://tvbythenumbers.com/2009/04/24/nfl-draft-viewership-up-62-over-6-years/17351. Retrieved May 22, 2010.

Graham, P. & Hearn, G. (2001). The coming of post-reflexive society: Commodification and language in digital capitalism. *Media International Australia Incorporating Culture and Policy, 98*, 79–90.

Gumperz, J. (1982). *Discourse strategies*. Cambridge: Cambridge University Press.

Hardin, M. (2005). Stopped at the gate: Women's sports, "reader interest," and decision making by editors. *Journalism and Mass Communication Quarterly, 82*, 62–77.

Horne, J. (2006). Sport in consumer culture. Basingstoke, UK and New York: Palgrave Macmillan.

Hutchins, B., Rowe, D., & Ruddock, A. (2009). "It's fantasy football made real": Networked media sport, the internet, and the hybrid reality of *MyFootballClub*. *Sociology of Sport Journal, 26*, 89–106.

Jansen, S.C. & Sabo, D. (1994). The sport/war metaphor: Hegemonic masculinity, the Persian Gulf War, and the new world order. *Sociology of Sport Journal, 11*, 1–17.

Jansson, A. (2002). The mediatization of consumption: Towards an analytical framework of image culture. *Journal of Consumer Culture, 2*, 5–31.

Kane, M.J. & Lenskyj, H.J. (1998). Media treatment of female athletes: Issues of gender and sexualities. In L.A. Wenner (Ed.), *MediaSport* (pp. 186–201). London: Routledge.

Klaassen, A. (January 5, 2009). ESPN.com redesigns to be more ad-friendly. *Advertising Age*, January 5, 2009. Retrieved from adage.com/article_id=133555.

Leonard, D.J. (2009). New media and global sporting cultures: Moving beyond the clichés and binaries. *Sociology of Sport Journal, 26*, 1–16.

Lindlof, T.R. (1988). Media audiences as interpretive communities. *Communication Yearbook, 11*, 108–26.

Lowry, T. (2005). ESPN.com: Guys and dollars. *Business Week* (cover story, October 17). Retrieved March 2, 2010.

McDavid, A. (July 21, 2008). ESPN audience high jumps over market obstacles. *Minonline.com*. (Retrieved from minonline.com/features/ESPN-Audience-High-Jumps-Over-Market-Obstacles_8219.html).

Meân, L.J. (2001). Identity and discursive practice: Doing gender on the football pitch. *Discourse & Society, 12*, 789–815.

Meân, L.J. (2003). Everyday discursive practices & the construction of gender: A study at the 'grass roots.' In A. Schorr, W. Campbell, & M. Schenk (Eds.), *Communication research in Europe and abroad* (pp. 497–515). Berlin: De Gruyter.

Meân, L.J. (2009). On the lite side? MillerLite's Men of the Square Table, Man Laws, and the making of masculinity. In L. Wenner & S. Jackson (Eds.), *Sport, beer and gender: Promotional culture and contemporary social life* (pp. 143–61). New York: Peter Lang.

Meân, L.J. (2010). Making masculinity and framing femininity: FIFA, soccer and World Cup websites. In H. Hundley & A. Billings (Eds.), *Examining identity in sports media* (pp. 65–86). Thousand Oaks, CA: Sage.

Meân, L.J. & Kassing, J. (2008) "I would just like to be known as an athlete": Managing hegemony, femininity, and heterosexuality in female sport. *Western Journal of Communication*, 72, 126–44.

Meân, L.J., Kassing, J.W., & Sanderson, J. (2010). The making of an epic (American) hero fighting for justice: Commodification, consumption, and intertextuality in the Floyd Landis defense campaign. *American Behavioral Scientist, 53*(11), 1590–609.

Mehus, I. (2005). Distinction through sport consumption. *International Review for the Sociology of Sport, 40*, 321–33.

Messner, M.A. (1988). Sports and male domination: The female athlete as contested ideological terrain. *Sociology of Sport Journal, 5*, 197–211.

Oates, T.P. (2009). New media and the repackaging of NFL fandom. *Sociology of Sport Journal, 26*, 31–49.

Pérez-Peña, R. (2007). The top player in this league? It may be the sports reporter. *New York Times* (December 24). Retrieved March 2, 2010. www.nytimes.com/2007/12/24/business/media/24sportswriters.html?_r=1&scp=1&sq=The%20top%20player%20in%20the%20league?&st=cse

Potter, J. (1996). *Representing reality: Discourse, rhetoric and social construction.* London: Sage.

Real, M. (2006). Sport online: The newest player in mediasport. In A. Raney & J. Bryant (Eds.), *Handbook of sports and media* (pp. 171–84). Mahwah, NJ: Lawrence Erlbaum.

Rowe, D. (2004). *Sport, culture and the media: The unruly trinity* (2nd Ed.). Maidenhead, UK and New York: Open University Press.

Scherer, J. (2007). Globalization, promotional culture and the production/consumption of online games: Engaging Adidas's "Beat Rugby" campaign. *New Media & Society, 9*, 475–96.

Sullivan, D.B. (2006). Broadcast television and the game of packaging sports. In A.A. Raney & J. Bryant (Eds.), *Handbook of sports and media* (pp. 131–45). Mahwah, NJ: Lawrence Erlbaum.

Vertinsky, P. (2006). Time gentlemen please: The space and place of gender in sport history. In M.G. Phillips (Ed.), *Deconstructing sport history: A postmodern analysis* (pp. 227–43). New York: SUNY Press.

Walsh, A.J. & Giulianotti, R. (2001). This sporting mammon: A normative critique of the commodification of sport. *Journal of the Philosophy of Sport, 29*, 53–77.

Wenner, L.A. (1991). One part alcohol, one part sport, one part dirt, stir gently: Beer commercial and television sports. In L.R. Vande Berg & L.A. Wenner (Eds.), *Television criticism: Approaches and applications* (pp. 388–407). New York: Longman.

Wenner, L.A. (1993). We are the world, we are the Quake: The redefinition of fans as interpretive community in sportswriting about the 1989 Bay Area World Series and earthquake disaster. *Journal of Sport & Social Issues, 17*, 181–205.

Wenner, L.A. (1998) Playing the MediaSport game. In L.A. Wenner (Ed.), *MediaSport* (pp. 3–13). New York: Routledge.

Wernick, A. (1991). *Promotional culture: Advertising, ideology and symbolic expression.* London: Sage.

11

REACTION TIME

Assessing the record and advancing a future of sports media scholarship

Andrew C. Billings

CLEMSON UNIVERSITY

If you wish to know the sports I tend to play at least moderately well, there is a common denominator to discerning what they are: reaction time. I have never been good at reacting immediately to a sporting situation occurring in front of me. I have always needed at least a second to process. I was decent at baseball until I got older and the pitches became a bit too speedy to grant me that second of reaction time. With tennis, I'm a decent baseline player, but not as efficient at the net, where reaction time is reduced. Golf and bowling require no reaction time and I still enjoy some success at both. Having the moment to cognitively process the variables at play is critical for me to even have a modicum of personal accomplishment in sports.

I mention this phenomenon when addressing the role of sports media in the 21st Century because sometimes the technology and overall modes of communication advance in such a swift manner that scholars lack the time to adapt and react. In Academe, reaction time is usually not measured in seconds but in years, as the process of researching, studying, presenting and publishing meaningful work is inevitably laborious. The works presented in this volume on *Sports Media: Transformation, Integration, Consumption* are jointly a measuring stick; a communicative gut check, so to phrase, assessing the quality and quantity of sports media research in the past, with an eye on how it informs us on the mediated transmission and impact of and on sport in the future.

When assessing the record of sports media scholarship, one conclusion seems abundantly clear: the amount of seminal sport communication scholarship produced over the past three decades is astounding and, moreover, exceeds the overarching systemic structures that should support it. A case in point would be the evolution of other disciplinary organizations that study sport as an influential and critical social phenomenon. The North American Society for the Sociology of Sport

(NASSS) recently celebrated its thirtieth year of annual conferences. The North American Society for Sport Historians (NASSH) offers a similar multi-decade lineage, as does the North American Society for Sports Management (NASSM). Most of these other disciplinary organizations attach a journal (e.g., *Sociology of Sport Journal, Journal of Sport History*) to their associative contributions as well.

In contrast, the National Communication Association (NCA) offers 58 divisions, sections and caucuses (as of the Summer of 2010) within a very layered structure, yet does not devote one to sport. The Association for Education in Journalism and Mass Communication (AEJMC) and Broadcast Education Association (BEA) only recently added a sport division, smartly coming to the realization that sports are no longer the "toy department" of media outlets, but rather are big business with quite real and serious consequences. One communication association, the International Association for Media and Communication Research (IAMCR) has had a section devoted to sport for more than a decade, and that group has not traditionally had the attendance or reach of some of the other national academic communication organizations.

The good news, of course, is that while communication scholars are 30 years behind organizationally this certainly is not the case in regard to scholarship. Seminal works of the 1970s and 1980s (consider the works of Bryant, Real, Parente, and Williams in the 1970s just to name a few that are listed in the Appendix) still contribute mightily to discussions and understandings of communication concepts today, and some of those forward-thinking foundational authors have offered contributions to this collection of scholarship. One advantage of the lack of scholarly communities devoted to the formal study of sports as communication-based phenomena is that the work has often necessitated interdisciplinarity, as communication scholars integrate theories, methodologies, and past research from other disciplines in order to publish in sport-specific journals that do not claim communication as central focal points. Conversely, scholars in other fields with more established links to sport have found communication to be a fruitful angle in which they, too, could explore interdisciplinary projects.

Much work must be done on the part of communication scholars to organizationally "catch up" with other disciplines, yet as it has been constructed in the past, we must do so with an eye to what these other areas of study contribute to the equation, asking: where does communication fit in with the larger puzzle? Just as other disciplines must re-examine their own fundamental conceptions by asking: what role does communication play in some of the assumptions we make about sport in society?

The mode of communication becomes essential to the conversation. Nearly every major technology innovation of the past several decades has been escalated, at least in part, by consumer demand for sports media content. Whether measured in quantity (number of sports media offerings) or quality (degree of informational and technical detail), the demand for sports product significantly influences everything from cable and satellite billing structures to high-definition television purchases to Internet-based applications and social media offerings. This volume considers the role that sports media scholarship has played in understanding the increasingly complex world of sports media. With an eye toward a future that is increasingly about hybrid forms of media offerings, *Sports Media: Transformation, Integration, Consumption* has assessed the past scholarship in the field while positing important future questions about the role sports media will increasingly play in the daily lives of billions of sports fans worldwide.

However, it is fair to say that the medium does not create the modern sports fan, or at least that it does not do so in a linear, cause and effect manner. Rather, sports media has evolved largely through a combination of immense consumer demand, capitalistic network opportunities, and the ability to attract highly desirable demographics in ways that frequently allow for cross-promotional appeals. Sports media in the 21st Century drives product lines, demands increasing hours of our attention, and becomes part and parcel of the consumer culture. Sport becomes interrelated with all other forms of media, personal interaction, and professional conversations. In doing so, the conversation regarding the sport–media–communication nexus has never been more relevant or more warranted.

So, we know that communication-based sports media scholarship has been occurring in quality form for decades and has even escalated both in terms of quantity and quality of publications (and publication outlets) in the past decade. We also know that sports fandom becomes the "straw that stirs the drink" (see Wenner & Jackson, 2009) of complex issues of identity, consumption, and the enactment of sport. Finally, we know that the role of sport within modern society (both for media entities and beyond) is of an expansive nature even as other forms of traditional media consumption contract. As a result, scholars at the forefront of sports media scholarship must be prepared to serve multiple purposes ranging from the informed advocate to the conscientious critic to the provocative educator. This leads me to an overview of the current trends in sports media and how sport scholarship can follow, analyze, and impart knowledge upon and about them in the coming years. Six themes appear particularly relevant to this discussion: (1) Sporting community in the age of fragmentation, (2) Primary consumption beyond the sporting performance, (3) Defining identity beyond one-shot variable analyses, (4) Recognizing the interdisciplinary nature of sport without losing sports media identity, (5) Stressing the impact factor, and (6) Emphasizing the value of distraction.

Theme #1: Sporting community in the age of fragmentation

The "water cooler" show is a concept that television networks consider the pot of gold at the end of the programming rainbow. However, the pot of gold is now rarely found. Given audience fragmentation and a rapidly increasing number of options available, it is difficult to find any one program that people view en masse – the media offering that prompts everyone at work to ask the next day: "Did you see that?" It is fair to say sport offers the majority of the meager number of water cooler moments that remain as the Super Bowl, Olympics, and other megasporting events remain vibrant parts of popular culture. As James Poiewozik (2010) observes, "the biggest shows are getting bigger."

Yet it is also fair to argue that even megasports are consumed quite differently. Robert S. Putnam's famous book *Bowling Alone* (2000) argued that, at the turn of the century, people were shirking previously held notions of community and belonging to instead create their own human existence. People in the 1960s gathered for bowling leagues; decades later, Putnam argued, they were "bowling alone." Similarly, many sports fans are "sporting alone" as it is not just that people are consuming sports in the private comfort of their own living rooms, but also that the sports selected in those living rooms are much less likely to mirror those of their neighbors. It is not that they're alone when they're bowling; it's that they can't even agree that bowling – or any sport for that matter – is the sport worthy of their time and attention. Increased fragmentation is the future – that much we know. What we need to explore within sport media scholarship is the impact on notions of the community of sport. Increasingly, media consumers won't be watching the same things, talking the same language, or bonding in the same droves that have made sport what Bob Costas refers to as a "vast mosaic" (Billings, 2008, p. 57) of interests and potential societal impact. Perhaps social media is the answer; perhaps it is something else in which we have not yet conceived. Still, as a column in *Time* magazine recently articulated: "The fall of watercooler TV has been playing out for years. When that happens, you can try to make better TV. Or you can find a better watercooler" (Poiewozik, 2010).

Theme #2: primary consumption beyond the sporting performance

The 21st-Century sports fan is a uniquely different breed. Being a fan used to be primarily enacted in the first person present tense: I watched it; I saw it; I loved it; I cared. Much as we hear that half of life is just showing up, half – if not more – of sports fandom used to involve being there. Season tickets. Active participation. Hoarse voices the next day. Now, with the plethora of sports media options seeping into the mainstream collective psyche, being a sport fan can be about many more forms of sports participation. A person can consume sports media for hours each day without ever seeing or hearing an enacted sporting event. Consider the person who wakes up, checks the Internet for their fantasy sports scores from the previous night, listens and even calls in to the local radio sports program, tweets their comments to a group of followers, watches opinion programs like *Pardon the Interruption* and *Around the Horn*, and gets sports updates on their cell phone in the evening. This, one would think, is a sports media addict – and yet, they never tuned in to an actual game or contest. Sports scholarship of the future must understand consumption from myriad points of view. Economics certainly enter the equation (see Gratton & Solberg, 2007) as it is not just the cost of attendance that is pricing out many fans of low- and middle-income status; it is also the cost of ESPN *Full Court* or NFL's *Sunday Ticket* that is marginalizing the avid fan from content they crave largely based on income. On the flip side of that coin, is it fair to say that the "common" or "true" fan has been priced out at a time in which college football stadiums – many of which reside in relatively small metropolitan areas – are expanding beyond 100,000 seat capacity (College Gridirons, 2010). The desire to witness sport in its live first-personness is still quite real, but the media offerings and concurrent economic values and choices fans must make offer ripe areas for sports media scholarship.

Theme #3: defining identity beyond one-shot variable analyses

When Stuart Hall (1996, p. 4) postulates that "identities are constructed within, not outside discourse," it is also important to note that he references identity in its plural form. Sports media scholars have accomplished a great deal in terms of the understanding of the role sport plays in the conveyance, discussion, and understanding of issues like gender, nationality, race, disability, religion, and age (see Hundley & Billings, 2010; Morris, 2006; Wenner, 1993). Identities are duplicitous, ubiquitous, and continually in flux (see Maguire, 1999); they are also constructed in much more fluid and nuanced manners than rudimentary empirical analyses have usually allowed.

Wenner (2006) elucidates the dilemma of single-variable identity analyses in his explication of the "super themes" present in a single communication artifact: the Justin Timberlake/Janet Jackson Super Bowl scandal of 2004. He points to 13 super themes that each are worthy of analysis, including race and ethnicity, deviance and distaste, and young and old. Yet, within the large majority of sports media analyses, a single identity variable is isolated and then extrapolated within mutually exclusive groups. Such analyses have a great deal of value; while gender certainly is defined by more than just chromosomes, the presence of gender differences that equate to mere division based on biological conceptions of sex are nonetheless insightful and indicative general conceptions of male vs. female issues (see Daddario, 1998; Tuggle, 1997). Such analyses are also understandable; it is difficult to draw generalizable conclusions about, for instance, Black female athletes at the Winter Games when the televised sample size is likely to be in the single digits.

Nonetheless, sports media scholarship must begin combining identity variables to gain insight on the manner in which they are interacting within media narratives and beyond. From a social scientific point of view, datasets could and should be combined and expanded to enable the understanding of, for instance, the aging female vs. the aging male athlete, the American Muslim vs. the Middle Eastern Muslim, and the disabled individual sport athlete vs. the disabled team athlete. From a rhetorical or critical/cultural view, even one-shot case studies of complex athlete identity narratives (think Muhammad Ali) could be more robust through the joint (as opposed to isolated) analyses of important figures and social issues. For example, consider the inherent value of addressing the Tiger Woods adultery scandal from the combined gender/race/religion viewpoint of a Buddhist Cablinasian athlete in a uniquely new form of public spectacle. These types of investigations, regardless of epistemology and viewpoint, will provide the necessary avenue for discovery in the years and decades ahead, particularly in a culture in which these identity lines are blurring far more than they are crystallizing.

Theme #4: recognizing the interdisciplinary nature of sport without losing sports media identity

If a dozen sports media scholars were asked to diagram a model explaining the disciplinary underpinnings that jointly constitute the field, each model would be so different that it would be an arduous task to synthesize what it is we purport to be analyzing when we say we are conducting sports media scholarship. In their preface to the *Handbook of Sports and Media*, Raney and Bryant (2006) note that with the exception of two groundbreaking edited works by Lawrence Wenner (*Media, Sports, and Society* and *MediaSport*) there has been little synthesis scholarship that asks foundational questions regarding the diversity and understanding of sports media as a worthy and critically important intellectual pursuit. As they articulated the issue, "Few have attempted to fashion a sports-media collage using the full pallet of colors offered in the extant eclectic literature, perhaps out of fear that the various intellectual traditions represented therein might clash" (Raney & Bryant, 2006, p. xi). The advent of convergence communication that incorporates everything from traditional media to new media to social media to user generated media has forced this clash to the fore – and sports media scholars would be both prescient and wise to embrace the collision of disciplinary epistemologies that have resulted.

Scholarship by Kassing et al. (2004) bridges necessary gaps between not just sports media and other disciplines, but even within the hybrid-based communication home discipline as well, suggesting that people enact, produce, consume, and organize sport primarily as a communicative activity regardless of the inevitable false dichotomous debates between human and mediated forms of communication. Still, more work must be done to offer theoretical grounding and practical understanding of where communication fits within the overlapping circles of social science and humanities work, not to mention within specific disciplinary silos which partition work that could be – indeed *must* be – more collaborative in nature. Consider, for instance, an analysis of the public persona of racing's Danica Patrick from a unified marketing/women's studies/sociological/communicative lens. With the subject of sport, many tendencies are natural – some may shy away from industry-based studies for fear that the academic nature of the analysis will be lost in the entertainment-based malaise; similarly, communication scholars sometimes diminish or underestimate the value of their work by deferring to other disciplines that have established "sport" in their program titles (e.g., sports management or sports marketing) or who have the proper entrenched notion that sport is not merely a context in which one studies enacted physical and cognitive phenomena but a separate and uniquely important intellectual pursuit. To be truly robust in scope and utility, communication scholars must transcend these boundaries (some real, some imagined) to ultimately advance the study of sports media in a way that does not simply attempt to legitimize the field but instead builds upon the already established legitimacy to proffer and answer more nuanced questions.

Theme #5: stressing the impact factor

Communication studies and, indeed, academia as a whole, continues to have a difficult time discerning what constitutes quality scholarship. One measure that has been adopted has been determining relative impact factors for academic journals. Such a gauge is necessary to uncover how our scholarship is disseminated and incorporated within the mass contributions of fields such as mass communication. How many people are consuming the work? What kind of impact is imbued within our educational dialogues? These become critical to what we value and, in turn, what gets promoted in future scholarly quests.

Debates remain as to whether sports media is a context, a subfield, or an entirely separate entity within the communication discipline, but no one can deny the impact factor sports media exerts. How can we understand family communication without discussing the role sports play on family gatherings, activities, and trips? How can we discuss workplace productivity without noting the transformation of the organizational environment during college basketball's March Madness? How can we not place sport at the forefront of understanding media uses and gratifications when so many of our media choices are directly related to what each form of media – traditional or new – offers people in terms of sports to consume? The impact factor is quite deep within a field that once was simply disregarded as the "toy department" (see Schultz, 2005) of newspaper and television newsrooms.

Within sports media (as a subset of sports communication), the impact factor can be quantified even more directly. Twenty-two of the top 25 television ratings of all time (88%) are sporting events. When culling through the most-viewed newspaper stories of the day, there are more sports-related stories than all other subjects (foreign and domestic) combined. Even aspects of sport that often are falsely dismissed as fringe or niche actually have tremendous impact factors. Consider fantasy sports, which has reached critical mass (an estimated 27 million Americans now play annually [Fantasy Sports Trade Association, 2009]) with $1.5 billion now being spent annually on fantasy sports (Klaassen, 2006). Some still consider it an activity that is far from mainstream, yet, as of January 2010, this means that five times as many Americans participate in fantasy sport than play the very popular and addictive online fantasy game "World of Warcraft" – a game that has gained a great deal of scholarly attention.

All of this is not an attempt to delegitimize online role playing games such as "World of Warcraft"; however, it is used to place even so-called sub-areas of sports in proper perspective. Impact factors ultimately tell us how people spend their time. What we systematically always find is that sport moves right to the top of that list, drawing comparisons to even the most fundamental of human experiences such as religion (see comparisons in Butterworth, 2005) and sex (see comparisons in Krizek, 2008).

Theme #6: emphasizing the value of distraction

It has been said that "Life is what happens when you are busy making other plans," but I would also argue that substance is what happens when you are busy being distracted. When people disregard sport as fluff or superfluous, educators, practitioners, and researchers must jointly rebut that it is when the receiver of media is in relative daydream – an aroused, elated, or suspended state brought about by sport (see Petty & Cacioppo, 1986) – that persuasion is perhaps most likely to occur. It is within distraction that we are more likely to suspend critical inquiry, making the study of the production, content and effects of these sport-oriented messages even more necessary.

Ironically, millions of people claim to be sports fans precisely because they wait in eager anticipation for the moments in which sports are no longer about sports. When a 59-year-old Tom Watson stands in the 18th fairway trying to win his sixth British Open Championship, the event is no longer about golf; it is about testing the boundaries of time and age to determine whether there is a point at which the legendary athlete must walk into the sunset. When Kerri Strug lands a one-legged vault in the 1996 Olympic team gymnastics competition, the event is no longer about gold medals; it is about whether a person can desire something badly enough to defy gravity if only for a few seconds. During the 2010 NCAA Basketball tournament, fans rooting for the Butler Bulldogs against the ever-powerful Duke Blue Devils were not just suddenly attached to a small school in Indianapolis who had stolen their sporting hearts; they were invested because of the common experience of being the downtrodden little guy presumed to be hopelessly overmatched against the large and entrenched corporate conglomerate. It becomes difficult to assess something strictly from a sport-centric focus on traditional constructs of fandom, audience, permeation, and demographics when sport sometimes takes on mythic quantities (see Real, 1975).

Sports fans are metaphorical surfers, always seeking the ultimate wave – the ride of a lifetime that was beyond what they have experienced before and transcending the action being performed. The ultimate distraction from career, health, and family stresses. We watch sports waiting for the magical moment when they're not really about sports anymore. When football resumed play after 9/11, it was not about sports. When Brett Favre threw four touchdowns in the first half one day after his father's passing, most people did not tear up because they were newfound Packers fans. It spoke to something larger. Distracting and yet quite important.

On January 8, 1994, my father passed away early in the morning. Needless to say, it was an extremely draining day. That night, I sat down and watched my Green Bay Packers defeat the Detroit Lions and I ate for the first time all day. Do not underestimate the power of distraction.

The tremendous potential for future sports scholarship

There are those in my field who are in it because they absolutely love sports and think sports are the greatest thing since sliced bread. There are others who study it because they see all of the negative impacts, arguing for things such as the abolishment of college athletics. I try to argue in the middle, because essentially both stances are based on the same premise: Sport wields power. Sport is, indeed, a double-edged sword that must be used with care and precision, but also with a great deal of passion and purpose. The future of sports media scholarship is bright, but only if scholars embrace industry ties without becoming beholden to them. Only if researchers consult prior research without merely replicating it. Only if insightful questions and useful analysis are offered instead of endless pontification, finger-pointing, and statements of the overly obvious. There is a great deal of work that has been accomplished (see the very elaborate set of references in the Appendix to this volume, which is by no means an exhaustive list), yet there is also a great deal of arduous work ahead as sports media scholars synthesize the past to challenge and analyze an uncertain media future.

References

Billings, A.C. (2008). *Olympic media: Inside the biggest show on television*. London: Routledge.
Butterworth, M.L. (2005). Ritual in the "church of baseball": Suppressing the discourse of democracy after 9/11. *Communication and Critical/Cultural Studies, 2*, 107–29.
College Gridirons (2010). Retrieved on May 6, 2010 from: www.collegegridirons.com/
Daddario, G. (1998). *Women's sport and spectacle*. Westport, CT: Praeger.
Fantasy Sports Trade Association (2009). Homepage. Retrieved on January 5, 2009 from www.fsta.org
Gratton, C. & Solberg, H.A. (2007). *The economics of sports broadcasting*. London: Routledge.
Hall, S. (1996). Introduction: Who needs "identity"? In S. Hall & P. du Gay (Eds.), *Questions of cultural identity* (pp. 1–17). London: Sage.
Hundley, H.L., & Billings, A.C. (Eds.). (2010). *Examining identity in sports media*. Thousand Oaks, CA: Sage.
Kassing, J.W., Billings, A.C., Brown, R.S., Halone, K.K., Harrison, K., Krizek, B., Meân, L.J., & Turman, P.D. (2004). Communication in the community of sport: The process of enacting, (re)producing, consuming, and organizing sport. *Communication Yearbook, 28*, 373–409.
Klaassen, A. (2006, August). That's real money – $1.5B – pouring into made-up leagues. *Advertising Age, 77*(32), 4–6.
Krizek, R.L. (2008). Introduction: Communication and the community of sport. *Western Journal of Communication, 72*(2), 103–6.
Maguire, J. (1999). *Global sport: Identities, societies, civilizations*. Cambridge, UK: Polity Press.
Morris, M. (2006). *Identity anecdotes: Translation and media culture*. London: Sage.

Petty, R.E. & Cacioppo, J.T. (1986). *Communication and persuasion: Central and peripheral routes to attitude change*. New York: Springer-Verlag.

Poiewozik, J. (2010, March 22). The world wide living room. Retrieved on May 6, 2010 at: www.time.com/time/magazine/article/0,9171,1971444,00.html

Putnam, R.D. (2000). *Bowling alone: The collapse and revival of the American community*. New York: Simon & Schuster.

Raney, A.A. & Bryant, J. (Eds.). (2006). *Handbook of sports and media*. Mahwah, NJ: Lawrence Erlbaum.

Real, M.R. (1975). Super Bowl: Mythic spectacle. *Journal of Communication, 75*, 31–43.

Schultz, B. (2005). *Sports media: Reporting, producing, and planning*. Burlington, MA: Focal Press.

Tuggle, C.A. (1997). Differences in television sports reporting of men's and women's athletics: ESPN *SportsCenter* and CNN *Sports Tonight*. *Journal of Broadcasting & Electronic Media, 41*(1), 14–24.

Wenner, L.A. (Ed.). (1989). *Media, sports, and society*. Newbury Park, CA: Sage.

Wenner, L.A. (1993). Men, women, and sports on television: Audience experiences and effects. In A. Yiannakis, T. McIntyre, & M. Melnick (Eds.), *Sport Sociology: Contemporary Themes* (pp. 208–16). Dubuque, IA: Kendall-Hunt.

Wenner, L.A. (Ed.). (1998). *MediaSport*. New York: Routledge.

Wenner, L.A. (2006). Sports and media through the super glass mirror: Placing blame, breast-beating, and a gaze to the future. In A. Raney & J. Bryant (Eds.), *Handbook of sports and media* (pp. 45–62). Mahwah, NJ: Lawrence Erlbaum.

Wenner, L.A. & Jackson, S.J. (Eds.). (2009). *Sport, beer, and gender: Promotional culture and contemporary social life*. New York: Peter Lang.

APPENDIX

Contributions to sports media scholarship: a comprehensive reference list

Adams, T. & Tuggle, C.A. (2004). ESPN's *SportsCenter* and coverage of women's athletics: It's a boy's club. *Mass Communication & Society, 7*, 237–48.

Alexander, S. (1994). Newspaper coverage of athletics as a function of gender. *Women's Studies International Forum, 17*(6), 655–62.

Allison, L. (Ed.). (1993). *The changing politics of sport* (pp. 58–83). Manchester, UK: Manchester University Press.

Allison, L. (2000). Sport and nationalism. In J. Coakley and E. Dunning (Eds.), *Handbook of Sports Studies* (pp. 344–55). London: Sage.

Anderson, D.A. (1994). *Contemporary sports reporting.* Chicago: Nelson-Hall.

Anderson, E. (2005). *In the game: Gay athletes and the cult of masculinity.* Albany, NY: SUNY Press.

Andrews, D. (2003). Sport and the transnationalizing media corporation. *Journal of Media Economics, 16*(4), 235–52.

Andrews, D.L. & Ritzer, G. (2007). The global in the sporting glocal. *Global Networks, 7*(2), 135–53.

Andrews, P. (2005). *Sports journalism: A practical guide.* London: Sage.

Angelini, J.R. (2008a). How did the sports make you feel? Looking at the three dimensions of emotion through a gendered lens. *Sex Roles: A Journal of Research, 58*(1), 127–35.

Angelini, J.R. (2008b). Television sports and athlete gender: The differences in watching male and female athletes. *Journal of Broadcasting & Electronic Media, 52*(1), 16–32.

Angelini, J.R. & Billings, A.C. (2010). Accounting for athletic performance: Race and sportscaster dialogue in NBC's 2008 Olympic telecast. *Communication Research Reports, 27*(1), 1–10.

Bairner, A. (2001). *Sport, nationalization, and globalization: European and North American perspectives.* Albany, NY: SUNY Press.

Baker, A. (2003). *Contesting identities: Sports in American film.* Urbana: University of Illinois Press.

Baker, A. & Boyd, T. (Eds.). (1997). *Out of bounds: Sports, media, and the politics of identity.* Bloomington: Indiana University Press.

Barnett, S. (1990). *Games and sets: The changing face of sport on television.* London: British Film Institute.

Barney, R.K., Wenn, S.R., & Martyn, S.G. (2002). *Selling the five rings: The International Olympic Committee and the rise of Olympic commercialism.* Salt Lake City: University of Utah Press.

Bass, A. (2002). *Not the triumph but the struggle: The 1968 Olympics and the making of the Black athlete.* Minneapolis: University of Minnesota Press.

Bellamy, R.V. (1993). Issues in the internationalization of U.S. sports media: The emerging European marketplace. *Journal of Sport & Social Issues, 17*(3), 168–80.

Bellamy, R.V. (2005). Whatever happened to synergy? MLB as media product. *NINE: A Journal of Baseball History & Culture, 13*(2), 19–30.

Bellamy, R. & Walker, J. (2001). Baseball and television origins: The case of the Cubs. *NINE, 10,* 31–48.

Bernache-Assollant, I., Lacassagne, M.F., & Braddock, J.H. (2007). Basking in reflected glory and blasting differences in identity-management strategies between two groups of highly identified soccer fans. *Journal of Language & Social Psychology, 26*(4), 381–88.

Bernhardt, P.C., Dabbs, J.M., Fielden, J.A., & Lutter, C.D. (1998). Testosterone changes during vicarious experience of winning and losing among fans at sporting events. *Physiology & Behaviors, 18,* 263–68.

Bernstein, A. (2002). Is it time for a victory lap? Changes in the media coverage of women in sport. *International Review for the Sociology of Sport, 37,* 415–28.

Bernstein, A. & Blain, N. (Eds.). (2003). *Sport, media, culture: Global and local dimensions.* Portland, OR: Frank Cass.

Berry, B. & Smith, E. (2000). Race, sport, and crime: The misrepresentations of African Americans in team sports and crime. *Sociology of Sport Journal, 17,* 171–97.

Billings, A.C. (2000). In search of women athletes: ESPN's list of the top 100 athletes of the Century. *Journal of Sport & Social Issues, 24*(4), 415–21.

Billings, A.C. (2003). Portraying Tiger Woods: Characterizations of a "Black" athlete in a "White" sport. *Howard Journal of Communications, 14*(1), 29–38.

Billings, A.C. (2004). Depicting the quarterback in Black and White: A content analysis of college and professional football broadcast commentary. *Howard Journal of Communications, 15*(4), 201–10.

Billings, A.C. (2007). From diving boards to pole vaults: Gendered athlete portrayals in the "big four" sports at the 2004 Athens Summer Olympics. *Southern Communication Journal, 72*(4), 329–44.

Billings, A.C. (2008). *Olympic media: Inside the biggest show on television.* London: Routledge.

Billings, A.C. (2010). *Communicating about sports media: Cultures collide.* Barcelona, Spain: Aresta.

Billings, A.C. & Angelini, J.R. (2007). Packaging the games for viewer consumption: Nationality, gender, and ethnicity in NBC's coverage of the 2004 Summer Olympics. *Communication Quarterly, 55*(1), 95–111.

Billings, A.C., Angelini, J.R., & Duke, A.H. (2010). Gendered profiles of Olympic history: Sportscaster dialogue in the 2008 Beijing Olympics. *Journal of Broadcasting & Electronic Media, 54*(1), 1–15.

Billings, A.C., Angelini, J.R., & Eastman, S.T. (2005). The hidden gender biases in televised golf announcing. *Mass Communication & Society, 8*(2), 155–71.

Billings, A.C., Angelini, J.R., & Eastman, S.T. (2008). Wie shock: Television commentary about playing on the PGA and LPGA tours. *Howard Journal of Communications, 19*(1), 64–84.

Billings, A.C., Brown, C.L., Crout, J.H., McKenna, K.E., Rice, B.A., Timanus, M.E., & Zeigler, J. (2008). The Games through the NBC lens: Gender, ethnic and national equity in the 2006 Torino Winter Olympics. *Journal of Broadcasting & Electronic Media, 52*(2), 215–30.

Billings, A.C., Craig, C.C., Croce, R., Cross, K.M., Moore, K.M., Vigodsky, W., & Watson, V.G. (2006). Just one of "the guys": An analysis of Annika Sorenstam at the 2003 PGA Colonial golf tournament. *Journal of Sport & Social Issues, 30*(1), 37–43.

Billings, A.C. & Eastman, S.T. (2002). Nationality, gender, and ethnicity: Formation of identity in NBC's 2000 Olympic coverage. *International Review for the Sociology of Sport, 37*(3), 349–68.

Billings, A.C. & Eastman, S.T. (2003). Framing identities: Gender, ethnic, and national parity in network announcing of the 2002 Winter Olympics. *Journal of Communication, 53*(4), 369–86.

Billings, A.C., Eastman, S.T., & Newton, G.D. (1998). Atlanta revisited: Primetime promotion in the 1996 Olympic Games. *Journal of Sport & Social Issues, 22*(1), 65–78.

Billings, A.C., Halone, K.K., & Denham, B.E. (2002). "Man" that was a "pretty" shot: An analysis of gendered broadcast commentary of the 2000 Mens' and Womens' NCAA Final Four basketball tournaments. *Mass Communication & Society, 5*(3), 295–315.

Billings, A.C., MacArthur, P.J., Licen, S., & Wu, D. (2009). Superpowers on the Olympic basketball court: U.S. v. China through four nationalistic lenses. *International Journal of Sport Communication, 2*(4), 380–97.

Billings, A.C. & Tambosi, F. (2004). Portraying the United States vs. portraying a champion: U.S. network bias in the 2002 World Cup. *International Review for the Sociology of Sport, 39*(2), 157–65.

Birrell, S. & McDonald, M. (Eds.). (2000). *Reading sport: Critical essays on power and representation.* Boston: Northeastern University Press.

Bishop, R. (2003). Missing in action: Feature coverage of women's sports in *Sports Illustrated. Journal of Sport & Social Issues, 27*(2), 184–94.

Bishop, R. (2009). It hurts the team even more: Differences in coverage by sports journalists of White and African-American athletes who engage in contract holdouts. *Journal of Sports Media, 4*(1), 55–84.

Bissell, K. & Birchall, K. (2008). Through the hoop: How sports participation displaces media use and is related to body self-esteem in competitive female athletes. *Journal of Sports Media, 3*(2), 25–59.

Bissell, K. & Porterfield, K. (2006). Who's got game? Exposure to entertainment and sports media and social physique anxiety in Division I female athletes. *Journal of Sports Media, 1*, 19–50.

Blain, N., Boyle, R., & O'Donnell, H. (1993). *Sport and national identity in the European media.* Leicester, UK: Leicester University Press.

Blinde, M.E., Greendorfer, S.L., & Shenker, R.J. (1991). Differential media coverage of men's and women's intercollegiate basketball: Reflection of gender ideology. *Journal of Sport and Social Issues, 15*, 98–114.

Boyle, R., Dinan, W., & Morrow, S. (2003). Doing the business? Newspaper reporting of the business of football. *Journalism, 3*, 161–81.

Boyle, R. & Haynes, R. (2002). New media sport. *Culture, Sport, Society, 5*, 95–114.

Boyle, R. & Haynes, R. (2009). *Power play: Sport, the media & popular culture.* (2nd Ed.) Edinburgh: Edinburgh University Press.

Brookes, R. (2002). *Representing sport.* New York: Oxford University Press.

Bruce, T. (1998). Audience frustration and pleasure: Women viewers confront televised women's basketball. *Journal of Sport & Social Issues, 22*, 373–97.

Bruce, T. (2004). Marking the bounds of the "normal" in televised sports: The play-by-play of race. *Media, Culture, and Society, 26*(6), 861–79.

Brummett, B. & Duncan, M.C. (1990). Theorizing about totalizing: Specularity and televised sports. *Quarterly Journal of Speech, 76*(3), 227–46.

Bryant, J. (1980). A two-year investigation of the female in sport as reported in the paper media. *Arena Review, 4*, 32–44.

Bryant, J., Brown, D., Comisky, P.W., & Zillmann, D. (1982). Sports and spectators: Commentary and appreciation. *Journal of Communication, 32*(1), 109–19.

Bryant, J., Comisky, P., & Zillmann, D. (1977). Drama in sports commentary. *Journal of Communication, 27*, 140–49.

Bryant, J., Comisky, P., & Zillmann, D. (1981). The appeal of rough-and-tumble play in televised professional football. *Communication Quarterly, 29*, 256–62.

Bryant, J. & Raney, A.A. (2000). Sports on the screen. In D. Zillmann & P. Vorderer (Eds.), *Media entertainment: The psychology of its appeal* (pp. 153–74). Mahwah, NJ: Lawrence Erlbaum Associates.

Bryant, J., Rockwell, S.C., & Owens, J.W. (1994). "Buzzer beaters" and "barn burners": The effects on enjoyment of watching the game go "down to the wire." *Journal of Sport & Social Issues, 18*, 326–39.

Bryant, J. & Zillmann, D. (1983). Sports violence and the media. In J.H. Goldstein (Ed.), *Sports violence* (pp. 195–211). New York: Springer-Verlag.

Buffington, D. (2005). Contesting race on Sundays: Making meaning out of the rise in the number of black quarterbacks. *Sociology of Sport Journal, 21*, 19–37.

Burroughs, A., Ashburn, L., & Seebohm, L. (1995). "Add sex and stir": Homophobic coverage of women's cricket in Australia. *Journal of Sport & Social Issues, 19*(3), 266–84.

Buscombe, E. (Ed.). (1974). *Football on television*. London: BFI.

Butterworth, M.L. (2005). Ritual in the "church of baseball": Suppressing the discourse of democracy after 9/11. *Communication and Critical/Cultural Studies, 2*, 107–29.

Butterworth, M.L. (2007). Race in "the race": Mark McGwire, Sammy Sosa, and heroic constructions of Whiteness. *Critical Studies in Media Communication, 24*, 228–44.

Butterworth, M. (2008a). Fox Sports, Super Bowl XLII, and the affirmation of American civil religion. *Journal of Sport & Social Issues, 32*, 318–23.

Butterworth, M.L. (2008b). "Katie was not only a girl, she was terrible": Katie Hnida, body rhetoric, and college football at the University of Colorado. *Communication Studies, 59*, 259–73.

Butterworth, M.L. (2008c). Purifying the body politic: Steroids, Rafael Palmeiro, and the rhetorical cleansing of Major League Baseball. *Western Journal of Communication, 72*(2), 145–61.

Butterworth, M.L. & Moskal, S.D. (2009). American football, flags, and "fun": The Bell Helicopter Armed Forces Bowl and the rhetorical production of militarism. *Communication, Culture & Critique, 2*(4), 411–33.

Byrd, J. & Utsler, M. (2007). Is stereotypical coverage of African-American athletes as "dead as disco"? An analysis of NFL quarterbacks in the pages of *Sports Illustrated*. *Journal of Sports Media, 2*(1), 1–28.

Capranica, L. & Aversa, F. (2002). Italian television sport coverage during the 2000 Sydney Olympic Games: A gender perspective. *International Review for the Sociology of Sport, 37*, 337–49.

Carrington, B. & McDonald, I. (Eds.). (2001). *"Race," sport and British society*. London and New York: Routledge.

Carrington, B. & McDonald, I. (Eds.). (2009). *Marxism, cultural studies and sport*. London and New York: Routledge.

Carroll, B. (2008). The Black press and the integration of professional baseball: A content analysis of shifts in coverage, 1945–48. *Journal of Sports Media, 3*(2), 61–87.

Carvalho, J. & Hawkins, L. (2006). We know the name; Do they know the game? "Celebrity" articles about the 1924 and 1932 World Series. *Journal of Sports Media, 1*, 73–93.

Cashmore, E. (2000). *Making sense of sport* (3rd Ed.). London: Routledge.

Catsis, J.R. (1996). *Sports broadcasting*. Chicago: Nelson-Hall.

Cheever, N. (2009). The uses and gratifications of viewing mixed martial arts. *Journal of Sports Media, 4*(1), 25–53.

Christopherson, N., Janning, M., & McConnell, E.D. (2002). Two kicks forward, one kick back: A content analysis of media discourses on the 1999 Women's World Cup Soccer Championship. *Sociology of Sport Journal, 19*(2), 170–88.

Cialdini, R.B., Borden, R.J., Thorne, A., Walker, M.R., Freeman, S., & Sloan, L.R. (1976). Basking in reflected glory: Three (football) field studies. *Journal of Personality and Social Psychology, 34*, 366–75.

Claringbould, I., Knoppers, A., & Elling, A. (2004). Exclusionary practices in sport journalism. *Sex Roles, 51*, 709–18.

Clarke, A. & Clarke, J. (1982). Highlights and action replays: Ideology, sport, and the media. In J. Hargreaves (Ed.), *Sport, culture, and ideology* (pp. 62–87). London: Routledge.

Coakley, J. (2004). *Sports in society: Issues and controversies.* Boston: McGraw-Hill.

Comiskey, P., Bryant, J., & Zillmann, D. (1977). Commentary as a substitute for action. *Journal of Communication, 27*(3), 150–53.

Cosgrove, A. & Bruce, T. (2005). "The way New Zealanders would like to see themselves": Reading white masculinity via media coverage of the death of Sir Peter Blake. *Sociology of Sport Journal, 22*(3), 236–55.

Coventry, B. (2004). On the sidelines: Sex and racial segregation in televised sports broadcasting. *Sociology of Sport Journal, 21*(4), 322–41.

Crawford, G. (2004). *Consuming sport: Fans, sport, and culture.* London: Routledge.

Creedon, P.J. (Ed.). (1994). *Women, media and sport: Challenging gender values.* Thousand Oaks, CA: Sage.

Cressman, D.L. & Swenson, L. (2007). The pigskin and the picture tube: The National Football League's first full season on the CBS television network. *Journal of Broadcasting & Electronic Media, 51*(3), 479–97.

Crosset, T. (1999). Male athletes' violence against women: A critical assessment of the athletic affiliation, violence against women debate. *Quest, 71,* 244–57.

Cuneen, J. & Branch, D. (2003). TV and sport's mutually beneficial partnership: 20th century summary and 21st century potential. *International Journal of Sports Management, 4,* 243–60.

Cuneen, J. & Sidwell, M.J. (1998). Gender portrayals in *Sports Illustrated for Kids* advertisements: A content analysis of prominent and supporting models. *Journal of Sport Management, 12*(1), 39–50.

Cunningham, G.B. & Bopp, T. (2010). Race ideology perpetuated: Media representations of newly hired football coaches. *Journal of Sports Media, 5*(1), 1–20.

Daddario, G. (1992). Swimming against the tide: *Sports Illustrated*'s imagery of female athletes in a swimsuit world. *Women's Studies in Communication, 15,* 49–64.

Daddario, G. (1994). Chilly scenes of the 1992 Winter Games: The mass media and the marginalization of female athletes. *Sociology of Sport Journal, 11*(3), 275–88.

Daddario, G. (1998). *Women's sport and spectacle.* Westport, CT: Praeger.

Daddario, G. & Wigley, B.J. (2007). Gender marking and racial stereotyping at the 2004 Athens Games. *Journal of Sports Media, 2*(1), 29–52.

Dart, J.J. (2009). Blogging the 2006 FIFA World Cup Finals. *Sociology of Sport Journal, 26,* 106–26.

Davis, L.R. (1997). *The swimsuit issue and sport: Hegemonic masculinity and* Sports Illustrated. Albany, NY: SUNY Press.

Davis, L.R. & Harris, O. (1998). Race and ethnicity in U.S. sports media. In L.A.Wenner (Ed.), *MediaSport* (1st Ed.) (pp. 154–69). New York: Routledge.

Delgado, F. (2003). The fusing of sport and politics: Media constructions of U.S. versus Iran at France '98. *Journal of Sport & Social Issues, 27*(3), 293–307.

DeNeui, D.L. & Sachau, D.A. (1996). Spectator enjoyment of aggression in intercollegiate hockey games. *Journal of Sport & Social Issues, 21,* 69–77.

Denham, B.E. (2004). Hero or hypocrite? United States and international media portrayals of Carl Lewis amid revelations of a positive drug test. *International Review for the Sociology of Sport, 39*(2), 167–85.

Denham, B.E. (2006). Effects of mass communication on attitudes toward anabolic steroids: An analysis of high school seniors. *Journal of Drug Issues, 36*(4), 809–830.

Denham, B.E., Billings, A.C., & Halone, K.K. (2002). Differential accounts of race in broadcast commentary of the 2000 mens' and womens' Final Four basketball tournaments. *Sociology of Sport Journal, 19,* 315–32.

Denham, B.E. & Cook, A.L. (2006). Byline gender and news source selection: Coverage of the 2004 Summer Olympics. *Journal of Sports Media, 1,* 1–17.

Dietz-Uhler, B. & Murrell, A. (1999). Examining fan reactions to game outcomes: A longitudinal study of social identity. *Journal of Sport Behavior, 22,* 15–27.

Dufur, M. (1998). Race logic and "being like Mike": Representations of athletes in advertising, 1985–94. In G.A. Sailes (Ed.), *African Americans in sport* (pp. 67–81). New Brunswick, NJ: Transaction Publishers.

Duncan, M.C. (1986). A hermeneutic of spectator sport: The 1976 and 1984 Olympic Games. *Quest, 58*, 50–77.

Duncan, M.C. (1990). Sports photographs and sexual difference: Images of women and men in the 1984 and 1988 Olympic Games. *Sociology of Sport Journal, 7*, 22–43.

Duncan, M.C. (1993). Representation and the gun that points backwards. *Journal of Sport & Social Issues, 17*(1), 42–46.

Duncan, M.C. & Brummett, B. (1987). The mediation of spectator sport. *Research Quarterly for Exercise and Sport, 58*, 168–77.

Duncan, M.C. & Brummett, B. (1989). Types and sources of spectating pleasure in televised sports. *Sociology of Sport Journal, 6*, 195–211.

Duncan, M. & Hasbrook, C. (1988). Denial of power in televised women's sport. *Sociology of Sport Journal, 5*, 1–21.

Duncan, M., Messner, M., Williams, L., Jensen, K., & Wilson, W. (Eds.). (1990). *Gender stereotyping in television sports.* Los Angeles, CA: The Amateur Athletic Foundation of Los Angeles.

Duncan, M.C. & Sayaovong, A. (1990). Photographic images and gender in *Sports Illustrated for Kids. Play and Culture, 3*, 91–316.

Dyer, K. (Ed.). (1989). *Sportswomen towards 2000: A celebration.* South Australia: Hyde Park.

Eastman, S.T. & Billings, A.C. (1999). Gender parity in the Olympics: Hyping women athletes, favoring men athletes. *Journal of Sport and Social Issues, 23*(2), 140–70.

Eastman, S.T. & Billings, A.C. (2000a). Promotion in and about sports programming. In S.T. Eastman (Ed.), *Research in Media Promotion* (pp. 203–30). Mahwah, NJ: Lawrence Erlbaum Associates.

Eastman, S.T. & Billings, A.C. (2000b). Sportscasting and sports reporting: The power of gender bias. *Journal of Sport and Social Issues, 24*(1), 192–212.

Eastman, S.T. & Billings, A.C. (2001). Biased voices of sports: Racial and gender stereotyping in college basketball announcing. *Howard Journal of Communications, 12*(4), 183–202.

Eastman, S.T. & Billings, A.C. (2004). Promotion's limited impact in the 2000 Sydney Olympics. *Television & New Media, 5*(1), 339–58.

Eastman, S.T., Brown, R.S., & Kovatch, K.J. (1996). The Olympics that got real? Television's story of Sarajevo. *Journal of Sport & Social Issues, 24*, 366–91.

Eastman, S.T., Newton, G.D., & Pack, L. (1996). Promoting primetime programs in megasporting events. *Journal of Broadcasting & Electronic Media, 40*, 366–88.

Eastman, S.T. & Otteson, J.L. (1994). Promotion increases ratings, doesn't it? The impact of program promotion in the 1992 Olympics. *Journal of Broadcasting & Electronic Media, 38*(3), 307–22.

Eitzen, D.S. (Ed.). (2001). *Sports in contemporary society: An anthology.* New York: Worth.

End, C.M., Kretschmar, J., Campbell, J., Mueller, D.G., & Dietz-Uhler, B. (2003). Sport fans' attitudes toward war analogies as descriptors of sport. *Journal of Sports Behavior, 26*, 356–67.

Espy, R. (1979). *The politics of the Olympic Games.* Berkeley: University of California Press.

Farrell, T. (1989). Media rhetoric as social drama: The Winter Olympics of 1984. *Critical Studies in Mass Communication, 6*(2), 158–82.

Ferguson, C.A. (1983). Sports announcer talk: Syntactic aspects of register variation. *Language in Society, 12*(2), 153–72.

Fink, J.S. & Kensicki, L.J. (2002). An imperceptible difference: Visual and textual constructions of femininity in *Sports Illustrated* and *Sports Illustrated for Women. Mass Communication & Society, 5*(3), 317–40.

Foley, D.E. (1990). The great American football ritual: Reproducing race, class, and gender inequality. *Sociology of Sport Journal, 7*, 111–35.

Fortunato, J. (2008). NFL agenda-setting: The NFL programming schedule: A study of agenda setting. *Journal of Sports Media, 3*(1), 26–49.

Fortunato, J. & Williams, J.D. (2010). Major League baseball and African-American participation: Is fee television part of the solution? *Journal of Sports Media, 5*(1), 79–84.

Fuller, L.K. (Ed.). (2006). *Sport, rhetoric, and gender.* New York: Palgrave Macmillan.

Fuller, L.K. (2008). *Sportscasters/sportscasting: Principles and practices.* New York: Routledge.

Gantz, W. (1981). An exploration of viewing motives and behaviors associated with television sports. *Journal of Broadcasting, 25,* 263–75.

Gantz, W., Wang, Z., Bryant, P., & Potter, R.F. (2006). Sports versus all comers: Comparing TV sports fans with fans of other programming genres. *Journal of Broadcasting & Electronic Media, 50*(1), 95–118.

Gantz, W. & Wenner, L. (1991). Men, women, and sports: Audience experiences and effects. *Journal of Broadcasting and Electronic Media, 35,* 233–43.

Gantz, W. & Wenner, L. (1995). Fanship and the television sports viewing experience. *Sociology of Sport Journal, 12,* 56–74.

Gantz, W., Wenner, L., Carrico, C., & Knorr, M. (1995). Televised sports and marital relationships. *Sociology of Sport Journal, 12,* 306–23.

Garland, J. (2004). The same old story? Englishness, the tabloid press, and the 2002 football World Cup. *Leisure Studies, 23*(1), 79–92.

Garland, J. & Rowe, M. (1999). War minus the shooting? Jingoism, the English press and Euro '96. *Journal of Sport & Social Issues, 23*(1), 80–95.

Garrison, B. (1990). *Sports reporting.* Ames: Iowa State University Press.

George, C., Hartley, A., & Paris, J. (2001). Focus on communication in sport: The representation of female athletes in textual and visual media. *Corporate Communications, 6,* 94–102.

Giacobbi, P.R., Jr. & DeSensi, J.T. (1999). Media portrayals of Tiger Woods: A qualitative deconstructive examination. *Quest, 51,* 408–17.

Gibson, R. (1991). *Radio and television reporting.* Boston: Allyn and Bacon.

Giulianotti, R. & Williams, J. (Eds.). (1994). *Game without frontiers: Football, identity, and modernity.* Aldershot, UK: Ashgate Publishing.

Goldberg, D.T. (1998). Call and response: Sports, talk radio, and the death of democracy. *Journal of Sport & Social Issues, 22*(2), 212–23.

Goldlust, J. (1987). *Playing for keeps: Sport, the media and society.* Melbourne, VIC: Longman Cheshire.

Good, H. (1997). *Diamonds in the dark: America, baseball, and the movies.* Lanham, MD: Scarecrow Press.

Gratton, C. & Solberg, H.A. (2007). *The economics of sports broadcasting.* London: Routledge.

Greendorfer, S.L. & Koehler, L.S. (1983). Sport and the mass media: Critique and prospectus. *Arena Review, 7*(3), 39–43.

Greer, J.D., Hardin, M., & Homan, C. (2009). "Naturally" less exciting? Visual production of men's and women's track and field coverage during the 2004 Olympics. *Journal of Broadcasting & Electronic Media, 53*(2), 173–89.

Guttman, A. (1988). *A whole new ball game: An interpretation of American sports.* Chapel Hill: University of North Carolina Press.

Haigh, M.M. (2008). The "cream," the "clear," BALCO and baseball: An analysis of MLB players' image. *Journal of Sports Media, 3*(2), 1–24.

Halbert, C. & Latimer, M. (1994). "Battling" gendered language: An analysis of the language used by sports commentators in a televised coed tennis competition. *Sociology of Sport Journal, 11,* 298–308.

Hallmark, J.R. & Armstrong, R.N. (1999). Gender equity in televised sports: A comparative analysis of men's and women's NCAA Division I basketball broadcasts, 1991–95. *Journal of Broadcasting and Electronic Media, 43*(2), 222–35.

Halone, K.K. (2008). The structuration of racialized sport organizing. *Journal of Communication Inquiry, 32,* 22–42.

Halone, K.K. & Billings, A.C. (in press, 2010). The temporal nature of racialized sport consumption. *American Behavioral Scientist.*

Hardin, B. & Hardin, M. (2003). Conformity and conflict: Wheelchair athletes discuss sport media. *Adapted Physical Activity Quarterly, 20,* 246–59.

Hardin, M. (2005). Stopped at the gate: Women's sports, "reader interest", and decision making by editors. *Journalism and Mass Communication Quarterly, 82,* 62–77.

Hardin, M. & Corrigan, T.C. (2008). Media and the business of high school sports: A case for closer scrutiny. *Journal of Sports Media, 3*(2), 89–94.

Hardin, M., Dodd, J.E., & Chance, J. (2005). On equal footing? The framing of sexual difference in *Runner's World. Women in Sport and Physical Activity Journal, 14*(2), 40–51.

Hardin, M., Dodd, J.E., & Lauffer, K. (2006). Passing it on: The reinforcement of male hegemony in sports journalism textbooks. *Mass Communication & Society, 9*(4), 429–46.

Hardin, M. & Greer, J.D. (2009). The influence of gender-role socialization, media use and sports participation on perceptions of sex-appropriate sports. *The Journal of Sport Behavior, 32*(2), 207–26.

Hardin, M., Kuehn, K.M., Jones, H., Genovese, J., & Balaji, M. (2009). "Have you got game?" hegemonic masculinity and neo-homophobia in U.S. newspaper sports columns. *Communication, Culture, and Critique, 2*(2), 182–200.

Hardin, M., Lynn, S., & Walsdorf, K. (2005). Challenge and conformity on "contested terrain": Images of women in four women's sport/fitness magazines. *Sex Roles: A Journal of Research, 52*(13–14), 105–17.

Hardin, M., Lynn, S., Walsdorf, K., & Hardin, B. (2002). The framing of sexual difference in *SI for Kids* editorial photos. *Mass Communication & Society, 5*(3), 341–60.

Hardin, M. & Shain, S. (2006a). Feeling much smaller than you know you are: The fragmented professional identity of female sports journalists. *Critical Studies in Media Communication, 23*(4), 322–38.

Hardin, M. & Shain, S. (2006b). Strength in numbers? The experiences and attitudes of women in sports media careers. *Journalism & Mass Communication Quarterly, 82*(4), 804–19.

Hardin, M., Simpson, S., Whiteside, E., & Garris, K. (2007). The "gender war" in U.S. sport: winners and losers in news coverage of Title IX. *Mass Communication & Society, 9*(4), 429–46.

Hardin, M., Walsdorf, S.L., Walsdorf, K., & Hardin, B. (2002). The framing of sexual difference in *Sports Illustrated for Kids* editorial photos. *Mass Communication & Society, 5*(3), 341–59.

Hardin, M. & Whiteside, E. (2009). Token responses to gendered newsrooms: Factors in the career-related decisions of female newspaper sports journalists. *Journalism, 10*(5), 627–46.

Hardin, M., Zhong, B., & Whiteside, E. (2009). Sports coverage: "toy department" or public service journalism? The relationship between reporters' ethics and attitudes toward the profession. *International Journal of Sport Communication, 2*(3), 319–39.

Hargreaves, J.A. (Ed.). (1982). *Sport, culture, and ideology.* London: Routledge & Kegan Paul.

Hargreaves, J.A. (1994). *Sporting females: Critical issues in the history and sociology of women's sports.* London: Routledge.

Hargreaves, J.A. (2000). *Heroines of sport.* London: Routledge.

Hargreaves, J.A. & McDonald, I. (2000). Cultural studies and the sociology of sport. In J. Coakley and E. Dunning (Eds.), *Handbook of sport studies* (pp. 48–60). London: Sage.

Hartmann, D. (1996). The politics of race and sport: Resistance and domination in the 1968 African American Olympic protest movement. *Ethnic and Racial Studies, 19*(3), 548–66.

Hartmann, D. (2003). *Race, culture and the revolt of the Black athlete: The 1968 Olympic protests and their aftermath.* Chicago: University of Chicago Press.

Hedrick, T. (2000). *The art of sportscasting: How to build a successful career.* South Bend, IN: Diamond Communications.

Helitzer, M. (1996). *The dream job: $port$ publicity, promotion and marketing*. Athens, OH: University Sports Press.

Higgs, C.T. & Weiller, K.H. (1994). Gender bias and the 1992 Summer Olympic Games: An analysis of television coverage. *Journal of Sport & Social Issues, 18*, 234–46.

Higgs, C., Weiller, K., & Martin, S. (2003). Gender bias in the 1996 Olympic Games: A comparative analysis. *Journal of Sport and Social Issues, 27*(1), 52–64.

Hilliard, D. (1984). Media images of male and female professional athletes: An interpretive analysis of magazine articles. *Sociology of Sport Journal, 1*, 251–62.

Hitchcock, J.R. (1989). *Sports and media*. Terre Haute, IN: ML Express.

Hitchcock, J.R. (1991). *Sportscasting*. Boston: Focal Press.

Hocking, J.E. (1982). Sports and spectators: Intra-audience effects. *Journal of Communication, 32*(1), 100–108.

Horne, J. (2006). *Sport in consumer culture*. New York: Palgrave.

Horne, J.D. & Manzenreiter, W. (2004). Accounting for mega-events. *International Review for the Sociology of Sport, 39*(2), 187–203.

Houlihan, B. (1994). *Sport and international politics*. Hemel Hempstead, UK: Harvester Wheatsheaf.

Hugenberg, L.W., Haridakis, P.M., & Earnheardt, A.C. (Eds.). (2008). *Sports mania: Essays on fandom and the media in the 21st century*. Jefferson, NC: McFarland.

Hundley, H.L. & Billings, A.C. (Eds.). (2010). *Examining identity in sports media*. Thousand Oaks, CA: Sage.

Hundley, H.L. & Billings, A.C. (2010). *Views from the fairway: Media explorations of identity in golf*. Cresskill, NJ: Hampton Press.

Hutchins, B. & Rowe, D. (2009) From broadcast rationing to digital plenitude: The changing dynamics of the media sport content economy. *Television & New Media, 10*(4), 354–70.

Hutchins, B., Rowe, D., & Ruddock, A. (2009). "It's fantasy football made real": Networked media sport, the Internet, and the hybrid reality of MyFootballClub. *Sociology of Sport Journal, 26*(1), 89–106.

Jackson, S.J. (1998). Life in the (mediated) fast lane: Ben Johnson, national affect and the 1988 crisis of Canadian identity. *International Review for the Sociology of Sport, 33*, 227–38.

Jensen, R. (1994). Banning Redskins from the sports page: The ethics and politics of Native American nicknames. *Journal of Mass Media Ethics, 9*, 16–25.

Johnson, T.C. & Schiappa, E. (2010). An exploratory study of the relationships between televised sports viewing habits and conformity to masculine norms. *Journal of Sports Media, 5*(1), 53–78.

Jones, R., Murrell, A.J., & Jackson, J. (1999). Pretty versus powerful in the sports pages: Print media coverage of U.S. Women's Olympic gold medal winning teams. *Journal of Sport & Social Issues, 23*(2), 183–92.

Kane, M.J. (1988). Media coverage of the female athlete before, during, and after Title IX: *Sports Illustrated* revisited. *Journal of Sports Management, 2*, 87–99.

Kane, M.J. (1989). The post-Title IX female athlete in the media: Things are changing, but how much? *Journal of Physical Education, Recreation, and Dance, 60*, 58–62.

Kane, M.J. (1996). Media coverage of the post-Title IX female athlete: A feminist analysis of sport, gender, and power. *Duke Journal of Gender Law & Policy, 3*(1), 95–127.

Kane, M.J. & Disch, L.J. (1993). Sexual violence and the reproduction of male power in the locker room: The "Lisa Olsen incident." *Sociology of Sport Journal, 10*, 331–52.

Kane, M.J. & Parks, J.B. (1992). The social construction of gender difference and hierarchy in sport journalism: A few twists on very old themes. *Women in Sport and Physical Activity Journal, 1*, 49–83.

Kassing, J.W., Billings, A.C., Brown, R.S., Halone, K.K., Harrison, K., Krizek, B., Meân, L., & Turman, P.D. (2004). Communication in the community of sport: The process of enacting, (re)producing, consuming, and organizing sport. *Communication Yearbook, 28*, 373–410.

Kassing, J. & Sanderson, J. (2008). "Is this a church? Such a big bunch of believers around here!": Fan expressions of social support on floydlandis.com. Third Summit on Communication and Sport (March 2008).

Keene, J.R. & Cummins, R.G. (2009). Sports commentators and source credibility: Do those who can't play ... commentate? *Journal of Sports Media, 4*(2), 57–83.

Kellner, D. (1996). Sports, media culture, and race: Some reflections on Michael Jordan. *Sociology of Sport Journal, 13*(4), 458–67.

Kennedy, E. (2000). Bad boys and gentlemen: Gendered narrative in televised sport. *International Review for the Sociology of Sport, 35*, 59–73.

Kian, E. & Hardin, M. (2009). Analyzing content based on the sex of sports writers: Female journalists counter the traditional gendering of media coverage. *International Journal of Sport Communication, 2*(2), 185–204.

Kian, E., Mondello, M., & Vincent, J. (2009). ESPN – The women's sports network? A content analysis of Internet coverage of March Madness. *Journal of Broadcasting & Electronic Media, 53*(3), 477–95.

King, C.R. (2007). Staging the Winter Olympics, or why sport matters to White power. *Journal of Sport & Social Issues, 31*, 89–94.

Kinnick, K.N. (1998). Gender bias in newspaper profiles of 1996 Olympic athletes: A content analysis of five major dailies. *Women's Studies in Communication, 21*(2), 212–37.

Klattell, D.A. & Marcus, N. (1988). *Sports for sale: Television, money, and the fans.* New York: Oxford University Press.

Knight, J.L. & Giuliano, T.A. (2001/2). He's a Laker; she's a "looker": The consequences of gender-stereotypical portrayals of male and female athletes by the print media. *Sex Roles, 45*(3/4), 217–29.

Koivula, N. (1999). Gender stereotyping in televised media sport coverage. *Sex Roles, 41* (7/8), 589–604.

Krein, M. (2008). If you build it, they will come: Developing a sports media major. *Journal of Sports Media, 3*(1), 77–82.

Kuiper, K. (1996). *Smooth talkers: The linguistic performance of auctioneers and sportscasters.* Mahwah, NJ: Lawrence Erlbaum Associates.

Kusz, K. (2007). *Revolt of the white athlete: Race, media and the emergence of extreme athletes in America.* New York: Peter Lang.

Lapchick, R.E. (1986). *Fractured focus: Sport as a reflection of society.* Lexington, MA: Lexington Books.

Larson, J.F. & Park, H.S. (1993). *Global television and the politics of the Seoul Olympics.* Boulder, CO: Westview.

Larson, J.F. & Rivenburgh, N.K. (1991). A comparative analysis of Australian, U.S., and British telecasts of the Seoul Olympic ceremony. *Journal of Broadcasting & Electronic Media, 35*, 75–94.

Lee, J. (1992). Media portrayals of male and female Olympic athletes: Analysis of newspaper accounts of the 1984 and 1988 Summer Games. *International Review for the Sociology of Sport, 27*, 197–219.

Lenskyj, H.J. (1994). Sexuality and femininity in sport contexts: Issues and alternatives. *Journal of Sport and Social Issues, 18*, 356–76.

Lenskyj, H.J. (2000). *Inside the Olympic industry: Power, politics, and activism.* Albany, NY: SUNY Press.

Lenskyj, H.J. (2002). *The best Olympics ever? Social impacts of Sydney 2000.* Albany, NY: SUNY Press.

Leonard, D. (2004). The next MJ or the next OJ? Kobe Bryant, race and the absurdity of colorblind rhetoric. *Journal of Sport and Social Issues, 28*(3), 284–313.

Leonard, D. (2007). Innocent until proven innocent: In defense of Duke lacrosse, White power (and against menacing black student-athletes, a black stripper, activists and the Jewish media). *Journal of Sport and Social Issues, 33*(1), 25–45.

Lindemann, K. & Cherney, J.L. (2008). Communicating in and through "Murderball": Masculinity and disability in wheelchair rugby. *Western Journal of Communication, 72*(2), 107–25.

Lines, G. (2001). Media sport audiences – young people and the summer of sport '96: Revisiting frameworks for analysis. *Media, Culture, & Society, 22*, 669–80.

Lule, J. (1995). The rape of Mike Tyson: Race, the press, and symbolic types. *Critical Studies in Mass Communication, 12*, 176–95.

Lumpkin, A. & Williams, L. (1991). An analysis of *Sport Illustrated* feature articles, 1954–87. *Sociology of Sport Journal, 8*, 16–32.

Lynn, S., Walsdorf, K., Hardin, M., & Hardin, B. (2002). Selling girls short: Advertising gender images in *Sports Illustrated for Kids. Women in Sport & Physical Activity Journal, 11*, 77–100.

MacNeill, M. (1996). Networks: Producing Olympic ice hockey for a national television audience. *Sociology of Sport Journal, 13*, 103–24.

Madan, M. (2000). It's not just cricket: World Series cricket: Race, nation, and diasporic Indian identity. *Journal of Sport & Social Issues, 24*, 24–35.

Madden, P.A. & Grube, J.W. (1994). The frequency and nature of alcohol and tobacco advertising in televised sports, 1990 through 1992. *American Journal of Public Health, 84*, 297–99.

Maguire, J. (1999). *Global sport: Identities, societies, civilizations.* Cambridge: Polity.

Maguire, J. (2005) *Power and global sport: Zones of prestige, emulation and resistance.* London: Routledge.

Maguire, J. (2006). Multimedia contracts in collegiate sports: A system theory perspective. *Journal of Sports Media, 1*, 51–71.

Maguire, J., Butler, K., Barnard, S., & Golding, P. (2008). Olympism and consumption: An analysis of advertising in the British media coverage of the 2004 Athens Olympic Games. *Sociology of Sport Journal, 25*(2), 167–86.

Maguire, J. & Lee, J.W. (2009). Global festival through national prism: Global and national nexus in South Korean media coverage of the 2004 Athens Olympic Games. *International Review for the Sociology of Sport, 44*(1), 5–24.

Maguire, J., Poulton, E., & Possamai, C. (1999). Weltkrieg III? Media coverage of England versus Germany in Euro '96. *Journal of Sport & Social Issues, 23*(4), 439–54.

Mahony, D.F., Madrigal, R., & Howard, D. (2000). Using the Psychological Commitment to Team (PCT) scale to segment sport consumers based on loyalty. *Sport Marketing Quarterly, 9*, 15–25.

Markula, P. (2009). *Olympic women and the media: International perspectives.* New York: Palgrave Macmillan.

Martin, R. & Miller, T. (1999). (Eds.). *SportCult.* Minneapolis: University of Minnesota Press.

Mason, D.S. (2002). Get the puck outta here! Media transnationalism and Canadian identity. *Journal of Sport & Social Issues, 26*, 140–67.

McAllister, M. (1998). College bowl sponsorship and the increased commercialization of amateur sports. *Critical Studies in Media Communication, 15*(4), 357–81.

McCleneghan, J.S. (1997). The myth makers and wreckers: Syndicated and non-syndicated sports columnists at 103 metro newspapers. *Social Science Journal, 34*, 337–49.

McDonald, M.G. (2005). Mapping whiteness in sport: An introduction. *Sociology of Sport Journal, 22*, 245–55.

McGregor, E. (1989). Mass media and sport: Influences on the public. *The Physical Educator, 46*(1), 52–55.

McKay, J. & Rowe, D. (1987). Ideology, the media and Australian sport. *Sociology of Sport Journal, 4*(3), 258–73.

Meân, L.J. (2001). Identity and discursive practice: Doing gender on the football pitch. *Discourse & Society, 12*, 789–815.

Mehus, I. (2005). Distinction through sport consumption: Spectators of soccer, basketball, and ski-jumping. *International Review for the Sociology of Sport, 40*, 321–33.

Mercurio, E. & Filak, V.F. (2010). Roughing the passer: The framing of Black and White quarterbacks prior to the NFL draft. *Howard Journal of Communications, 21*(1), 56–71.

Messner, M. (1993). *Power at play: Sports and the problem of masculinity*. Boston: Beacon.

Messner, M. (2002). *Taking the field: Women, men and sports*. Minneapolis: University of Minnesota Press.

Messner, M.A., Dunbar, M., & Hunt, D. (2000). The televised sports manhood formula. *Journal of Sport & Social Issues, 24*, 380–94.

Messner, M.A., Duncan, M.C., & Cooky, C. (2003). Silence, sports bras, and wrestling porn: Women in televised sports news and highlight shows. *Journal of Sport & Social Issues, 27*, 38–51.

Messner, M.A., Duncan, M.C., & Jensen, K. (1993). Separating the men from the girls: The gendered language of televised sports. In D.S. Eitzen (Ed.), *Sport in contemporary society* (pp. 219–33). New York: St. Martin's Press.

Messner, M.A., Duncan, M.C., & Wachs, F.L. (1996). The gender of audience building: Televised coverage of women's and men's NCAA basketball. *Sociological Inquiry, 66*(4), 422–40.

Messner, M.A. & Montez de Oca, J. (2005). The male consumer as loser: Beer and liquor ads in mega sports media events. *Signs, 30*, 1879–1909.

Miller, T. (2001). *Sportsex*. Philadelphia, PA: Temple University Press.

Miller, T., Lawrence, G., McKay, J., & Rowe, D. (2001). *Globalization and sport: Playing the world*. London: Sage.

Miller, T., Rowe, D., Lawrence, G., & McKay, J. (2003). The over production of U.S. sport and the new international division of cultural labour. *International Review for the Sociology of Sport, 38*(4), 427–40.

Moragas Spà, M., Rivenburgh, N.K., & Larson, J.F. (1995). *Television in the Olympics*. London: J. Libbey.

Morris, B. & Nydahl, J. (1985). Sports spectacle as drama: Image, language, and technology. *Journal of Popular Culture, 18*(4), 101–10.

Mullen, L.J. & Mazzocco, D.W. (2000). Coaches, drama, and technology: Mediation of Super Bowl broadcasts from 1969–97. *Critical Studies in Media Communication, 17*(3), 347–63.

Murrell, A.J. & Curtis, E.M. (1994). Causal attributions of performance for black and white quarterbacks in the NFL: A look at the sports pages. *Journal of Sport and Social Issues, 18*(3), 224–33.

Newton, G.D., Williams, G.C., Billings, A.C., & Eastman, S.T. (2009). Prime-time promotion pays off: The Athens exemplar. *Journal of Promotion Management, 15*(1–2), 137–49.

Nichols, W., Moynahan, P., Hall, A., & Taylor, J. (2002). *Media relations in sport*. Morgantown, WV: Fitness Information Technology.

Nylund, D. (2004). When in Rome: Heterosexism, homophobia, and sports talk radio. *Journal of Sport and Social Issues, 28*(2), 136–68.

Nylund, D. (2007). *Beer, babes, and balls: Masculinity and sports talk radio*. Albany, NY: SUNY Press.

Oates, T.P. (2009). New media and the repackaging of NFL fandom. *Sociology of Sport Journal, 26*, 31–49.

O'Donnell, H. (1994). Mapping the mythical: A geopolitics of national sporting stereotypes. *Discourse and Society, 4*(3), 345–80.

O'Reilly, J. & Cahn, S.K. (2007). *Women and sports in the United States*. Boston: Northeastern University Press.

Owens, J. (2003). *Television sports production*. Salt Lake City, UT: International Sports Broadcasting.

Parente, D.E. (1977). The interdependence of sports and television. *Journal of Communication, 27*(3), 128–32.

Pearson, D.W. (2000). The depiction and characterization of women in sport theme feature films after Title IX. *Research Quarterly for Exercise and Sport, 71*(1), A-102.

Pedersen, P.M. (2003). Examining stereotypical written and photographic reporting on the sports page: An analysis of newspaper coverage of interscholastic athletics. *Women in Sport & Physical Activity Journal, 12*, 67–75.

Pedersen, P.M., Miloch, K.S., & Laucella, P.C. (2007). *Strategic sport communication.* Champaign, IL: Human Kinetics.

Peterson, E.M. & Raney, A.A. (2008). Reconceptualizing and reexamining suspense as a predictor of mediated sports enjoyment. *Journal of Broadcasting & Electronic Media, 52*(4), 544–62.

Phillips, M.G. (Ed.). (2006). *Deconstructing sport history: A postmodern analysis.* New York: SUNY Press.

Pound, D. (2004). *Inside the Olympics.* Ontario, Canada: Wiley & Sons.

Powers, R. (1984). *Supertube: The rise of television sports.* New York: Coward-McCann.

Puijk, R. (1997). *Global spotlights on Lillehammer: How the world viewed Norway during the 1994 Winter Olympics.* Luton, UK: University of Luton Press.

Rada, J. (1996). Color blind-sided: Racial bias in network television's coverage of professional football games. *Howard Journal of Communications, 7*(3), 231–40.

Rada, J. & Wulfemeyer, K.T. (2005). Color coded: Racial descriptors in television coverage of intercollegiate sports. *Journal of Broadcasting & Electronic Media, 49*, 65–85.

Rader, B.G. (1983). *American sports.* Englewood Cliffs, NJ: Prentice-Hall.

Rader, B.G. (1984). *In its own image: How television has transformed sports.* New York: Free Press.

Rainville, R.E. & McCormick, E. (1977). Extent of covert racial prejudice in pro football announcers' speech. *Journalism Quarterly, 54*, 20–26.

Raney, A.A. (2003a). Enjoyment of sports spectatorship. In J. Bryant, D. Roskos-Ewoldsen, & J. Cantor (Eds.), *Communication and emotion: Essays in honor of Dolf Zillmann* (pp. 397–416). Mahwah, NJ: Lawrence Erlbaum Associates.

Raney, A.A. (2003b). Professional wrestling and human dignity: Questioning the boundaries of entertainment. In H. Good (Ed.), *Desperately seeking ethics* (pp. 161–76). Lanham, MD: Scarecrow Press.

Raney, A.A. & Bryant, J. (Eds.). (2006). *Handbook of sports and media.* Mahwah, NJ: Lawrence Erlbaum Associates.

Raney, A.A. & Depalma, A. (2006). The effect of viewing varying levels of aggressive sports programming on enjoyment, mood, and perceived violence. *Mass Communication & Society, 9*, 321–38.

Raney, A.A. & Kinnally, W. (2009). Examining perceived violence in and enjoyment of televised rivalry sports contests. *Mass Communication & Society, 12*(3), 311–31.

Real, M.R. (1975). Super Bowl: Mythic spectacle. *Journal of Communication, 75*, 31–43.

Real, M.R. (1995). Sport as spectacle. In J. Downing (Ed.), *Questioning the media: A critical introduction.* Newbury Park, CA: Sage.

Real, M.R. (1996a). A look back – and ahead at the televised Olympics. *TV Quarterly, 28*(3), 9–12.

Real, M.R. (1996b). The post-modern Olympics: Technology and the commodification of the Olympic movement. *Quest, 48*(1), 9–24.

Real, M.R. (2009). Gold for whom? Canadian sports, mega-events and the 2010 Olympics. In L.R. Shade, *Mediascapes: New patterns in Canadian communication, 3rd Edition* (pp. 165–78). Toronto: Thomson Nelson.

Real, M.R. & Mechikoff, R. (1992). Deep fan: Mythic identification, technology, and advertising in spectator sports. *Sociology of Sport Journal, 9*, 323–39.

Reaser, J. (2003). A quantitative approach to (sub)registers: The case of sports announcer talk. *Discourse Studies, 5*(3), 303–21.

Rein, I., Kotler, P., & Shields, B. (2006). *The elusive fan: Reinventing sports in a crowded marketplace.* New York: McGraw-Hill.

Reinardy, S. (2009). Back to basics: Teaching the teachers of sports journalism and media. *Journal of Sports Media, 4*(2), 85–91.

Riggs, K.E., Eastman, S.T., & Golobic, T.S. (1993). Manufactured conflict in the 1992 Olympics: The discourse of television and politics. *Critical Studies in Mass Communication, 10*, 253–72.

Rintala, J. & Birrell, S. (1984). Fair treatment for the active female: A content analysis of *Young Athlete* magazine. *Sociology of Sport Journal, 1*(1), 235–45.

Roche, M. (2000). *Mega-events and modernity: Olympics and expos in the growth of global culture.* London and New York: Routledge.

Rowe, D. (1996). The global love-match: Sport and television. *Media, Culture & Society, 18*(4), 565–82.

Rowe, D. (1998). If you film it, will they come? Sports on film. *Journal of Sport & Social Issues, 22*(4), 350–59.

Rowe, D. (Ed.). (2004a). *Critical readings: Sport, culture, and the media.* Maidenhead, UK: Open University Press.

Rowe, D. (2004b). *Sport, culture, and the media* (2nd Ed.). Buckingham, UK: Open University Press.

Rowe, D. (2004c). Watching brief: Cultural citizenship and viewing rights. *Sport in Society, 7*(3), 385–402.

Rowe, D. (2007). Sports journalism: Still the "toy department" of the news media? *Journalism, 8*(4), 385–405.

Rowe, D. (2008a). The east–west balance in 21st century media sport. In *Asian Communication and Media Studies 2007: Sports Globalization Communication* (pp. 14–27). Beijing: Communication University of China Press.

Rowe, D. (2008b). History of sports and the media. In W. Donsbach (Ed.), *The international encyclopedia of communication* (pp. 4798–4802). Oxford: Blackwell.

Rowe, D. (2008c). Time and timelessness in sport film. *Sport in Society, 11*(2/3), 146–58.

Rowe, D. (2011). Sport and its audiences. In V. Nightingale (Ed.), *Handbook of media audiences,* pp. 509–26. Forthcoming, Oxford: Blackwell.

Rowe, D. & Gilmour, C. (2008). Contemporary media sport: De- or re-Westernization? *International Journal of Sport Communication, 1*(2), 177–94.

Rowe, D. & Gilmour, C. (2009). Getting a ticket to the world party: Televising soccer in Australia. *Soccer & Society, 10*(1), 9–26.

Rowe, D. & Lawrence, G. (Eds.). (1998). *Tourism, leisure, sport: Critical perspectives.* Melbourne, VIC: Cambridge University Press.

Sabo, D. & Jansen, S.C. (1992). Images of men in sport media: The social reproduction of gender order. In S. Craig (Ed.), *Men, masculinity, and the media* (pp. 169–84). Newbury Park, CA: Sage.

Sabo, D., Jansen, S.C., Tate, D., Duncan, M.C., & Leggett, S. (1996). Televising international sport: Race, ethnicity, and nationalistic bias. *Journal of Sport & Social Issues, 20*, 7–21.

Salwen, M. & Wood, N. (1994). Depictions of female athletes on *Sports Illustrated* covers, 1957–89. *Journal of Sports Behavior, 17*(2), 98–108.

Sargent, S.L., Zillmann, D., & Weaver, J.B. (1998). The gender gap in the enjoyment of televised sports. *Journal of Sport & Social Issues, 22*, 46–64.

Scannell, P. (1991). *Broadcast talk.* London: Sage.

Schaffer, K. & Smith, S. (Eds.). (2000). *The Olympics at the millennium: Power politics and the Games.* Piscataway, NJ: Rutgers University Press.

Schell, L.A. & Duncan, M.C. (1999). A content analysis of CBS's coverage of the 1996 Paralympic Games. *Adapted Physical Activity Quarterly, 16*, 27–47.

Scherer, J. (2007). Globalization, promotional culture and the production/consumption of online games: Engaging Adidas's "Beat Rugby" campaign. *New Media & Society, 9*, 475–96.

Scherer, J. & Whitson, D. (2009). Public broadcasting, sport, and cultural citizenship: The future of sport on the Canadian Broadcasting Corporation? *International Review for the Sociology of Sport, 44*(2–3), 213–129.

Schultz, B. (2005). *Sports media: Reporting, producing, and planning.* Burlington, MA: Focal Press.

Schultz, B. & Sheffer, M.L. (2008). Left behind: Local television and the community of sport. *Western Journal of Communication, 72*(2), 180–95.

Schultz, B. & Sheffer, M.L. (2009). Resisting change: Blogging and local sports media. *Journal of Communication Studies, 1*, 372–85.

Schweitzer, K., Zillmann, D., Weaver, J., & Luttrell, E. (1992). Perception of threatening events in the emotional aftermath of a televised college football game. *Journal of Broadcasting and Electronic Media, 36*(1), 75–82.

Scraton, S. & Flintoff, F. (Eds.). (2002). *Gender and sport: A reader.* New York: Routledge.

Seltzer, T. & Mitrook, M. (2009). The role of expert opinion in framing media coverage of the Heisman Trophy race. *Journal of Sports Media, 4*(2), 1–29.

Sheffer, M.L. & Schultz, B. (2007). Double standard: Why women have trouble getting jobs in local television sports. *Journal of Sports Media, 2*, 77–101.

Shifflet, B. & Revelle, R. (1994). Gender equity in sports media coverage: A review of the *NCAA News. Journal of Sport & Social Issues, 18*(2), 144–50.

Slater, M.D., Rouner, D., Domenech-Rodriguez, M., Beauvais, R., Murphy, K., & Van Leuven, J.K. (1997). Adolescent responses to TV beer ads and sports content/context: Gender and ethnic differences. *Journalism and Mass Communication Quarterly, 74*, 108–22.

Smith, R.A. (2001). *Play by play: Radio, television, and big-time college sport.* Baltimore, MD: Johns Hopkins University Press.

Smith, R. & Schwarz, N. (2003). Language, social comparison, and college football: Is your school less similar to the rival school than the rival school is to your school? *Communication Monographs, 70*(4), 351–60.

Sowell, M. (2008). The birth of national sports coverage: An examination of the *New York Herald's* use of the telegraph to report America's first "championship" boxing match in 1849. *Journal of Sports Media, 3*(1), 51–75.

Spinda, J.S.W., Earnheardt, A.C., & Hugenberg, L. (2009). Checkered flags and mediated friendships: Parasocial interaction among NASCAR fans. *Journal of Sports Media, 4*(2), 31–55.

Staples, R. & Jones, T. (1985). Culture, ideology and Black television images. *The Black Scholar, 16*(3), 10–20.

Stempel, C. (2006). Televised sports, masculinist moral capital, and support for the U.S. invasion in Iraq. *Journal of Sport & Social Issues, 30*(1), 79–106.

Su-lin Gan, Tuggle, C.A., Mitrook, M.A., Coussement, S.H., & Zillmann, D. (1997). The thrill of a close game: Who enjoys it and who doesn't? *Journal of Sport & Social Issues, 21*(1), 53–64.

Sugden, J. & Tomlinson, A. (Eds.). (1994). *Hosts and champions: Soccer culture, national identity and the World Cup.* Aldershot, UK: Arena.

Sullivan, D.B. (1991). Commentary and viewer perception of player hostility: Adding punch to televised sport. *Journal of Broadcasting & Electronic Media, 35*, 487–504.

Theberge, N. (1991). A content analysis of print media coverage of gender, women, and physical activity. *Journal of Applied Sport Psychology, 3*, 36–48.

Theberge, N. & Cronk, A. (1986). Work routines in newspaper sports departments and the coverage of women's sports. *Sociology of Sport Journal, 3*, 195–203.

Thorpe, H. (2008). Foucault, technologies of self, and the media: Discourses of femininity in snowboarding culture. *Journal of Sport & Social Issues, 32*(2), 199–229.

Tomlinson, A. (1996). Olympic spectacle: Opening ceremonies and some paradoxes of globalization. *Media, Culture and Society, 18*, 583–602.

Tomlinson, A. (Ed.). (2007). *The sports studies reader.* London: Routledge.

Tomlinson, A. & Fleming, S. (Eds.). (1997). *Ethics, sport, and leisure: Crises and critiques.* Aachen, Germany: Meyer & Meyer Verlag.

Toohey, K. (1997). Australian television, gender and the Olympic Games. *International Review for the Sociology of Sport, 31*(1), 19–29.

Toohey, K. & Veal, A.J. (2000). *The Olympic Games: A social science perspective.* Oxfordshire, UK: Cabi.

Tremblay, S. & Tremblay, W. (2001). Mediated masculinity at the millennium: The *Jim Rome Show* as a male bonding speech community. *Journal of Radio Studies, 8*(2), 271–91.

Trujillo, N. (1991). Hegemonic masculinity on the mound: Media representations of Nolan Ryan and American sports culture. *Critical Studies in Mass Communication, 9,* 290–308.

Trujillo, N. (1995). Machines, missiles and men: Images of the male body on ABC's *Monday Night Football. Sociology of Sport Journal, 12*(4), 403–23.

Tudor, A. (1998). Sports reporting: Race, difference and identity. In K. Brants, J. Hermes, & L.V. Zoonen (Eds.), *The media in question: Popular cultures and public interests* (pp. 147–56). London/Thousand Oaks, CA/New Delhi: Sage.

Tuggle, C.A. (1997). Differences in television sports reporting of men's and women's athletics: ESPN *SportsCenter* and CNN *Sports Tonight. Journal of Broadcasting & Electronic Media, 41*(1), 14–24.

Tuggle, C.A., Huffman, S., & Rosengard, D.S. (2002). A descriptive analysis of NBC's coverage of the 2000 Summer Olympics. *Mass Communication & Society, 5,* 361–75.

Tuggle, C.A., Huffman, S., & Rosengard, D.S. (2007). A descriptive analysis of NBC's coverage of the 2004 Summer Olympics. *Journal of Sports Media, 2*(1), 53–76.

Tuggle, C.A. & Owen, A. (1999). A descriptive analysis of NBC's coverage of the centennial Olympics. *Journal of Sport & Social Issues, 23*(2), 171–83.

Turner, P. (1999). Television and Internet convergence: Implications for sports broadcasting. *Sports Marketing Quarterly, 8,* 43–49.

Urquhart, J. & Crossman, J. (1999). The *Globe and Mail* coverage of the Winter Olympic Games: A cold place for women athletes. *Journal of Sport and Social Issues, 23*(2), 193–202.

van Sterkenburg, J. & Knoppers, A. (2004). Dominant discourses about race/ethnicity and gender in sport practice and performance. *International Review for the Sociology of Sport, 39,* 301–21.

Vincent, J. (2004). Game, sex, match: The construction of gender in British newspaper coverage of the 2000 Wimbledon Championships. *Sociology of Sport Journal, 21,* 435–56.

Von der Lippe, G. (2002). Media image: Sport, gender, and national identities in five European countries. *International Review for the Sociology of Sport, 37,* 371–95.

Wachs, F.L. & Dworkin, S.L. (1997). "There's no such thing as a gay hero": Sexual identity and media framing of HIV-positive athletes. *Journal of Sport & Social Issues, 21,* 327–47.

Wann, D.L. (1995). Preliminary validation of the Sports Fan Motivational Scale. *Journal of Sport & Social Issues, 19,* 377–96.

Wann, D.L. & Branscombe, N.R. (1990). Die-hard and fair-weather fans: Effects of identification on BIRGing and CORFing tendencies. *Journal of Sport & Social Issues, 14*(2), 103–17.

Wann, D.L., Carlson, J.D., Holland, L.C., Jacob, B.E., Owens, D.A., & Wells, D.D. (1999). Beliefs in symbolic catharsis: The importance of involvement with aggressive sports. *Social Behavior and Personality, 27*(2), 155–64.

Wann, D.L., Melnick, M.J., Russell, G.W., & Pease, D.G. (2001). *Sports fans: The psychology and social impact of spectators.* New York: Routledge.

Wann, D.L., Peterson, R.R., Cothran, C., & Dykes, M. (1999). Sport fan aggression and anonymity: The importance of team identification. *Social Behavior and Personality, 27*(6), 597–602.

Wann, D.L., Schrader, M.P., Allison, J.A., & McGeorge, K.K. (1998). The inequitable newspaper coverage of men's and women's athletics at small, medium, and large universities. *Journal of Sport & Social Issues, 22,* 79–87.

Wanta, W. & Kunz, W.M. (1997). The impact of the baseball strike on newspapers. *Journalism & Mass Communication Quarterly, 74*, 184–94.

Wanta, W. & Leggett, D. (1988). "Hitting paydirt": Capacity theory and sports announcers' use of clichés. *Journal of Communication, 38*(4), 82–89.

Wanta, W. & Leggett, D. (1989). Gender stereotypes in wire service sports photos. *Newspaper Research Journal, 10*, 105–14.

Wearden, S.T. & Creeden, P.J. (2002). "We got next": Images of women in television commercials during the inaugural WNBA season. *Culture, Sport, and Society, 5*, 189–210.

Weaver, D.H. & Mauro, J.B. (1978). Newspaper readership patterns. *Journalism Quarterly, 55*, 84–91, 134.

Weiller, K.H. & Higgs, C.T. (1999). Television coverage of professional golf: A focus on gender. *Women in Sport and Physical Activity Journal, 8*, 83–100.

Wenner, L.A. (Ed.). (1989). *Media, sports, and society.* Newbury Park, CA: Sage.

Wenner, L.A. (1990). Therapeutic engagement in mediated sports. In G. Gumpert & S. Fish (Eds.), *Talking to strangers: Mediated therapeutic communication* (pp. 221–42). Norwood, NJ: Ablex.

Wenner, L.A. (1991). One part alcohol, one part sport, one part dirt, stir gently: Beer commercial and television sports. In L.R. Vande Berg & L.A. Wenner (Eds.), *Television criticism: Approaches and applications.* New York: Longman.

Wenner, L.A. (1993a). Men, women, and sports on television: Audience experiences and effects. In A. Yiannakis, T. McIntyre, and M. Melnick (Eds.), *Sport sociology: Contemporary themes* (pp. 208–16). Dubuque, IA: Kendall-Hunt.

Wenner, L.A. (1993b). We are the world, we are the quake: The redefinition of fans as interpretive community in sportswriting about the 1989 Bay Area World Series and earthquake disaster. *Journal of Sport and Social Issues, 17*, 181–205.

Wenner, L.A. (1994). The dream team, communicative dirt, and the marketing of synergy: USA basketball and cross-merchandising in television commercials. *Journal of Sport and Social Issues, 18*, 27–47.

Wenner, L.A. (Ed.). (1998a). *MediaSport.* New York: Routledge.

Wenner, L.A. (1998b). The sports bar: Masculinity, alcohol, sports, and the mediation of public space. In G. Rail and J. Harvey (Eds.), *Sport and postmodern times: Gender, sexuality, the body, and sport* (pp. 301–32), Albany, NY: SUNY Press.

Wenner, L.A. (2004). Recovering (from) Janet Jackson's breast: Ethics and the nexus of media, sports, and management. *Journal of Sport Management, 18*, 315–34.

Wenner, L.A. (2007). Towards a dirty theory of narrative ethics. Prolegomenon on media, sport and commodity value. *International Journal of Media and Cultural Politics, 3*, 111–29.

Wenner, L.A. (2008). Super-cooled sports dirt: Moral contagion and Super Bowl commercials in the shadows of Janet Jackson. *Television and New Media, 9*(2), 131–54.

Wenner, L.A. (2009). The unbearable dirtiness of being: On the commodification of mediasport and the necessity of ethical criticism. *Journal of Sports Media, 4*(1), 85–94.

Wenner, L.A., Gantz, W., Carrico, C., & Knorr, M. (1995). Television sports and marital relations. *Sociology of Sport Journal, 12*, 306–23.

Wenner, L.A. & Jackson, S.J. (Eds.). (2009). *Sport, beer, and gender: Promotional culture and contemporary social life.* New York: Peter Lang.

Whannel, G. (1992). *Fields in vision: Television sport and cultural transformation.* London: Routledge.

Whannel, G. (2000). Sport and the media. In J. Coakley & E. Dunning (Eds.), *Handbook of sports studies* (pp. 291–308). London: Sage.

Whannel, G. (2002). *Media sport stars: Masculinities and modernities.* London: Routledge.

Whannel, G. (2008). Winning and losing respect: Narratives of identity in sport films. *Sport in Society: Cultures, Media, Politics, 11*(2/3), 195–208.

Whiteside, E. & Hardin, M. (2010). Public relations and sport: Work force demographics in the intersection of two gendered industries. *Journal of Sports Media, 5*(1), 21–52.

Wigley, S. & Meirick, P.C. (2008). Interactive media and sports journalists: The impact of interactive media on sports journalists. *Journal of Sports Media, 3*(1), 1–25.

Williams, B.R. (1977). The structure of televised football. *Journal of Communication, 27*(3), 133–39.

Williams, C., Lawrence, G., & Rowe, D. (1985). Women and sport: A lost ideal. *Women's Studies International Forum, 8*(6), 639–45.

Williams, J. (1994). Sport, postmodernism and global TV. In S. Earnsham (Ed.), *Postmodern surroundings*. Amsterdam: Rodopi.

Wonsek, P.L. (1992). College basketball on television: A study of racism in the media. *Media, Culture and Society, 14*, 449–61.

Woods, R.B. (2007). *Social issues in sport*. Champaign, IL: Human Kinetics.

Zillmann, D., Bryant, J., & Sapolsky, B.S. (1979). The enjoyment of watching sports contests. In J.H. Goldstein (Ed.), *Sports, games and play: Social and psychological viewpoints* (pp. 297–335). Hillsdale, NJ: Erlbaum.

Zillmann, D., Bryant, J., & Sapolsky, B. (1989). Enjoyment from sports spectatorship. In J.H. Goldstein (Ed.), *Sports, games, and play: Social and psychological viewpoints* (pp. 241–78). Hillsdale, NJ: Lawrence Erlbaum Associates.

Zillmann, D. & Paulus, P.B. (1993). Spectators: Reactions to sports events and effects on athletic performance. In R.N. Singer, M. Murphey, & L.K. Tennant (Eds.), *Handbook of research on sports psychology* (pp. 600–619). New York: Macmillan.

Zwarun, L. & Farrar, K.M. (2005). Doing what they say, saying what they mean: Self-regulatory compliance and depictions of drinking in alcohol commercials in televised sports. *Mass Communication & Society, 8*, 347–71.

INDEX